The individual struggling with overwhelming emotions and DBT therapists will benefit significantly from this workbook. McKay, Wood and Brantley have expanded and translated DBT Skills, making Linehan's iconic work on emotional skill building even more accessible and easy to apply to everyday life.

—Kate Northcott, MA, MFT, is a DBT therapist in private practice with Mindfulness Therapy Associates and is director of New Perspectives Center for Counseling, a non-profit counseling center, in San Francisco, CA

The Dialectical Behavior Therapy Skills Workbook

Practical DBT Exercises for
Learning Mindfulness, Interpersonal
Effectiveness, Emotion Regulation
& Distress Tolerance

MATTHEW McKAY, PH.D. • JEFFREY C. WOOD, PSY.D.
JEFFREY BRANTLEY, MD

New Harbinger Publications, Inc.

Publisher's Note

This publication is designed to provide accurate and authoritative information in regard to the subject matter covered. It is sold with the understanding that the publisher is not engaged in rendering psychological, financial, legal, or other professional services. If expert assistance or counseling is needed, the services of a competent professional should be sought.

Library of Congress Cataloging-in-Publication Data

The dialectical behavior therapy skills workbook : practical DBT exercises for learning mindfulness, interpersonal effectiveness, emotion regulation, and distress tolerance / Matthew McKay ... [et al.].
    p. cm.
  ISBN-13: 978-1-57224-513-6
  ISBN-10: 1-57224-513-1
  1. Dialectical behavior therapy--Problems, exercises, etc. I. McKay, Matthew.
  RC489.B4D52 2007
  616.89'142--dc22

          2007013007

14 13 12

20 19 18 17 16 15

In memory of my mother, Louise Long LaBrash, who was always there for me in the hard times.

—Matthew McKay

To my students and clients at Fresno City College and Reedley College, 2005–2006, whose strength, hope, and resilience inspired me while writing this book.

—Jeffrey C. Wood

This work is dedicated to all who struggle with intense and unpredictable emotions in their inner and outer lives. May you find peace and happiness, and may all living beings benefit from your efforts.

—Jeffrey Brantley

Contents

Dialectical Behavior Therapy: An Overview of the Treatment

Dialectical behavior therapy, developed by Marsha Linehan (1993a, 1993b), is extraordinarily effective at helping people manage overwhelming emotions. Research shows that dialectical behavior therapy strengthens a person's ability to handle distress without losing control or acting destructively.

A lot of people struggle with overwhelming emotions. It's as if the knob is turned to maximum volume on much of what they feel. When they get angry or sad or scared, it shows up as a big, powerful wave that can sweep them off their feet.

If you've faced overwhelming emotions in your life, you know what we're talking about. There are days when your feelings hit you with the force of a tsunami. And when that happens, it makes you—understandably—afraid to feel things because you don't want to get swept away by your emotions. The trouble is, the more you try to suppress or put a lid on your emotions, the more overwhelming they can get. We'll talk about that in chapters 6 and 7 on emotional regulation. What's important to know right now is that trying to stop your feelings doesn't work.

There's a fair amount of research to suggest that the likelihood of developing intense, overwhelming emotions may be hardwired from birth. But it can also be greatly affected by trauma or neglect during childhood. Trauma at critical points in our development can literally alter our brain structure in ways that make us more vulnerable to intense, negative emotions. However, the fact that a propensity to intense emotions is often rooted in genetics or trauma doesn't mean the problem can't be overcome. Thousands of people have used the skills you'll learn in this book to achieve better emotional control. They have changed their lives—and you can too.

So what are these skills, and how will they help you? Dialectical behavior therapy teaches four critically important skills that can both reduce the size of emotional waves and help you keep your balance when those emotions overwhelm you.

1. *Distress tolerance* will help you cope better with painful events by building up your resiliency and giving you new ways to soften the effects of upsetting circumstances.

2. *Mindfulness* will help you experience more fully the present moment while focusing less on painful experiences from the past or frightening possibilities in the future. Mindfulness will also give you tools to overcome habitual, negative judgments about yourself and others.

3. *Emotion regulation* skills help you to recognize more clearly what you feel and then to observe each emotion without getting overwhelmed by it. The goal is to modulate your feelings without behaving in reactive, destructive ways.

4. *Interpersonal effectiveness* gives you new tools to express your beliefs and needs, set limits, and negotiate solutions to problems—all while protecting your relationships and treating others with respect.

This book is structured to make learning easier. Each of the key skills is covered in two chapters—basic and advanced—except mindfulness, which has a third, more advanced chapter. The basic skills chapters teach necessary concepts, identify the components of the new skill, and lead you through initial steps for acquiring the skill. The advanced skills chapters take you through the remaining components of the skill, building level by level. There will be examples to make each step clear as well as assessments, exercises, and worksheets to help you practice each thing you learn. Then in the final chapter, Putting It All Together, you'll learn how to integrate all those skills, in order to make them a regular part of your life.

The Dialectical Behavior Therapy Skills Workbook is written to make learning easy. The hard part will be making the commitment to *do* the exercises and put your new skills into practice. Nothing will change by just reading. The words on these pages will have no impact on your life unless you implement—behaviorally—the new techniques and strategies you will learn here. So now is a good time to think about why you are reading this book and what you want to change. Right here, on this page, write down three ways you currently react to your emotions that you want to change. In other words, what three things do you do when upset or overwhelmed that are damaging—and that you are committed to replace with better ways to cope?

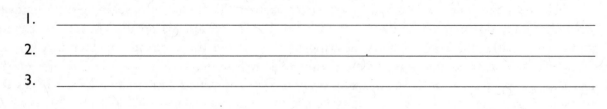

1. _____

2. _____

3. _____

WHO THIS BOOK IS FOR

There are two intended audiences for *The Dialectical Behavior Therapy Skills Workbook*. The first is people who are in dialectical behavior therapy (either group or individual) and need a workbook to help learn the four key skills. We also wrote this book so it could be used independently by *anyone* who struggles with overwhelming feelings. All the tools are here to achieve significant changes in your ability to control emotion. With that said, if you are reading this workbook on your own and are having a hard time implementing the new skills, we strongly recommend seeking the services of a qualified dialectical behavior therapist.

THERE IS HOPE

Life is hard. You already know that. But you are not stuck or helpless in your struggle with your emotions. You can expect, if you really do the work to implement these skills, that how you react to feelings will change. That's because—regardless of genetics or early pain—the key skills you'll learn here can affect the outcome of every conflict and every upset and can literally alter the course of your relationships. There is every reason to hope. All you have to do is turn the page and begin. Then keep working at it.

CHAPTER 1

Basic Distress Tolerance Skills

DISTRESS TOLERANCE SKILLS: WHAT ARE THEY?

At some point in our lives, we all have to cope with distress and pain. Either it can be physical, like a bee sting or a broken arm, or it can be emotional, like sadness or anger. In both cases, the pain is often unavoidable and unpredictable. You can't always anticipate when the bee will sting you or when something will make you sad. Often, the best you can do is to use the coping skills that you have and hope that they work.

But for some people, emotional and physical pain feels more intense and occurs more frequently than it does for other people. Their distress comes on more quickly and feels like an overwhelming tidal wave. Often, these situations feel like they'll never end, and the people experiencing them don't know how to cope with the severity of their pain. For the purposes of this book, we'll call this problem *overwhelming emotions*. (But remember, emotional and physical pain often occur together.)

People struggling with overwhelming emotions often deal with their pain in very unhealthy, very unsuccessful ways because they don't know what else to do. This is understandable. When a person is in emotional pain, it's hard to be rational and to think of a good solution. Nevertheless, many of the coping strategies used by people with overwhelming emotions only serve to make their problems worse.

Here's a list of some common coping strategies used by people dealing with this problem. Check (✓) the ones that you use to cope with your stressful situations:

_____ You spend a great deal of time thinking about past pains, mistakes, and problems.

_____ You get anxious worrying about possible future pains, mistakes, and problems.

_____ You isolate yourself from other people to avoid distressing situations.

_____ You make yourself feel numb with alcohol or drugs.

_____ You take your feelings out on other people by getting excessively angry at them or trying to control them.

_____ You engage in dangerous behaviors, such as cutting, hitting, picking at, or burning yourself or pulling out your own hair.

_____ You engage in unsafe sexual activities, such as having sex with strangers or having frequent unprotected sex.

_____ You avoid dealing with the causes of your problems, such as an abusive or dysfunctional relationship.

_____ You use food to punish or control yourself by eating too much, not eating at all, or by throwing up what you do eat.

_____ You attempt suicide or engage in high-risk activities, like reckless driving or taking dangerous amounts of alcohol and drugs.

_____ You avoid pleasant activities, such as social events and exercise, maybe because you don't think that you deserve to feel better.

_____ You surrender to your pain and resign yourself to living a miserable and unfulfilling life.

All of these strategies are paths to even deeper emotional pain, because even the strategies that offer temporary relief will only cause you more suffering in the future. Use the Cost of Self-Destructive Coping Strategies worksheet to see how. Note the strategies that you use as well as their costs, and then include any additional costs that you can think of. At the end of the worksheet, feel free to add any of your own strategies that aren't included as well as their costs.

THE COST OF SELF-DESTRUCTIVE COPING STRATEGIES

Self-Destructive Coping Strategy	Possible Costs
1. You spend a great deal of time thinking about past pain, mistakes, and problems.	Miss good things that might be happening now and then regret missing those things, too; depression about the past Other: _____ _____
2. You get anxious worrying about possible future pain, mistakes, and problems.	Miss good things that might be happening now; anxiety about the future Other: _____ _____
3. You isolate yourself to avoid possible pain.	Spend more time alone and, as a result, feel even more depressed Other: _____ _____
4. You use alcohol and drugs to numb yourself.	Addiction; loss of money; work problems; legal problems; relationship problems; health consequences Other: _____ _____
5. You take your painful feelings out on others.	Loss of friendships, romantic relationships, and family members; other people avoid you; loneliness; feel bad about hurting other people; legal consequences of your actions Other: _____ _____
6. You engage in dangerous behaviors, like cutting, pulling out hair, and self-mutilation.	Possible death; infection; scarring; disfigurement; shame; physical pain Other: _____ _____

7.	You engage in unsafe sexual activity, like unprotected sex or frequent sex with strangers.	Sexually transmitted diseases, some life threatening; pregnancy; shame; embarrassment Other: _____ _____
8.	You avoid dealing with the causes of your problems.	Put up with destructive relationships; get burned-out doing things for other people; don't get any of your own needs met; depression Other: _____ _____
9.	You eat too much, restrict what you eat, or throw up what you eat.	Weight gain; anorexia; bulimia; health consequences; medical treatment; embarrassment; shame; depression Other: _____
10.	You have attempted suicide or engaged in other nearly fatal activities.	Possible death; hospitalization; embarrassment; shame; depression; long-term medical complications Other: _____ _____
11.	You avoid pleasant activities, like social events and exercise.	Lack of enjoyment; lack of exercise; depression; shame; isolation Other: _____ _____
12.	You surrender to your pain and live an unfulfilling life.	Lots of pain and distress; regrets about your life; depression Other: _____ _____
13.		_____ _____ _____
14.		_____ _____ _____

The costs of these self-destructive coping strategies are clear. All of them lead to your pain being prolonged into long-term suffering. Remember, sometimes pain can't be avoided, but many times suffering can.

Take, for example, an argument between friends Maria and Sandra. For Maria, who doesn't have overwhelming emotions, the argument was initially painful. But after a few hours, she began to realize that she and Sandra were both to blame for the argument. So by the next day, Maria was no longer upset or mad at Sandra. But for Sandra, who struggles with overwhelming emotions, the argument was replayed in her memory over and over again for three days. Each word and gesture was remembered as an insult from Maria. So the next time Sandra saw Maria, three days later, Sandra was still angry and she restarted the argument just where it had ended. Both women experienced the initial pain of the argument, but only Sandra was suffering. Clearly, Sandra carried her emotional pain with her for days, and it made her life more of a struggle. While we can't always control the pain in our lives, we can control the amount of suffering we have in response to that pain.

To avoid this type of long-term suffering, chapters 1 and 2 will teach you *distress tolerance skills*. These skills will help you endure and cope with your pain in a new, healthier way so that it doesn't lead to suffering. The new plan outlined in these two chapters will teach you to "distract, relax, and cope."

ABOUT THIS CHAPTER

The first distress tolerance skills you'll learn in this chapter will help you distract yourself from the situations that are causing you emotional pain. Distraction skills are important because (1) they can temporarily stop you from thinking about your pain and, as a result, (2) they give you time to find an appropriate coping response. Remember how Sandra carried her pain with her for three days? She couldn't stop thinking about her argument with Maria. Distraction can help you let go of the pain by helping you think about something else. Distraction also buys you time so that your emotions can settle down before you take action to deal with a distressing situation.

However, do not confuse distraction with avoidance. When you avoid a distressing situation, you choose not to deal with it. But when you distract yourself from a distressing situation, you still intend to deal with it in the future, when your emotions have calmed down to a tolerable level.

The second group of distress tolerance skills you'll learn in this chapter are self-soothing skills (Johnson, 1985; Linehan, 1993b). It's often necessary to soothe yourself before you face the cause of your distress because your emotions might be too "hot." Many people with overwhelming emotions panic when faced with an argument, rejection, failure, or other painful events. Before you can address these problems with your new emotion regulation skills (chapters 6 and 7) or your new interpersonal effectiveness skills (chapters 8 and 9), it's often necessary to soothe yourself to regain your strength. In situations like these, distress tolerance skills are similar to refilling the gas in your car so that you can keep going. Self-soothing is meant to bring you some amount of peace and relief from your pain so that you can figure out what you're going to do next.

Self-soothing skills also serve another purpose. They'll help you learn to treat yourself compassionately. Many people with overwhelming emotions have been abused or neglected as children. As a result, they were taught more about how to hurt than to help themselves. The second purpose of the self-soothing skills, therefore, is to teach you how to treat yourself kindly and lovingly.

HOW TO USE THIS CHAPTER

As you read the following groups of skills, mark the ones that are helpful to you. This will make it easier to create a distraction plan for emergencies when you get to the end of this chapter. You'll also be shown how to create a list of relaxation skills to help soothe yourself, both at home and when you're away. Then, in the next chapter, you'll learn more advanced distress tolerance skills.

RADICAL ACCEPTANCE

Increasing your ability to tolerate distress starts with a change in your attitude. You're going to need something called *radical acceptance* (Linehan, 1993a). This is a new way of looking at your life. In the next chapter, you'll be given some key questions to help you examine your experiences using radical acceptance. But for now, it will be sufficient to cover this concept briefly.

Often, when a person is in pain, his or her first reaction is to get angry or upset or to blame someone for causing the pain in the first place. But unfortunately, no matter who you blame for your distress, your pain still exists and you continue to suffer. In fact, in some cases, the angrier you get, the worse your pain will feel (Greenwood, Thurston, Rumble, Waters, & Keefe, 2003; Kerns, Rosenberg, & Jacob, 1994).

Getting angry or upset over a situation also stops you from seeing what is really happening. Have you ever heard the expression "being blinded by rage"? This often happens to people with overwhelming emotions. Criticizing yourself all the time or being overly judgmental of a situation is like wearing dark sunglasses indoors. By doing this, you're missing the details and not seeing everything as it really is. By getting angry and thinking that a situation should never have happened, you're missing the point that it *did* happen and that you have to deal with it.

Being overly critical about a situation prevents you from taking steps to change that situation. You can't change the past. And if you spend your time fighting the past—wishfully thinking that your anger will change the outcome of an event that has already happened—you'll become paralyzed and helpless. Then, nothing will improve.

So, to review—being overly judgmental of a situation or overly critical of yourself often leads to more pain, missed details, and paralysis. Obviously, getting angry, upset, or critical doesn't improve a situation. So what else can you do?

The other option, which radical acceptance suggests, is to acknowledge your present situation, whatever it is, without judging the events or criticizing yourself. Instead, try to recognize that your present situation exists because of a long chain of events that began far in the past. For example, some time ago, you (or someone else) thought you needed help for the emotional pain you were experiencing. So, a few days later, you went to the bookstore and bought this book. Then today you thought about reading this chapter, and eventually you sat down, opened the book, and began reading. Now, you are up to the words you see here. Denying this chain of events does nothing to change what has already happened. Trying to fight this moment or say that it shouldn't be only leads to more suffering for you. Radical acceptance means looking at yourself and the situation and seeing it as it really is.

Keep in mind that radical acceptance does *not* mean that you condone or agree with bad behavior in others. But it does mean that you stop trying to change what's happened by getting angry and blaming the situation. For example, if you're in an abusive relationship and you need to get out, then get out. Don't waste your time and continue to suffer by blaming yourself or the other person. That won't help you. Refocus your attention on what you can do now. This will allow you to think more clearly and figure out a better way to cope with your suffering.

Radical Acceptance Coping Statements

To help you begin using radical acceptance, it's often helpful to use a coping statement to remind yourself. Below are a few examples and spaces to create your own. Check (✓) the statements that you would be willing to use to remind yourself that you should accept the present moment and the chain of events that created it. Then, in the next exercise, you'll begin using the statements that you chose.

_____ "This is the way it has to be."

_____ "All the events have led up to now."

✓ "I can't change what's already happened."

_____ "It's no use fighting the past."

_____ "Fighting the past only blinds me to my present."

_____ "The present is the only moment I have control over."

_____ "It's a waste of time to fight what's already occurred."

_____ "The present moment is perfect, even if I don't like what's happening."

_____ "This moment is exactly as it should be, given what's happened before it."

_____ "This moment is the result of over a million other decisions."

_____ Other ideas: _____

_____

Exercise: Radical Acceptance

Now, using the coping statements that you checked, begin radically accepting different moments in your life without judging them. Naturally, it will be difficult to accept very painful situations, so start with smaller events. Here are some suggestions. Check (✓) the ones you're willing to do, and add any of your own ideas. Then use your coping statements to radically accept the situation without being judgmental or critical.

_____ Read a controversial story in the newspaper without being judgmental about what has occurred.

_____ The next time you get caught in heavy traffic, wait without being critical.

_____ Watch the world news on television without being critical of what's happening.

_____ Listen to a news story or a political commentary on the radio without being judgmental.

_____ Review a nonupsetting event that happened in your life many years ago, and use radical acceptance to remember the event without judging it.

_____ Other ideas: _____

_____

DISTRACT YOURSELF FROM SELF-DESTRUCTIVE BEHAVIORS

One of the most important purposes of dialectical behavior therapy is to help you stop engaging in self-destructive behaviors, such as cutting, burning, scratching, and mutilating yourself (Linehan, 1993a). No one can deny the amount of pain you are in when you engage in one of these behaviors. Some people with overwhelming emotions say that self-injury temporarily relieves them of some of the pain they're feeling. This might be true, but it's also true that these actions can cause serious permanent damage and even death if taken to an extreme.

Think about all the pain you've already been through in your life. Think about all the people who have hurt you physically, sexually, emotionally, and verbally. Does it make sense to continue hurting yourself even more in the present? Doesn't it make more sense to start healing yourself and your wounds? If you really want to recover from the pain you've already experienced, stopping these self-destructive behaviors is the first step you should take. This can be very hard to do. You might be addicted to the rush of natural painkillers called *endorphins* that are released when you hurt yourself. However, these types of self-destructive actions are highly dangerous and certainly deserve your best efforts to control them.

Exercise: Distract Yourself from Self-Destructive Behaviors

Here are some safer actions that you can use to distract yourself from your self-destructive emotions and thoughts. Check (✓) the ones you're willing to do, and then add any healthy, nonharming activities that you can think of:

_____ Instead of hurting yourself, hold an ice cube in one hand and squeeze it. The sensation from the cold ice is numbing and very distracting.

_____ Write on yourself with a red felt-tip marker instead of cutting. Draw exactly where you would cut. Use red paint or nail polish to make it look like you're bleeding. Then draw stitches with a black marker. If you need to make it even more distracting, squeeze an ice cube in the other hand at the same time.

_____ Snap a rubber band on your wrist each time you feel like hurting yourself. This is very painful, but it causes less permanent damage than cutting, burning, or mutilating yourself.

_____ Dig your fingernails into your arm without breaking the skin.

_____ Draw faces of people you hate on balloons and then pop them.

_____ Write letters to people you hate or to people who have hurt you. Tell them what they did to you and tell them why you hate them. Then throw the letters away or save them to read later.

_____ Throw foam balls, rolled-up socks, or pillows against the wall as hard as you can.

_____ Scream as loud as you can into a pillow or scream some place where you won't draw the attention of other people, like at a loud concert or in your car.

_____ Stick pins in a voodoo doll instead of hurting yourself. You can make a voodoo doll with some rolled-up socks or a foam ball and some markers. Or you can buy a doll in a store for the specific purpose of sticking pins in it. Buy one that's soft and easy to stick.

_____ Cry. Sometimes people do other things instead of crying because they're afraid that if they start to cry they'll never stop. This never happens. In fact, the truth is that crying can make you feel better because it releases stress hormones.

_____ Other healthy, nonharming ideas: _____

_____

_____

Here's an example of using alternative actions to distract your self-destructive emotions. Lucy often cut herself when she felt upset or angry. She had dozens of scars on her wrists and forearms. She wore long-sleeve shirts even in the hot summer because she was embarrassed when other people saw what she had done to herself. But after getting some ideas from this workbook, she made a distraction plan. So the next time she got angry with herself and felt like cutting, she looked at her plan for alternative actions. She had written down the idea of drawing on herself with a red marker. She drew a line exactly where she would have cut herself. She even used red paint to make it look like she was bleeding. She carried the mark on her arm for the rest of the day to remind herself how sad and overwhelmed she felt. But then, before she went to sleep, she was able to erase the "scar" and "blood" from her arm, unlike the rest of the marks from her permanent injuries.

DISTRACT YOURSELF WITH PLEASURABLE ACTIVITIES

Sometimes doing something that makes you feel good is the best way to distract yourself from painful emotions. But remember, you don't have to wait until you feel overwhelmed by painful emotions in order to do one of these activities. It's also helpful to engage in these types of activities on a regular basis. In fact, you should try to do something pleasurable every day. Exercise is also especially important because not only is it good for your overall physical health but it's also been shown to be an effective treatment for depression in some cases (Babyak et al., 2000). Plus, exercise makes you feel good almost immediately by releasing natural painkillers in your body called *endorphins* (the same painkillers that are released when you cut yourself).

Following is a list of over one hundred pleasurable activities you can use to distract yourself.

THE BIG LIST OF PLEASURABLE ACTIVITIES

Check (✓) the ones you're willing to do, and then add any activities that you can think of:

_____ Talk to a friend on the telephone.

_____ Go out and visit a friend.

_____ Invite a friend to come to your home.

_____ Text message your friends.

_____ Organize a party.

_____ Exercise.

_____ Lift weights.

_____ Do yoga, tai chi, or Pilates, or take classes to learn.

_____ Stretch your muscles.

_____ Go for a long walk in a park or someplace else that's peaceful.

_____ Go outside and watch the clouds.

_____ Go jog.

_____ Ride your bike.

_____ Go for a swim.

_____ Go hiking.

_____ Do something exciting, like surfing, rock climbing, skiing, skydiving, motorcycle riding, or kayaking, or go learn how to do one of these things.

_____ Go to your local playground and join a game being played or watch a game.

_____ Go play something you can do by yourself if no one else is around, like basketball, bowling, handball, miniature golf, billiards, or hitting a tennis ball against the wall.

_____ Get a massage; this can also help soothe your emotions.

_____ Get out of your house, even if you just sit outside.

_____ Go for a drive in your car or go for a ride on public transportation.

_____ Plan a trip to a place you've never been before.

_____ Sleep or take a nap.

_____ Eat chocolate (it's good for you!) or eat something else you really like.

_____ Eat your favorite ice cream.

_____ Cook your favorite dish or meal.

_____ Cook a recipe that you've never tried before.

_____ Take a cooking class.

_____ Go out for something to eat.

_____ Go outside and play with your pet.

_____ Go borrow a friend's dog and take it to the park.

_____ Give your pet a bath.

_____ Go outside and watch the birds and other animals.

_____ Find something funny to do, like reading the Sunday comics.

_____ Watch a funny movie (start collecting funny movies to watch when you're feeling overwhelmed with pain).

_____ Go to the movie theater and watch whatever's playing.

_____ Watch television.

_____ Listen to the radio.

_____ Go to a sporting event, like a baseball or football game.

_____ Play a game with a friend.

_____ Play solitaire.

_____ Play video games.

_____ Go online to chat.

_____ Visit your favorite Web sites.

_____ Visit crazy Web sites and start keeping a list of them.

_____ Create your own Web site.

_____ Create your own online blog.

_____ Join an Internet dating service.

_____ Sell something you don't want on the Internet.

_____ Buy something on the Internet.

_____ Do a puzzle with a lot of pieces.

_____ Call a crisis or suicide hotline and talk to someone.

_____ Go shopping.

_____ Go get a haircut.

_____ Go to a spa.

_____ Go to a library.

_____ Go to a bookstore and read.

_____ Go to your favorite café for coffee or tea.

_____ Visit a museum or local art gallery.

_____ Go to the mall or the park and watch other people; try to imagine what they're thinking.

_____ Pray or meditate.

_____ Go to your church, synagogue, temple, or other place of worship.

_____ Join a group at your place of worship.

_____ Write a letter to God.

_____ Call a family member you haven't spoken to in a long time.

_____ Learn a new language.

_____ Sing or learn how to sing.

_____ Play a musical instrument or learn how to play one.

_____ Write a song.

_____ Listen to some upbeat, happy music (start collecting happy songs for times when you're feeling overwhelmed).

_____ Turn on some loud music and dance in your room.

_____ Memorize lines from your favorite movie, play, or song.

_____ Make a movie or video with your camcorder.

_____ Take photographs.

_____ Join a public-speaking group and write a speech.

_____ Participate in a local theater group.

_____ Sing in a local choir.

_____ Join a club.

_____ Plant a garden.

_____ Work outside.

_____ Knit, crochet, or sew—or learn how to.

_____ Make a scrapbook with pictures.

_____ Paint your nails.

_____ Change your hair color.

_____ Take a bubble bath or shower.

_____ Work on your car, truck, motorcycle, or bicycle.

_____ Sign up for a class that excites you at a local college, adult school, or online.

_____ Read your favorite book, magazine, paper, or poem.

_____ Read a trashy celebrity magazine.

_____ Write a letter to a friend or family member.

_____ Write things you like about yourself on a picture of your body or draw them on a photograph of yourself.

_____ Write a poem, story, movie, or play about your life or someone else's life.

_____ Write in your journal or diary about what happened to you today.

_____ Write a loving letter to yourself when you're feeling good and keep it with you to read when you're feeling upset.

_____ Make a list of ten things you're good at or that you like about yourself when you're feeling good, and keep it with you to read when you're feeling upset.

_____ Draw a picture.

_____ Paint a picture with a brush or your fingers.

_____ Masturbate.

_____ Have sex with someone you care about.

_____ Make a list of the people you admire and want to be like—it can be anyone real or fictional throughout history. Describe what you admire about these people.

_____ Write a story about the craziest, funniest, or sexiest thing that has ever happened to you.

_____ Make a list of ten things you would like to do before you die.

_____ Make a list of ten celebrities you would like to be friends with and describe why.

_____ Make a list of ten celebrities you would like to have sex with and describe why.

_____ Write a letter to someone who has made your life better and tell them why. (You don't have to send the letter if you don't want to.)

_____ Create your own list of pleasurable activities.

_____ Other ideas: _____

_____

_____

Here's an example of using pleasurable activities to distract yourself. Karen was feeling lonely and had nothing to do. As she sat alone at home, she began to think about how lonely she'd been her whole life and how she was hurt by her father when she was growing up. Very quickly, Karen was overwhelmed with very painful emotions. In fact, the memories also triggered physical pain in her shoulder. Karen began to cry and didn't know what to do. Luckily, she remembered the distraction plan she had created. Exercise had always been a powerful tool for Karen, so she went for a long walk in the park while she listened to some of her favorite music. The activity didn't erase her memories or remove her pain completely, but the long walk did soothe her and prevent her from being overwhelmed with sadness.

DISTRACT YOURSELF BY PAYING ATTENTION TO SOMEONE ELSE

Another great way to distract yourself from pain is to put your attention on someone else. Here are some examples. Check (✓) the ones you're willing to do, and then add any activities that you can think of:

_____ *Do something for someone else.* Call your friends and ask if they need help doing something, such as a chore, grocery shopping, or housecleaning. Ask your parents, grandparents, or siblings if you can help them with something. Tell them you're feeling bored and you're looking for something to do. Call up someone you know and offer to take them out to lunch. Go outside and give money to the first needy person you see. If you can plan ahead for moments like these when you're overwhelmed with pain, call your local soup kitchen, homeless shelter, or volunteer organization. Plan to participate in activities that help other people. Join a local political activities group, environmental group, or other organization, and get involved helping other people.

_____ *Take your attention off yourself.* Go to a local store, shopping center, bookstore, or park. Just sit and watch other people or walk around among them. Watch what they do. Observe how they dress. Listen to their conversations. Count the number of buttons they're wearing on their shirts. Observe as many details about these other people as you can. Count the number of people with blue eyes versus the number of people with brown eyes. When your thinking returns to your own pain, refocus on the details of the people you're watching.

_____ *Think of someone you care about.* Keep a picture of them in your wallet or in your purse. This could be your husband, wife, parent, boyfriend, girlfriend, children, or friend, or it could be someone else you admire, such as Mother Teresa, Gandhi, Jesus, the Dalai Lama, Ganesha, and so on. It could even be a movie star, an athlete, or someone you've never met. Then, when you're feeling distressed, take out the picture and imagine a healing, peaceful conversation you would have with that person if you could talk to them at that moment when you're feeling hurt. What would they say to you that would help make you feel better? Imagine them saying those words to you.

_____ . Other ideas: _____

_____

_____

Here's an example of distracting yourself by paying attention to someone else. Louis got upset by a fight he had with his boyfriend, Roger. Very quickly, Louis became overwhelmed by sadness as he started to remember all the other fights he and Roger had had in the past. Louis went to his desk, where he kept a picture of his mother. He sat down and started to talk to his mother as if she were there with him. He asked for strength and guidance to handle the situation with Roger. Then he imagined what she would say to him, and he started to feel better. Later, when he was able to think more clearly, he returned to what he needed to do that day.

DISTRACT YOUR THOUGHTS

The human brain is a wonderful thought-producing machine. It turns out millions of thoughts every day. Most of the time, this makes our lives much easier. But unfortunately, we can't fully control what our brain thinks about. Here's an example. Imagine a picture of your favorite cartoon character, such as Bugs Bunny, Snoopy, Superman, or whomever. Close your eyes and see the character in vivid detail in your mind's eye. Remember exactly what it looks like. Think about the character for about fifteen seconds. Got it? Now, for the next thirty seconds do your best not to think about the character. Try to block the character from your thoughts. But be honest with yourself and notice how often the character pops into your thoughts. It's impossible not to think about the character. In fact, the harder you try not to think about it, the more power you give to the image and the more your brain keeps bringing it into your thoughts. It's almost as if the harder you try to forget something, the harder your brain tries to remember it. This is why forcing yourself to forget about something that happened to you is impossible. It's also why you can't simply force yourself to get rid of emotions that you don't want.

So, instead of trying to force yourself to forget a memory or thought, try to distract your thoughts with other memories or creative images. Here are some examples. Check (✓) the ones you're willing to do, and then add any activities that you can think of:

_____ Remember events from your past that were pleasant, fun, or exciting. Try to remember as many details as possible about these happy memories. What did you do? Who were you with? What happened?

_____ Imagine sexual thoughts that make you excited. Create sexual fantasies involving you and someone you know or someone you would like to know. Try to think of as many details as possible. What happens that's so exciting?

_____ Look outside at the natural world around you. Observe the flowers, trees, sky, and landscape as closely as you can. Observe any animals that are around. Listen to the sounds that they make. Or if you live in a city without much nature around you, either do your best to observe what you can or close your eyes and imagine a scene you've observed in the past.

_____ Imagine yourself as a hero or heroine correcting some past or future event in your life. How would you do it? What would people say to you?

_____ Imagine yourself getting praise from someone whose opinion matters to you. What did you do? What does this person say to you? Why does this person's opinion matter to you?

_____ Imagine your wildest fantasy coming true. What would it be? Who else would be involved? What would you do afterwards?

_____ Keep a copy of your favorite prayer or favorite saying with you. Then, when you feel distressed, pull it out and read it to yourself. Imagine the words calming and soothing you. Use imagery (such as a white light coming down from heaven or the universe) that soothes you as you read the words.

_____ Other ideas: _____

_____

_____

Here's an example of using distracting thoughts. Joel was in a bad relationship that often reminded him of the way he was treated by his mother. She was always criticizing him and telling him he was wrong. When these memories overwhelmed him, Joel never knew what to do. Sometimes he would just scream at his friends or whoever else was around. But after creating a distraction plan, Joel thought of other ideas. The next time he had memories of his mother berating him, he went to his bedroom to lie down. Then he started to imagine himself as a child confronting his mother about her abusive language. He told her all the things he wished he could have said to her years ago. He told her she was wrong and that she should stop criticizing him. Joel controlled the details of the fantasy in the way he wished it could have happened years ago. Afterwards, he slowly felt better. He had escaped the cycle of letting his painful emotions overwhelm him.

DISTRACT YOURSELF BY LEAVING

Sometimes the best thing that you can do is leave. If you're in a very painful situation with someone and you recognize that your emotions are going to overwhelm you and possibly make the situation worse than it is already, then often it's best to just leave. Remember, if you're already overwhelmed by your emotions, it will be harder for you to think of a healthy resolution to your problem. Maybe it's best to put some distance between you and the situation in order to give yourself time to calm your emotions and think of what to do next. Just walk away if that's the best you can do. It will be better than adding fuel to the emotional fire.

Here's an example of leaving to distract yourself. Anna was in a large department store shopping for a blouse. She wanted one of the clerks to help her find her size, but the store clerk was busy with other customers. Anna waited as long as she could and kept trying to get the clerk's attention, but nothing worked. Anna recognized that she was getting angry very quickly. She was ready to tear the blouse in half. She didn't know what else to do. In the past, she would have stayed in the store and gotten angrier, but this time she remembered to leave. She walked out of the store, did some shopping elsewhere, and returned to get the blouse later, when the store was less crowded and when she was feeling more in control of her behaviors.

DISTRACT YOURSELF WITH TASKS AND CHORES

Strangely, many people don't schedule enough time to take care of themselves or their living environments. As a result, tasks and chores go uncompleted. Here, then, is the perfect opportunity to do something to take care of yourself and your environment. The next time you're in a situation in which your emotions become too painful, temporarily distract yourself by engaging in one of the following activities. Check (✓) the ones you're willing to do, and then add any activities that you can think of:

_____ Wash the dishes.

_____ Make phone calls to people you haven't spoken to recently but not someone you're angry with.

_____ Clean your room or house, or go help a friend with their cleaning or gardening project.

_____ Clean out your closet and donate your old clothes.

_____ Redecorate a room or at least the walls.

_____ Organize your books, CDs, computer desktop, and so forth.

_____ Make a plan for getting a job if you don't already have one, or make a plan for finding a better job.

_____ Go get a haircut.

_____ Go get a manicure or pedicure, or both.

_____ Go get a massage.

_____ Wash your or someone else's car.

_____ Mow the lawn.

_____ Clean your garage.

_____ Wash the laundry.

_____ Do your homework.

_____ Do work that you've brought home from your job.

_____ Polish your shoes.

_____ Polish your jewelry.

_____ Clean the bathtub and then take a bath.

_____ Water your plants or work in the garden.

_____ Cook dinner for yourself and some friends.

_____ Pay the bills.

_____ Go to a support meeting, like Narcotics Anonymous, Alcoholics Anonymous, or Overeaters Anonymous.

_____ Other ideas: _____

_____

_____

Here's an example of using tasks and chores to distract yourself. Mike called his girlfriend Michelle to go to a movie. Michelle had already made plans with her friends to do something else. Mike felt incredibly rejected and abandoned. He started yelling at Michelle, who hung up on him. This made Mike feel worse. He didn't know what to do. Quickly, he began to feel light-headed and confused, and his emotions became very angry. But this time, instead of calling Michelle back and arguing, he opened his wallet and pulled out the distraction plan he had made (which you'll also create at the end of this chapter). He had written down "get a haircut," so he walked a half mile to his barber. Getting out of his house helped soothe his anger, and when he returned home, he had cooled down enough to call Michelle back to see if she was busy the next day.

DISTRACT YOURSELF BY COUNTING

Counting is a simple skill that can really keep your mind busy and help you focus on something other than your pain. Here are some examples. Check (✓) the ones you're willing to do, and then add any activities that you can think of:

_____ *Count your breaths.* Sit in a comfortable chair, put one hand on your belly, and take slow, long breaths. Imagine breathing into your stomach instead of your lungs. Feel your belly expand like a balloon with each inhalation. Start counting your breaths. When you inevitably start thinking about whatever it is that's causing you pain, return your focus to counting.

_____ *Count anything else.* If you're too distracted by your emotions, simply count the sounds that you're hearing. This will take your attention outside of yourself. Or try counting the number of cars that are passing by, the number of sensations that you're feeling, or anything else you can put a number on, such as the branches of a tree you're looking at.

Count or subtract by increments of seven. For example, start with one hundred and subtract seven. Now take that answer and subtract seven more. Keep going. This activity will really distract you from your emotions because it requires extra attention and concentration.

_____ Other counting ideas: _____

_____

_____

Here's an example of using counting to distract yourself. Dawn became upset when her mother told her to help set the table for dinner. "She's always telling me what to do," Dawn thought. She could feel her anger getting worse, so she went to her room and remembered that the last time this happened, counting her breaths had helped soothe her emotions. She sat down and did it again. After ten minutes, she felt calmer, so she went back to the dining room.

CREATE YOUR DISTRACTION PLAN

Now identify those distraction skills that you're willing to use the next time you're in a situation that's causing you pain and discomfort. These chosen skills will make up your distraction plan. Remember, these are the first steps you will use in your plan to distract, relax, and cope. Write your chosen distraction techniques below. When you're done, write them down again on a 3 x 5 inch note card or a sticky note to carry around with you in your wallet or purse. Then the next time you're in a distressing situation, you can pull out the card to remind yourself of your distraction plan.

MY DISTRACTION PLAN

1. _____

2. _____

3. _____

4. _____

5. _____

6. _____

7. _____

8. _____

9. _____

10. _____

RELAX AND SOOTHE YOURSELF

Now that you've learned some healthy and effective ways to distract yourself when you become overwhelmed by painful emotions, you'll need to learn new ways to help soothe yourself (Johnson, 1985; Linehan, 1993b). Remember, these next skills will give you the second step in your plan to distract, relax, and cope. The activities in this section will help you relax. Then, later in this book, you'll learn specific skills to cope with problematic situations. These will include emotion regulation skills, mindfulness skills, and interpersonal effectiveness skills.

Learning to relax and soothe yourself is very important for many reasons. When you're relaxed, your body feels better. It also functions in a healthier way. In a state of relaxation, your heart beats more slowly and your blood pressure is reduced. Your body is no longer in a state of constant emergency, preparing to either confront a stressful situation or run away from it. As a result, it's easier for your brain to think of healthier ways to cope with your problems.

Included here are some simple relaxation and soothing activities that utilize your five senses of smell, sight, hearing, taste, and touch. These activities are meant to bring you a small amount of peace in your life. So if one of these activities doesn't help you feel relaxed, or makes you feel worse, don't do it. Try something else. And remember, each one of us is different. For example, some people will become more relaxed by listening to music and others will find that taking a hot bubble bath works for them. As you explore this list, think about what works best for you and be willing to try something new if it sounds exciting.

Self-Soothing Using Your Sense of Smell

Smell is a very powerful sense that can often trigger memories and make you feel a certain way. Therefore, it's very important that you identify smells that make you feel good, not bad. Here are some ideas. Check (✓) the ones you're willing to do, and then add any activities that you can think of:

_____ Burn scented candles or incense in your room or house. Find a scent that's pleasing to you.

_____ Wear scented oils, perfume, or cologne that makes you feel happy, confident, or sexy.

_____ Cut out perfumed cards from magazines and carry them with you in your handbag or wallet.

_____ Go someplace where the scent is pleasing to you, like a bakery or restaurant.

_____ Bake your own food that has a pleasing smell, like chocolate chip cookies.

_____ Lie down in your local park and smell the grass and outdoor smells.

_____ Buy fresh-cut flowers or seek out flowers in your neighborhood.

_____ Hug someone whose smell makes you feel calm.

_____ Other ideas: _____

_____

_____

Self-Soothing Using Your Sense of Vision

Vision is very important to humans. In fact, a large portion of our brain is devoted solely to our sense of sight. The things you look at can often have very powerful effects on you, for better or for worse. That's why it's important to find images that have a very soothing effect on you. And again, for each person, it comes down to individual taste and preference. Here are some ideas. Check (✓) the ones you're willing to do, and then add any activities that you can think of:

_____ Go through magazines and books to cut out pictures that you like. Make a collage of them to hang on your wall or keep some of them with you in your handbag or wallet to look at when you're away from home.

_____ Find a place that's soothing for you to look at, like a park or a museum. Or find a picture of a place that's soothing for you to look at, like the Grand Canyon.

_____ Go to the bookstore and find a collection of photographs or paintings that you find relaxing, such as the nature photographs of Ansel Adams.

_____ Draw or paint your own picture that's pleasing to you.

_____ Carry a picture or photograph of someone you love, someone you find attractive, or someone you admire.

_____ Other ideas: _____

_____

_____

Self-Soothing Using Your Sense of Hearing

Certain sounds can soothe us. Listening to gentle music, for example, may be relaxing. In fact, this entire chapter was written while listening to classical music. However, each one of us has our own tastes. You have to find what works best for you. Use these examples to identify the sounds that help you relax. Check (✓) the ones you're willing to do, and then add any activities that you can think of:

_____ Listen to soothing music. This can be classical, opera, oldies, new age, Motown, jazz, Celtic, African, or anything else that works for you. It might be music with singing or without. Go to a music store that lets you listen to music before you buy it, and listen to a wide variety of genres to determine what helps you relax. If you have a portable radio or an MP3 player, carry it with you to listen to music when you're away from home.

_____ Listen to books on tape or compact discs. Many public libraries will let you borrow books on tape. Take some out to see if it helps you relax. You don't even have to pay attention to the story line. Sometimes just listening to the sound of someone talking can be very relaxing. Again, keep some of these recordings with you in your car or loaded in your portable stereo.

_____ Turn on the television and just listen. Find a show that's boring or sedate, not something like Jerry Springer that's just going to get you angry. Sit in a comfortable chair or lie down, and then close your eyes and just listen. Make sure you turn the volume down to a level that's not too loud. Years ago there was a show on public television featuring a painter named Bob Ross. His voice was so soothing and relaxing that many people reported falling asleep while watching him. Find a show like this that will help you relax.

_____ Listen to a gentle talk show on the radio. Remember—a _gentle_ talk show, not something that's going to make you upset or angry. Stay away from political talk shows and the news. Find something neutral in discussion, like *Car Talk* on National Public Radio or a gardening show. Again, sometimes just listening to someone else talk can be relaxing. Carry a portable radio with you to listen to when you're feeling upset or angry.

_____ Open your window and listen to the peaceful sounds outside. Or, if you live in a place without relaxing sounds outside, go visit a place with relaxing sounds, such as a park.

_____ Listen to a recording of nature sounds, such as birds and other wildlife. You can often buy these in a music store and then take them with you to listen to on your portable compact disc player, cassette player, or MP3 device.

_____ Listen to a white-noise machine. *White noise* is a sound that blocks out other distracting sounds. You can buy a machine that makes white noise with circulating air, or you can turn on a fan to block out distracting sounds. Other white-noise machines have recorded sounds on them, such as the sounds of birds, waterfalls, and rain forests. Many people find these machines very relaxing.

_____ Listen to the sound of a personal water fountain. These small electronic fountains can be bought in most department stores, and many people find the sound of the trickling water in their homes to be very soothing.

_____ Listen to a recording of a relaxation exercise. Exercises such as these will help you imagine yourself relaxing in many different ways. Other recorded exercises can even teach you self-hypnosis techniques to help you relax. Recordings like these can be bought at some bookstores and online at self-help publishers, such as New Harbinger Publications. Go to www.newharbinger.com and look under "Audio Programs." Then you can take the programs with you to listen to when you're feeling overwhelmed.

_____ Listen to the sound of rushing or trickling water. Maybe your local park has a waterfall, or the nearby mall has a fountain. Or maybe just sit in your bathroom with the water running.

_____ Other ideas: _____

_____

_____

Self-Soothing Using Your Sense of Taste

Taste is also a very powerful sense. Our tongue has distinct regions of taste buds on it to differentiate flavors and tastes of food. These sensations can also trigger memories and feelings, so again, it's important that you find the tastes that are pleasing to you. However, if eating is a problem for you, such as eating too much, bingeing, purging, or restricting what you eat, talk to a professional counselor about getting help for yourself. If the process of eating can make you upset or nervous, use your other senses to calm yourself. But if food soothes you, use some of these suggestions. Check (✓) the ones you're willing to do, and then add any activities you can think of:

_____ Enjoy your favorite meal, whatever it is. Eat it slowly so you can enjoy the way it tastes.

_____ Carry lollipops, gum, or other candy with you to eat when you're feeling upset.

_____ Eat a soothing food, like ice cream, chocolate, pudding, or something else that makes you feel good.

_____ Drink something soothing, such as tea, coffee, or hot chocolate. Practice drinking it slowly so you can enjoy the way it tastes.

_____ Suck on an ice cube or an ice pop, especially if you're feeling warm, and enjoy the taste as it melts in your mouth.

_____ Buy a piece of ripe and juicy fresh fruit and then eat it slowly.

_____ Other ideas: _____

_____

_____

Self-Soothing Using Your Sense of Touch

We often forget about our sense of touch, and yet we're always touching something, such as the clothes we're wearing or the chair we're sitting in. Our skin is our largest organ, and it's completely covered with nerves that carry feelings to our brain. Certain tactile sensations can be pleasing, like petting a soft dog, while other sensations are shocking or painful in order to communicate danger, like touching a hot stove. Again, each of us prefers different sensations. You have to find the ones that are most pleasing for you. Here are some suggestions. Check (✓) the ones you're willing to do, and then add any activities that you can think of:

_____ Carry something soft or velvety in your pocket to touch when you need to, like a piece of cloth.

_____ Take a hot or cold shower and enjoy the feelings of the water falling on your skin.

_____ Take a warm bubble bath or a bath with scented oils and enjoy the soothing sensations on your skin.

_____ Get a massage. Many people who have survived physical and sexual abuse do not want to be touched by anyone. This is understandable. But not all types of massage require you to take off your clothes. Some techniques, such as traditional Japanese shiatsu massage, simply require you to wear loose-fitting clothes. A shoulder and neck massage, received while seated in a massage chair, can also be done without removing any clothes. If this is a concern for you, just ask the massage therapist what kind of massage would be best to have while wearing your clothes.

_____ Massage yourself. Sometimes just rubbing your own sore muscles is very pleasing.

_____ Play with your pet. Owning a pet can have many health benefits. Pet owners often have lower blood pressure, lower cholesterol levels, and reduced risk for heart disease (Anderson, Reid, & Jennings, 1992), and they experience other general health improvements (Serpell, 1991). In addition, playing with your pet and stroking the animal's fur or skin can provide you with a soothing tactile experience. If you don't have a pet, consider getting one. Or if you can't afford one, visit a friend who has a pet or volunteer at your local animal shelter where you can play with the rescued animals.

_____ Wear your most comfortable clothes, like your favorite worn-in T-shirt, baggy sweat suit, or old jeans.

_____ Other ideas: _____

_____

_____

CREATE A RELAXATION PLAN

Now that you've read the suggestions to help you relax and soothe yourself using your five senses, construct a list of techniques you're willing to use. For ideas, review the activities that you checked. Be specific about what you're going to do. Make a list of ideas to try at home and a list of ideas you can take with you when you're away from home.

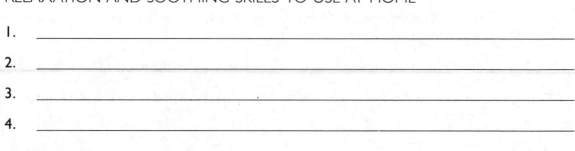

RELAXATION AND SOOTHING SKILLS TO USE AT HOME

1. _____

2. _____

3. _____

4. _____

5. _____

6. _____

7. _____

8. _____

9. _____

10. _____

Keep this list in a convenient place that's easy to remember. You might even want to copy this list and put it in places where you see it all the time, such as on your refrigerator, above your desk, on the mirror in your bathroom, or next to your bed. This way you'll remind yourself to relax and soothe yourself as often as possible. It will also make it easier to soothe yourself when your painful emotions overwhelm you and prevent you from thinking clearly.

Now create a similar list to use when you're away from home. Again, review the soothing skills you checked in the last few pages to give you ideas. But make sure that it's possible to use these skills when you're away from home. For example, don't list "take a hot bath" because, most likely, there won't be a hot bath available to you when you're not at home.

RELAXATION AND SOOTHING SKILLS TO USE AWAY FROM HOME

1. _____

2. _____

3. _____

4. _____

5. _____

6. _____

7. _____

8. _____

9. _____

10. _____

Now copy these last ten ideas on an index card to remind you what to do when you're away from home. Keep this list with you, in your car, in your wallet, or in your handbag. Then make sure you have whatever's needed with you, such as candy, a portable radio, pictures, and so forth. This way you can practice relaxing when you're not at home, especially when your painful emotions overwhelm you and prevent you from thinking clearly.

CONCLUSION

You've now learned some basic distraction and relaxation skills. You should begin using these skills immediately when you become overwhelmed with painful emotions. The next chapter will build on these skills and teach you more advanced distraction and relaxation skills.

CHAPTER 2

Advanced Distress Tolerance Skills:
Improve the Moment

In the last chapter, you learned many important skills that you can use in a crisis. These skills will distract you from painful situations and then help you soothe yourself and relax so that you can deal with the situation in a more effective way. Remember, your plan for handling a crisis is to distract, relax, and cope.

Now that you've been practicing the distress tolerance skills from the last chapter, you'll be ready for the advanced distress tolerance skills found in this chapter. These techniques will help you feel more empowered when you encounter painful situations in the future, and they'll help you build a more relaxing and fulfilling life for yourself.

After trying each technique, mark the ones that are helpful so you can identify them later.

SAFE-PLACE VISUALIZATION

Safe-place visualization is a powerful stress-reduction technique. Using it, you can soothe yourself by imagining a peaceful, safe place where you can relax. The truth is, your brain and body often can't tell the difference between what's really happening to you and what you're just imagining. So if you can successfully create a peaceful, relaxing scene in your thoughts, your body will often respond to those soothing ideas.

Make sure you conduct this exercise in a quiet room where you'll be free from distractions. Turn off your phone, television, and radio. Tell the people in your home, if there are any, that you can't be disturbed for the next twenty minutes. Allow yourself the time and the freedom to relax. You deserve it. Read the following directions before you begin. If you feel comfortable remembering them, close your eyes and begin the visualization exercise. Or, if you would prefer, use an audio-recording device to record the directions for yourself. Read them aloud using a slow, soothing voice. Then close your eyes and listen to the guided visualization you created.

Before you begin the exercise, think of a real or imaginary place that makes you feel safe and relaxed. It can be a real place that you've visited in the past, such as the beach, a park, a field, a church/temple, your room, and so on. Or it can be a place that you've completely made up, such as a white cloud floating in the sky, a medieval castle, or the surface of the moon. It can be anywhere. If you have trouble thinking of a place, think of a color that makes you feel relaxed, such as pink or baby blue. Just do your best. In the exercise, you'll be guided through exploring this place in more detail. But before you begin, make sure you already have a place in mind, and remember—thinking of it should make you feel safe and relaxed.

Complete the following sentences about your safe place before beginning the visualization:

- My safe place is _____

- My safe place makes me feel _____

Instructions

To begin, sit in a comfortable chair with your feet flat on the floor and your hands resting comfortably, either on the arms of the chair or in your lap. Close your eyes. Take a slow, long breath in through your nose. Feel your belly expand like a balloon as you breathe in. Hold it for five seconds: 1, 2, 3, 4, 5. Then release it slowly through your mouth. Feel your belly collapse like a balloon losing its air. Again, take a slow, long breath in through your nose and feel your stomach expand. Hold it for five seconds: 1, 2, 3, 4, 5. Then exhale slowly through your mouth. One more time: take a slow, long breath in through your nose and feel your stomach expand. Hold it for five seconds: 1, 2, 3, 4, 5. Then exhale slowly through your mouth. Now begin to take slow, long breaths without holding them, and continue to breathe smoothly for the rest of this exercise.

Now, with your eyes closed, imagine that you enter your safe place using all of your senses to ground yourself in the scene.

First, look around using your imaginary sense of sight. What does this place look like? Is it daytime or nighttime? Is it sunny or cloudy? Notice the details. Are you alone or are there other people or animals? What are they doing? If you're outside, look up and notice the sky. Look out at the horizon. If you're inside, notice what the walls and the furniture look like. Is the room light or dark? Choose something soothing to look at. Then continue looking for a few seconds using your imaginary sense of sight.

Next, use your imaginary sense of hearing. What do you hear? Do you hear other people or animals? Do you hear music? Do you hear the wind or the ocean? Choose something soothing to hear. Then listen for a few seconds using your imaginary sense of hearing.

Then use your imaginary sense of smell. If you're inside, what does it smell like? Does it smell fresh? Do you have a fire burning that you can smell? Or, if you're outside, can you smell the air, the grass, the ocean, or the flowers? Choose to smell something soothing in your scene. Then take a few seconds to use your imaginary sense of smell.

Next, notice if you can feel anything with your imaginary sense of touch. What are you sitting or standing on in your scene? Can you feel the wind? Can you feel something you're touching in the scene? Choose to touch something soothing in your scene. Then take a few seconds to use your imaginary sense of touch.

Last, use your imaginary sense of taste. Are you eating or drinking anything in this scene? Choose something soothing to taste. Then take a few seconds to use your imaginary sense of taste.

Now take a few more seconds to explore your safe place using all of your imaginary senses. Recognize how safe and relaxed you feel here. Remember that you can come back to this place in your imagination whenever you need to feel safe and relaxed. You can also come back whenever you're feeling sad, angry, restless, or in pain. Look around one last time to remember what it looks like.

Now keep your eyes closed and return your focus to your breathing. Again, take some slow, long breaths in through your nose and exhale through your mouth. Then, when you feel ready, open your eyes and return your focus to the room.

CUE-CONTROLLED RELAXATION

Cue-controlled relaxation is a quick and easy technique that will help you reduce your stress level and muscle tension. A *cue* is a trigger or command that helps you relax. In this case, your cue will be a word, like "relax" or "peace." The goal of this technique is to train your body to release muscle tension when you think about your cue word. Initially, you'll need the help of the guided instructions to help you release muscle tension in different sections of your body. But after you've been practicing this technique for a few weeks, you'll be able to relax your whole body at one time simply by taking a few slow breaths and thinking about your cue word. With practice, this can become a very quick and easy technique to help you relax. Before you begin, choose a cue word that will help you relax.

■　My cue word is _____

To begin this exercise, you'll need to find a comfortable chair to sit in. Later, after you've practiced this exercise for a few weeks, you'll be able to do it wherever you are, even if you're standing. You'll also be able to do it more quickly. But to begin, choose a comfortable place to sit in a room where you won't be disturbed. Make sure you'll be free from distractions. Turn off your phone, television, and radio. Tell the people in your home, if there are any, that you can't be disturbed for the next twenty minutes. Allow yourself the time and the freedom to relax. You deserve it. Read the following directions before you begin. If you feel comfortable remembering them, close your eyes and begin the relaxation exercise. Or, if you would prefer, use an audio-recording device to record the directions for yourself. Then close your eyes and listen to the guided relaxation technique that you created.

Instructions

To begin, sit in a comfortable chair with your feet flat on the floor and your hands resting comfortably, either on the arms of the chair or in your lap. Close your eyes. Take a slow, long breath in through your nose. Feel your belly expand like a balloon as you breathe in. Hold it for five seconds: 1, 2, 3, 4, 5. Then release it slowly through your mouth. Feel your belly collapse like a balloon losing its air. Again, take a slow, long breath in through your nose and feel your stomach expand. Hold it for five seconds: 1, 2, 3, 4, 5. Then exhale slowly through your mouth. One more time: take a slow, long breath in through your nose and feel your stomach expand. Hold it for five seconds: 1, 2, 3, 4, 5. Then exhale slowly through your mouth. Now begin to take slow, long breaths without holding them, and continue to breathe smoothly for the rest of this exercise.

Now, with your eyes still closed, imagine that a white beam of light shines down from the sky like a bright laser and lands on the very top of your head. Notice how warm and soothing the light makes you feel. This could be a light from God, the universe, or whatever power makes you feel comfortable. As you continue to breathe smoothly, taking slow, long breaths, notice how the light makes you feel more and more relaxed as it continues to shine on the top of your head. Now, slowly, the warm, white light begins to spread over the top of your head like soothing water. And as it does, the light begins to loosen any muscle tension that you're feeling on the top of your head. Slowly the light begins to slide down your body, and as it moves across your forehead, all the muscle tension there is released. Then the white light continues down past your ears, the back of your head, your eyes, nose, mouth, and chin, and it continues to release any tension you're holding there. Notice how pleasantly warm your forehead feels. Now, slowly, imagine that the light begins to move down your neck and over your shoulders, releasing any muscle tension. Then the light slowly proceeds down both of your arms and the front and back of your torso. Feel the muscles in your upper and lower back release. Notice the soothing sensation of the white light as it moves across your chest and stomach. Feel the muscles in your arms release as the light moves down to your forearm and then across both sides of your hands to your fingertips. Now notice the light moving down through your pelvis and buttocks and feel the tension being released. Again, feel the light move like soothing water across your upper and lower legs until it spreads across both the upper and lower surfaces of your feet. Feel all of the tension leaving the muscles of your body as the white light makes your body feel warm and relaxed.

Continue to notice how peaceful and calm you feel as you continue to take slow, long, smooth breaths. Observe how your stomach continues to expand as you inhale, and feel it deflate as you exhale. Now, as you continue breathing, silently think to yourself "breathe in" as you inhale, and then silently think your cue word as you exhale. (If your cue word is something other than "relax," use that word in the following instructions.) Slowly inhale and think: "breathe in." Slowly exhale and think: "relax." As you do, notice your entire body feeling relaxed at the same time. Feel all the muscle tension in your body being released as you focus on your cue word. Again, inhale and think: "breathe in." Exhale and think: "relax." Notice your entire body releasing any muscle tension. Again, inhale … "breathe in." Exhale … "relax." Feel all the tension in your body releasing.

Continue breathing and thinking these words at your own pace for several minutes. With each breath, notice how relaxed your entire body feels. When your mind begins to wander, return your focus to the words "breathe in" and "relax."

Practice the cue-controlled relaxation technique twice a day, and record how long it takes you to feel relaxed. With daily practice, this technique should help you relax more quickly each time. Again, remember that the ultimate goal of this technique is to train your entire body to relax simply when you think of your cue word, such as "relax." This will only come with regular practice. Initially, you might also have to think of the white-light imagery and engage in slow, deep breathing to help yourself relax. But with practice this technique can help you relax in many distressing situations. You can also combine this exercise with the previous safe-place visualization. Engaging in cue-controlled relaxation first will help you feel even more safe and calm in that visualization process.

REDISCOVER YOUR VALUES

The word "values" can be defined as your ethics, principles, ideals, standards, or morals. These are literally the ideas, concepts, and actions that fill your life with worth and importance. Remembering what you value in life can be a very powerful way to help you tolerate a stressful situation. It can also be particularly helpful when you find yourself upset over and over again in the same situation or with the same person. Sometimes we forget why we're doing something that's hard, and this makes it difficult for us to continue. Maybe you have a job that you don't like and you wonder why you keep going to work. Perhaps you're going to school, and you don't remember what your goals are. Or maybe you're in a relationship that isn't fulfilling, and you wonder why you keep maintaining that relationship. In cases like these, remembering what you value can help you tolerate stressful situations and also help you create a more fulfilling life for yourself. Use the following exercises to explore what you value in life.

Exercise: Valued Living Questionnaire

This first exercise will ask you to identify how you value ten different components of your life using the Valued Living Questionnaire (Wilson, 2002; Wilson & Murrell, 2004). As you read each component, ask yourself how important each of these areas is to your life—regardless of how much time or effort you now put into fulfilling the needs of that area. For example, maybe you highly value "self-care" regardless of the fact that you devote little time to it. Rate the importance of each component on a scale of 0 to 10, with 0 being not important at all and 10 being extremely important. Do your best to rate them honestly, according to your own true feelings, not to what you think you *should* rate them. You'll then use your responses to the Valued Living Questionnaire in the following exercise, which will help you move toward engaging in what you value.

VALUED LIVING QUESTIONNAIRE
(Wilson, 2002)

Life Component	Not Important at All					Moderately Important				Extremely Important	
Family (other than romantic relationships or parenting)	0	1	2	3	4	5	6	7	8	9	10
Romantic relationships (marriage, life partners, dating, and so on)	0	1	2	3	4	5	6	7	8	9	10
Parenting	0	1	2	3	4	5	6	7	8	9	10
Friends and social life	0	1	2	3	4	5	6	7	8	9	10
Work	0	1	2	3	4	5	6	7	8	9	10
Education and training	0	1	2	3	4	5	6	7	8	9	10
Recreation and fun	0	1	2	3	4	5	6	7	8	9	10
Spirituality and religion	0	1	2	3	4	5	6	7	8	9	10
Citizenship and community life	0	1	2	3	4	5	6	7	8	9	10
Self-care (exercise, diet, relaxation, and so on)	0	1	2	3	4	5	6	7	8	9	10

Exercise: Committed Action

This next exercise will help you create a more fulfilling life for yourself by formulating intentions and committed actions based on your values (Olerud & Wilson, 2002). Maybe you already dedicate a lot of time to the components of your life that you value, or maybe you don't. Either way, this exercise will help you think about ways to make your life feel more fulfilling based on what you think is important.

First, using the Valued Living Questionnaire, identify the components of your life that you rated between 5 and 10, from moderately important to extremely important. Then fill in the names of those areas on the Committed Action Worksheet that follows the questionnaire. (Make additional photocopies of this worksheet if you need more space.)

Next, identify one intention for each of those valued components, which will help make your life feel more fulfilling. For example, if you rated education highly, maybe your intention would be "to go back to school." Or if you rated romantic relationships highly, maybe your intention would be "to spend more time with my spouse or partner."

Then, finally, identify several actions you are willing to commit to doing that will move you toward your intention. Also, note when you're willing to begin that commitment. For example, if your intention is to go back to school, the actions you list might include "getting a catalog of classes next week" and "signing up for a class within the next three weeks." If your intention is to spend more time with your spouse, your committed actions might include "not working overtime for the next month" and "spending less time with friends for the next two weeks."

Again, the purpose of these exercises is to fill your life with activities that are important to you. Creating a life that you value can often help you deal with other situations that are distressing and less desirable. Having a fulfilling life can give you something to look forward to when you're doing something you don't like, and it can make you feel stronger during times of distress.

COMMITTED ACTION WORKSHEET

(Adapted from Olerud & Wilson, 2002)

1. A component of my life that I value is _____

    My intention for this component is _____

    The committed actions that I'm willing to take include the following (be sure to note when you'll begin these actions):

    - ▪ _____

    - ▪ _____

    - ▪ _____

2. A component of my life that I value is _____

    My intention for this component is _____

    The committed actions that I'm willing to take include the following (be sure to note when you'll begin these actions):

    - ▪ _____

    - ▪ _____

    - ▪ _____

3. A component of my life that I value is _____

    My intention for this component is _____

    The committed actions that I'm willing to take include the following (be sure to note when you'll begin these actions):

    - ▪ _____

    - ▪ _____

    - ▪ _____

IDENTIFY YOUR HIGHER POWER
... AND MAKE YOURSELF FEEL MORE *POWERFUL*

Whether you believe in one God, many gods, a divine universe, or the goodness that exists within each human being, having faith in something bigger and more powerful than yourself can often make *you* feel empowered, safe, and calm. This is what people mean when they talk about believing in a "higher power" or seeing "the big picture" in life. Believing in something divine, holy, or special can help you endure stressful situations as well as help you soothe yourself.

At some point in life, we all feel hopeless or powerless. We've all experienced unfortunate situations during which we felt alone and needed strength. Sometimes unexpected circumstances hurt us or the people we care about. These situations often include being the victim of a crime, getting into an accident, having someone close to us die, or being diagnosed with a serious illness. Having faith in something special during times like these can often help you feel connected to a bigger purpose in life. And remember, your faith doesn't have to involve God if that's not what you believe in. Some people only put their faith in the goodness of the people they love. Yet basic beliefs like these are often powerful enough to help people find the strength and comfort to lead happy, healthy lives.

While you're exploring your spirituality, remember that your spiritual beliefs can change over time. Sometimes a person is raised in a spiritual tradition that no longer makes sense or feels helpful. Yet, despite these feelings, a person will sometimes continue to attend the services of that tradition because he or she thinks "it's the right thing to do." The truth is, if your spiritual tradition is no longer giving you peace and strength, it's okay to reexamine that faith and to change traditions if necessary.

Connect to Your Higher Power

Use the following questions to help you identify your beliefs and to identify some ways in which you can strengthen and use your beliefs on a regular basis:

■ What are some of your beliefs about a higher power or a big picture that give you strength and comfort? _____

_____

_____

_____

■ Why are these beliefs important to you? _____

_____

_____

_____

■ How do these beliefs make you feel? _____

_____

_____

_____

■ How do these beliefs make you think about others? _____

_____

_____

_____

■ How do these beliefs make you think about life in general? _____

_____

_____

■ How do you acknowledge your beliefs throughout your daily life? For example, do you go to church, synagogue, or temple? Do you pray? Do you talk to other people about your beliefs? Do you read books about your beliefs? Do you help other people?

_____

_____

■ What else would you be willing to do in order to strengthen your beliefs? _____

_____

_____

_____

■ What can you do to remind yourself of your beliefs on a regular basis? _____

_____

_____

_____

■ What can you say or do to remind yourself of your beliefs the next time you're feeling distressed? _____

_____

_____

_____

Exercise: Higher-Power Activities

Here are some additional activities to help you feel more connected to your higher power, the universe, and the big picture. Check (✓) the ones that you're willing to do:

_____ *If you do believe in the teachings of a particular religion or faith, find related activities that make you feel more empowered and calm.* Go to your church, synagogue, or temple for services. Talk to the man or woman who runs your services. Talk to other members of your faith about how they've handled difficult experiences. Join discussion groups formed at your place of worship. Read the books that are important to your faith. Find passages that give you strength, and mark them or copy them to keep with you in your wallet or purse so you can read them no matter where you are.

_____ *Remember that your higher power can also be something other than God.* Your higher power can be a person who makes you feel stronger and more confident to deal with the challenges that you face. Think of someone you admire who can be your higher power. Describe that person. What makes that person special? Then, the next time you're in a difficult or distressing situation, act as if you are that person, and notice how you handle the situation differently.

_____ *Look up at the stars.* The light you're seeing is millions of years old, and it has traveled from stars that are billions of miles away. In fact, each time you look up at the stars, you're looking through a time machine and seeing the universe as it looked billions of years ago. Strangely, many of the stars you're looking at have already died, but their light is just reaching your eyes on the Earth. Look up at the stars and recognize that whatever created them also created you, whether it was God or a cosmic accident. You are connected to the stars. Imagine yourself connecting with the universe. Sit in a comfortable chair, close your eyes, and imagine a white beam of light shining down from the universe. Like a laser beam, the white light shines on the top of your head and fills you with a feeling of peace. Now imagine the white light spreading all over your body, relaxing every muscle. Now imagine your legs stretching down through the floor like giant tree trunks, going all the way down into the center of the Earth. Imagine these roots tapping into the energy that drives the planet. Feel your body fill with confidence as your legs absorb the golden energy flowing up from the Earth.

_____ *Think about our planet Earth.* Water is the most important substance for sustaining life on our planet. Yet if we were much closer to the sun, all the water on our planet would evaporate because the temperature would be too hot, and if we were much farther away, all the water would freeze because the temperature would be too cold. Somehow, we've been lucky enough to be in just the right place for life to form. Even if you don't believe in a religious purpose, ask yourself what it means that you live on a planet with just the right climate and elements for life to exist. How did this happen, and what does it mean about your life?

_____ *Go to the beach.* Try to count the grains in a handful of sand. Now try to imagine how many handfuls of sand there are in the world, on all the beaches and in all the deserts. Try to imagine how many billions of years must have passed to create so many grains of sand. And again, recognize that the chemical elements that make up the sand also exist in you. Stand with your feet in the sand and imagine feeling connected to the planet.

_____ *Go to a park or to a field and observe the trees, the grass, and the animals.* Again, recognize that whatever created all of that also created you. Remember that all living things are made of the same chemical elements. On a subatomic scale, there isn't much difference between you and many other life forms. Yet you are still different and special. What is it that makes you unique from other life?

_____ *Think about the human body, especially your own.* Each human being is more wonderful than a piece of artwork and more complex than any computer ever invented. Everything about you is largely determined by your *DNA* (deoxyribonucleic acid), the instructions that are found in every cell of your body. Yet amazingly, each set of instructions that creates every part of your body is composed of just four chemical elements that are repeated in different combinations. These different combinations are called *genes*, and these are the instructions you inherit from your parents that determine everything from your eye color to the structure of your heart. Incredibly, it only takes an estimated thirty to forty thousand genes to design a human being. Imagine trying to write so few instructions in order to create a body that thinks, breathes, eats, moves, and does everything else you do. Plus, remember that this same number of instructions is also responsible for creating approximately 100 billion neurons in your brain, 60,000 miles (!) of blood vessels throughout your body, 600 skeletal muscles, 206 bones, 32 teeth, and 11 pints of blood.

TAKE A TIME-OUT

Time-outs aren't just for kids. We all need to relax in order to refresh our bodies, minds, and spirits. Yet many people don't take time out for themselves because they feel like they'd be disappointing someone else, like their boss, spouse, family, or friends. Many people struggle with the constant need to please others, and as a result, they neglect to take care of themselves. But people who don't take care of themselves lead very unbalanced lives. Many people ignore their own needs because they feel guilty or selfish about doing anything for themselves. But how long can you continue to take care of someone else without taking care of yourself? Imagine a woman who stands on a street corner on a hot, summer day holding a jug of cold water. She pours drinks for every pedestrian who walks by and, of course, everyone is grateful. But what happens when she's thirsty and goes to get a drink? After a long day of helping everyone else and neglecting herself, the jug is now empty. How often do you feel like this woman? How often do you run out of time for yourself because you've spent all of it taking care of other people? Helping others is a good thing to do as long as it doesn't come at the expense of sacrificing your own health. You need to take care of yourself, and that doesn't mean you're selfish.

Exercise: Time-Out

Here are some simple ideas you can use to take time out for yourself. Check (✓) the ones you're willing to do.

_____ Treat yourself as kindly as you treat other people. Do one nice thing for yourself that you've been putting off.

_____ Take time to devote to yourself, even if it's just a few hours during the week, by doing things like taking a walk or preparing your favorite meal.

_____ Or if you're feeling really brave, take a half day off from work. Go someplace beautiful, like a park, the ocean, a lake, the mountains, a museum, or even someplace like a shopping center.

_____ Take time to do things for your own life, like shopping, errands, doctor's appointments, and so on.

_____ Other ideas: _____

_____

_____

LIVE IN THE PRESENT MOMENT

Time travel is possible. We all do it occasionally, but some people do it more often than others. People who time travel spend a large portion of each day thinking about all the things they should've done yesterday, all the things that went wrong in the past, and all the things they're supposed to do tomorrow. As a result, that's where they live, in the past or in the future. They rarely pay attention to what's happening to them right now, so they miss living in the present moment—the only true moment in which anyone can really live. For example, notice what's happening to you right now as you read this. Are you thinking of something else? Are you thinking of something that happened in the past or something that's coming up in the future? What does your body feel like right now? Pay attention to it. Do you notice any spots of tension or physical pain? How are you breathing? Are you taking full, deep breaths, or are you breathing very shallowly?

Often, we don't pay attention to what's happening to us. We don't pay attention to what people are saying to us or to the things that we read. We don't even pay attention to who's around us while we're walking. And to make it even more problematic, we often try to do more than one thing at the same time, like driving, eating, and talking on the phone simultaneously. As a result, we miss a lot of what life has to offer and we often make easy situations more difficult.

But even worse, not living in the present moment can also make life more painful. For example, maybe you anticipate that the person with whom you're talking is going to say something insulting, which makes you feel angry—even though the person hasn't even said anything yet! Or maybe just thinking about past events makes you feel physically or emotionally upset, which then interferes with whatever you're trying to do at the moment. Obviously, both types of time traveling can make any event unnecessarily painful.

In chapters 3 through 5 on mindfulness skills, you'll learn advanced skills to help you stay in the moment. But for now, try the following exercises to help you live in the moment and tolerate distressing events more skillfully.

Exercise: "Where Are You Now?"

The next time you're in a distressing situation, ask yourself the following questions:

- Where am I right now?

- Am I time traveling in the future, worrying about something that might happen, or planning something that might happen?

- Am I time traveling in the past, reviewing mistakes, reliving bad experiences, or thinking about how my life could have been under different circumstances?

- Or am I in the present, really paying attention to what I'm doing, thinking, and feeling?

If you're not in the present moment, refocus your attention on what's happening to you now by using the following steps:

- Notice what you're thinking about and recognize if you're time traveling. Bring your focus back to the present moment.

- Notice how you're breathing. Take slow, long breaths to help you refocus on the present.

- Notice how your body feels and observe any tension or pain you might be feeling. Recognize how your thoughts might be contributing to how you're feeling. Use cue-controlled relaxation to release any tension.

- Notice any painful emotions you might be feeling as a result of time traveling, and use one of the distress tolerance skills to help you relieve any immediate pain.

Exercise: Listening to Now

Another exercise to help you refocus on the present moment is the Listening to Now exercise. Dedicate at least five minutes to help yourself refocus.

Instructions

Sit in a comfortable chair. Turn off any distractions, like your phone, radio, and television. Take slow, long breaths, in through your nose and out through your mouth. Feel your stomach expand like a balloon each time you breathe in and feel it deflate each time you exhale. Now, as you continue to breathe, simply listen. Listen to any sounds you hear outside your home, inside your home, and inside your own body. Count each sound that you hear. When you get distracted, return your focus to listening. Maybe you hear cars, people, or airplanes outside. Perhaps you hear a clock ticking or a fan blowing inside. Or maybe you hear the sound of your own heart beating inside your body. Actively and carefully listen to your environment and count as many sounds as you can. Try this exercise for five minutes and notice how you feel afterwards.

A variation of this listening exercise will help you stay focused on the present moment while you're in a conversation with another person. If you notice that your attention is beginning to wander and you start thinking about your past or future, focus your attention on something that the person is wearing, like a button on their shirt, a hat they're wearing, or their collar. Note to yourself what color the item is and what it looks like. Sometimes this can snap you out of your time traveling. Now continue to listen, and if your mind begins to wander again, do the same thing and try to keep listening.

Exercise: Mindful Breathing

Another exercise that will help you stay focused in the present moment is breathing. It sounds simple, but we often don't breathe as well as we should. Think about it: who ever taught you how to breathe? If you're like the rest of us, probably no one. And yet, you do it about fifteen times a minute or almost 22,000 times a day! Everyone knows that we breathe air to take in oxygen. But how much of the air you breathe is actually oxygen—100 percent, 75 percent? The correct answer is that the air you breathe is only about 21 percent oxygen, and when your body doesn't get enough oxygen it can knock your biological system off balance. For this reason alone, taking full, slow breaths is important. But another benefit of breathing fully is that this simple technique can help you relax and focus. Many spiritual traditions combine slow breathing techniques with guided meditations to help people focus and relax.

Here's a breathing exercise that many people find helpful. This type of breathing is also called *diaphragmatic breathing* because it activates the diaphragm muscle at the bottom of your lung cavity. Engaging the diaphragm helps you take fuller, deeper breaths, which also helps you relax.

Read the instructions before beginning the exercise to familiarize yourself with the experience. If you feel more comfortable listening to the instructions, use an audio-recording device to record the directions in a slow, even voice so that you can listen to them while practicing this technique. Set a kitchen timer or an alarm clock for five minutes and practice breathing until the alarm goes off. Then as you get more accustomed to using this technique to help you relax, you can set the alarm for longer periods of time, like ten or fifteen minutes. But don't expect to be able to sit still that long when you first start. In the beginning, five minutes is a long time to sit still and breathe.

When using this new form of breathing, many people often feel as if they become "one" with their breathing, meaning that they feel a deep connection to the experience. If that happens for you, great. If not, that's okay, too. Just keep practicing. Also, some people feel light-headed when they first begin practicing this technique. This may be caused by breathing too fast, too deeply, or too slowly. Don't be alarmed. If you begin to feel light-headed, stop if you need to, or return your breathing to a normal rate and begin counting your breaths.

Instructions

To begin, find a comfortable place to sit in a room where you won't be disturbed for as long as you've set your timer. Turn off any distracting sounds. Take a few slow, long breaths and relax. Place one hand on your stomach. Now slowly breathe in through your nose and then slowly exhale through your mouth. Feel your stomach rise and fall as you breathe. Imagine your belly filling up with air like a balloon as you breathe in, and then feel it deflate as you breathe out. Feel the breath moving in across your nostrils, and then feel your breath blowing out across your lips. As you breathe, notice the sensations in your body. Feel your lungs fill up with air. Notice the weight of your body resting on whatever you're sitting on. With each breath, notice how your body feels more and more relaxed.

Now, as you continue to breathe, begin counting your breaths each time you exhale. You can count either silently to yourself or aloud. Count each exhalation until you reach "4" and then begin counting at "1" again. To begin, breathe in slowly through your nose and then exhale slowly through your mouth. Count "1." Again, breathe in slowly through your nose and slowly out through your mouth. Count "2." Repeat, breathing in slowly through your nose, and then slowly exhale. Count "3." Last time—breathe in through your nose and out through your mouth. Count "4." Now begin counting at "1" again.

When your mind begins to wander and you catch yourself thinking of something else, return your focus to counting your breaths. Try not to criticize yourself for getting distracted. Just keep taking slow breaths into your belly, in and out. Imagine filling up your belly with air like a balloon. Feel it rising with each inhalation and falling with each exhalation. *Keep counting each breath, and with each exhale, feel your body relaxing, deeper and deeper.*

Keep breathing until your alarm goes off, and then slowly return your focus to the room you're in.

USE SELF-ENCOURAGING COPING THOUGHTS

There are many distressing times in life when we all need to hear some encouraging words to keep us motivated or to help us endure the pain that we're experiencing. But there are many distressing times like these when you are also alone, and you need to encourage yourself to stay strong. Often, this can be done with self-encouraging coping thoughts. Coping thoughts are reminders of how strong you've been in the past when you survived distressing situations, and they're also reminders of encouraging words that have given you strength. Coping thoughts are especially helpful when you first notice that you're feeling agitated, nervous, angry, or upset. If you can recognize your distress early on, you'll have a better chance of using one of these thoughts to help soothe yourself. Maybe there are even situations in your life that occur on a regular basis, when you can predict that one of these coping thoughts might be useful.

List of Coping Thoughts

Here is a list of some coping thoughts that many people have found to be helpful (McKay, Davis, & Fanning, 1997). Check (✓) the ones that are helpful to you and create your own.

_____ "This situation won't last forever."

_____ "I've already been through many other painful experiences, and I've survived."

_____ "This too shall pass."

_____ "My feelings make me uncomfortable right now, but I can accept them."

_____ "I can be anxious and still deal with the situation."

_____ "I'm strong enough to handle what's happening to me right now."

_____ "This is an opportunity for me to learn how to cope with my fears."

_____ "I can ride this out and not let it get to me."

_____ "I can take all the time I need right now to let go and relax."

_____ "I've survived other situations like this before, and I'll survive this one too."

_____ "My anxiety/fear/sadness won't kill me; it just doesn't feel good right now."

_____ "These are just my feelings, and eventually they'll go away."

_____ "It's okay to feel sad/anxious/afraid sometimes."

_____ "My thoughts don't control my life, I do."

_____ "I can think different thoughts if I want to."

_____ "I'm not in danger right now."

_____ "So what?"

_____ "This situation sucks, but it's only temporary."

_____ "I'm strong and I can deal with this."

_____ Other ideas: _____

_____

_____

Coping thoughts can help you tolerate distressing situations by giving you strength and motivation to endure those experiences. Now that you know about coping thoughts, you can begin using them immediately. Write your five favorite coping thoughts on an index card or a sticky note and keep it with you in your wallet or purse. Or put your coping thoughts in conspicuous places where you can see them every day, like on your refrigerator or mirror. The more you see your coping thoughts, the more quickly they will become part of your automatic thought process.

Use the following worksheet to record stressful situations in which you use your coping thoughts to give you strength. Make copies of the worksheet, and keep one with you so that you can record the experience as soon as it happens. Recording the experience quickly might be awkward or inconvenient for you, but doing it this way will help you remember to use your self-encouraging coping thoughts more often. Read the example worksheet for ideas about when coping thoughts might be helpful to you.

EXAMPLE: USING COPING THOUGHTS

Distressing Situation	New Coping Thought
1. My boss yelled at me.	"This job stinks, but it's only temporary."
2. The weatherperson on television said that there is a really bad storm approaching that might cause some minor flooding.	"I can keep taking deep breaths and remind myself that this will pass soon. I can cope."
3. I couldn't get my gardening done before my friends came over, and I really wanted them to see how nice my backyard looks.	"It's disappointing, but I can cope. I'll talk about my plans for the backyard."
4. My sister called me "selfish" for not leaving work early to take her shopping.	"She lives in a world of pain herself; that's how she copes with disappointment."
5. I got sad while watching a movie.	"These are just my feelings, and eventually they'll go away. I can use my skills to cope."
6. I heard police sirens coming down the street, and it made me nervous.	"I'm not in danger right now. I'm safe and I'm comfortable behind the closed doors of my house."
7. The store clerk gave me the wrong change, and I have to go back and ask for more money.	"I can deal with this. I can say what I want, and deal with the disappointment if I don't get it."
8. My daughter is leaving for college, and I'm really going to miss her.	"My sadness won't kill me; it just doesn't feel good right now."
9. I get nervous when I don't have anything to keep me busy.	"I can take all the time I need right now to let go and relax."
10. I really hate to fly, but I need to go visit my grandmother in Tulsa.	"This is an opportunity for me to learn how to cope with my fears. I'll use my breathing and visualization skills."

COPING THOUGHTS WORKSHEET

Distressing Situation	New Coping Thought
1.	
2.	
3.	
4.	
5.	
6.	
7.	
8.	
9.	
10.	
11.	

RADICAL ACCEPTANCE

The word *dialectic* (in *dialectical behavior therapy*) means to balance and compare two things that appear very different or even contradictory. In dialectical behavior therapy, the balance is between change and acceptance (Linehan, 1993a). You need to change the behaviors in your life that are creating more suffering for yourself and others while simultaneously also accepting yourself the way you are. This might sound contradictory, but it's a key part of this treatment. Dialectical behavior therapy depends on acceptance *and* change, not acceptance *or* change. Most of this book will focus on skills you can develop to change your life. But this section will focus on how to accept your life. In fact, it will teach you how to *radically* accept your life.

Radical acceptance is one of the hardest skills in this chapter to master because it will require you to look at yourself and the world in a different way. However, it's also one of the most important skills in dialectical behavior therapy (Linehan, 1993a). (You'll be exploring it further in chapters 3 through 5 on mindfulness skills.) *Radical acceptance* means that you accept something completely, without judging it. For example, radically accepting the present moment means that you don't fight it, get angry at it, or try to change it into something that it's not. To radically accept the present moment means that you must acknowledge that the present moment is what it is due to a long chain of events and decisions made by you and other people *in the past*. The present moment never spontaneously leaps into existence without being caused by events that have already taken place. Imagine that each moment of your life is connected like a line of dominoes that knock each other down.

But remember, radically accepting something doesn't mean that you give up and simply accept every bad situation that happens to you. Some situations in life are unjust, such as when someone abuses or assaults you. But for other situations in life, you share at least some responsibility. There's a balance between what you created and what others have created. However, many people struggling with overwhelming emotions often feel like life just "happens" to them, not recognizing their own role in creating a situation. As a result, their first reaction is to get angry. In fact, one woman said that anger was her "default emotion," meaning that when she was just being herself, she was angry. Her excessive hostility caused her to hurt herself—by drinking heavily, cutting herself, and constantly berating herself—and it also led to her hurting the people she cared about by constantly fighting with them.

In contrast, radically accepting the present moment opens up the opportunity for you to recognize the role that you have played in creating your current situation. And as a result, it also creates an opportunity to respond to that situation in a new way that's less painful for yourself and others. In many ways, radical acceptance is like the Serenity Prayer, which says: "Grant me the serenity to accept the things I cannot change, courage to change the things I can, and the wisdom to know the difference." In the exercise below, you will find some questions to ask yourself when you want to use radical acceptance. But first, let's look at an example of how radical acceptance can help a person in a distressing situation.

Example: Using Radical Acceptance

Christine and her boyfriend John had a difficult relationship. John spent a lot of his free time at the bar drinking with his friends, and in response, Christine would get mad, threaten to leave him, and then do something destructive to "piss him off." This occurred regularly for five years. Then one night Christine came home from work angry, and when John wasn't around to talk to, she suddenly felt hopeless about their relationship. So she called John at the bar to tell him that she was going to kill herself because she couldn't put up with his behavior any longer. John raced home to find Christine swallowing a handful of pills, and he made her spit them out. Then he made her promise that she wouldn't do it again. She promised, and then John left, taking the keys to Christine's car so that she couldn't go anywhere. Now Christine got even angrier and called the police to report that her keys had been stolen. Then she walked up to the bar, found John's car, and smashed his windshield with a brick. She would have broken the other windows too, but the police stopped her and arrested her. Needless to say, neither Christine nor John gave any consideration to using radical acceptance in this situation. Both of them were angry at each other, and by acting on their anger, they both ended up hurting themselves and the other person.

So how could this situation have occurred differently if radical acceptance had been used? Let's consider the situation from Christine's point of view. Instead of threatening to kill herself, maybe she could have used one of the distress tolerance skills you learned in the last chapter. Remember your strategy for dealing with distressing situations is to distract, relax, and cope. Maybe Christine could have screamed into a pillow and then gone outside for a long walk. Or maybe she could have called one of her friends to talk for a little while. Then after she'd cooled off a bit, maybe she could have asked herself the following questions and used radical acceptance to reexamine her situation.

- *What events led up to Christine's situation?* She and John had been behaving and fighting like this for years. This night was nothing new. But she had come home angry about work, and she became even angrier with John because he wasn't around.

- *What role did Christine play in creating this situation?* Instead of trying to cope with her anger and frustration in a healthy way, she took her emotions out on herself and John. Also, Christine had had many reasons and opportunities in the past to end this relationship if she wanted to, but she had chosen to stay in this destructive relationship.

- *What role did John play in creating this situation?* John had an alcohol addiction that had been interfering with their relationship for five years. This night, he also didn't take the time to discuss Christine's suicidal behaviors with her. Instead, he chose to return to the bar, which made her even angrier.

- *What does Christine have control of in this situation?* She can end the relationship if she wants to, or she can choose a different way to cope with this distressing situation.

- *What doesn't Christine have control of in this situation?* Ultimately, it is John who has to seek help to stop his alcohol addiction. Christine can't make him stop drinking. She also doesn't have control of how John chooses to behave toward her in this situation.

- *What was Christine's response to this situation?* She tried to kill herself, and then she smashed John's windshield.

- *How did her response affect her own thoughts and feelings?* Her actions made her feel worse about herself and her relationship, and she kept thinking about why she was still in this destructive relationship.

- *How did her response affect the thoughts and feelings of other people?* Christine and John were arrested, which made both of them feel worse than they already did about themselves and their relationship.

- *How could Christine have changed her response to this situation so that it led to less suffering for herself and John?* She could have used other distress tolerance skills to cope with her pain and anger. She could also have used radical acceptance to reevaluate the situation so that she could choose to react in a different way. And perhaps she could even have chosen to leave John that evening, even temporarily, which might have been less painful for the both of them.

- *How could the situation have occurred differently if Christine had decided to radically accept the situation?* If she had used some type of distress tolerance skills that evening, maybe she could have waited until the next morning to talk to John about how angry she felt at work and how upset his drinking made her feel. Or maybe if she had ended the relationship, she could have made space in her life for a healthier relationship or simply spared herself the reoccurring pain of a destructive relationship.

Exercise: Radical Acceptance

Now answer the same questions for yourself. Think of a distressing situation that you experienced recently. Then answer these questions that will help you radically accept the situation in a new way:

- What happened in this distressing situation? _____

_____

_____

■ What past events happened that led up to this situation? _____

_____

_____

■ What role did you play in creating this situation? _____

_____

_____

■ What roles did other people play in creating this situation? _____

_____

_____

■ What *do* you have control of in this situation? _____

_____

_____

■ What *don't* you have control of in this situation? _____

_____

_____

■ What was your response to this situation? _____

_____

_____

■ How did your response affect your own thoughts and feelings? _____

_____

_____

■ How did your response affect the thoughts and feelings of other people? _____

_____

_____

- How could you have changed your response to this situation so that it led to less suffering for yourself and others? _____

_____

_____

- How could the situation have occurred differently if you had decided to radically accept the situation? _____

_____

_____

It's very important to remember that radical acceptance also applies to accepting yourself. In this case, radical acceptance means embracing who you are without judging or criticizing yourself. Or, to put it another way, radically accepting yourself means loving yourself just the way you are, with all of your goodness and all of your faults. Finding the goodness inside of yourself might be a difficult challenge, especially if you're struggling with overwhelming emotions. Many people with this problem often think of themselves as being defective, bad, or unlovable. As a result, they overlook their good qualities and add more pain to their lives. This is why radically accepting yourself is so extremely important.

SELF-AFFIRMING STATEMENTS

To begin building a healthier self-image, many people find it helpful to use self-affirming statements. The purpose of these statements is to remind yourself of the good qualities you possess in order to give you strength and resilience when confronted with distressing situations. This type of statement will remind you that hidden underneath your sometimes overwhelming emotions is a caring, loving person who is capable of handling a distressing situation in a healthier way.

Example: Self-Affirming Statements

Here are some examples of self-affirming statements. Check (✔) the ones you're willing to use, and then create your own:

_____ "I might have some faults, but I'm still a good person."

_____ "I care about myself and other people."

_____ "I accept who I am."

_____ "I love myself."

_____ "I'm a good person, not a mistake."

_____ "I'm good and nobody's perfect."

_____ "I embrace both my good and bad qualities."

_____ "Today I take responsibility for everything I do and say."

_____ "I'm becoming a better person every day."

_____ "I'm a sensitive person who experiences the world differently."

_____ "I'm a sensitive person with rich emotional experiences."

_____ "Each day I do the best I can."

_____ "Even though I forget sometimes, I'm still a good person."

_____ "Even though bad things happened to me in the past, I'm still a good person."

_____ "Even though I've made mistakes in the past, I'm still a good person."

_____ "I'm here for a reason."

_____ "There's a purpose to my life, even though I might not always see it."

_____ "I radically accept myself."

_____ Other ideas: _____

_____

Some people find it helpful to write their self-affirming statements on index cards and then post them throughout their homes. One woman wrote her statement on her bathroom mirror with an erasable marker so it was the first thing she saw in the morning. One man wrote his on a sticky note and kept it posted on his computer as he worked. You can choose to remind yourself of your self-affirming statement in any way that works. But choose a technique that will remind you many times throughout the day. The more often you can see the statement, the more it will help change the way you think about yourself.

CREATE NEW COPING STRATEGIES

Now that you're familiar with all the distress tolerance skills, you can create new coping strategies for your future. The easiest way to do this is to examine some of the distressing situations you've experienced in the past and to identify how you've coped with them. Often, people with overwhelming emotions go through similar distressing situations over and over again. So in some ways these situations are predictable. In this exercise, you'll identify what those past situations were, how you coped with them, and what the unhealthy consequences were. Then you'll identify what new coping strategies you can use in the future if you experience similar situations and what the healthier consequences might be as a result of using those new strategies.

But as you'll notice, you've been given two different New Coping Strategies worksheets. This is because you'll need different coping strategies to use in situations when you're alone or when you're with someone else. For example, when you're alone and feel overwhelmed, it might be most effective to use cue-controlled relaxation or mindful breathing techniques to soothe yourself. But these techniques might be awkward or impossible to use when you're with someone else. So you'll need to be prepared with other skills for those situations.

Here's an example of preparing for both kinds of situations. Carl identified a distressing situation that occurred when he was with someone else. He wrote: "When I'm with my brother, he always corrects everything I do." This is a good situation for Carl to examine because it's predictable that the next time he's with his brother, Carl will experience a similar distressing situation. Next, Carl identified how he usually coped with that situation with his brother, using his old coping strategies. He wrote: "We fight. I eat too much. I scratch myself. I think about all the times he's insulted me in the past." Then Carl recorded the unhealthy consequences of his actions: "We both get angry. I gain weight. I get cuts all over my face and arms. I feel horrible for days thinking about the past." Obviously, none of Carl's strategies has had any long-term benefits. Next, Carl identified new distress tolerance skills he could use the next time this situation arose with his brother. Under "New Coping Strategies," Carl wrote the most appropriate distress tolerance skills for this type of situation. He chose them from the skills he found helpful in the last two chapters. He wrote: "Take a time-out. Use my new coping thought: 'I'm strong and I can deal with him.' Radically accept myself and the situation in a new way." Then he predicted what the healthier possible consequences of these new strategies would be: "We won't fight as much. I won't eat as much. I'll feel stronger. Maybe I can deal with the situation better in the future." Obviously, the consequences of using his new distress tolerance skills would have been much healthier for Carl.

But these coping strategies are probably different from the strategies he might choose when he's in a distressing situation by himself. So Carl also filled out the worksheet for coping with distressing situations when he's alone. The situation he selected was: "Sometimes I feel scared when I'm alone." Again, this is a good situation for Carl to examine because it's predictable that he will experience this same overwhelming feeling the next time he's alone. The old coping strategies that Carl used to deal with this situation were: "I smoke pot. I go to the bar and drink. I cut myself. I spend money on my credit card." And the unhealthy consequences of these actions were: "I feel sick after smoking or drinking too much. I get into fights at the bar. I bleed. I spend too much money for things I don't need." Next, in order to prepare for the future, Carl chose new coping strategies to deal with this situation: "Use mindful breathing. Remember my connection to the universe. Use safe-place visualization. Remember what I value." And finally, the healthier possible consequences that he predicted were: "I won't feel as anxious. I won't hurt myself. I'll have more money. I'll feel more relaxed." Again, it's easy to see that Carl's new distress tolerance skills are much healthier for him than his old coping strategies. The same results can also benefit you if you take the time to prepare for predictable situations in your own future.

CREATE NEW COPING STRATEGIES FOR DISTRESSING SITUATIONS WHEN YOU'RE WITH SOMEONE ELSE

Distressing Situation	Old Coping Strategies	Unhealthy Consequences	New Coping Strategies	Healthier Possible Consequences
Example: When I'm with my brother, he always corrects everything I do.	We fight. I eat too much. I scratch myself. I think about all the times he's insulted me in the past.	We both get angry. I gain weight. I get cuts all over my face and arms. I feel horrible for days thinking about the past.	Take a time-out. Use my new coping thought: "I'm strong and I can deal with him." Radically accept myself and situation in a new way.	We won't fight as much. I won't eat as much. I'll feel stronger. Maybe I can deal with the situation better in the future.
1.				
2.				
3.				
4.				

CREATE NEW COPING STRATEGIES FOR
DISTRESSING SITUATIONS WHEN YOU'RE ALONE

Distressing Situation	Old Coping Strategies	Unhealthy Consequences	New Coping Strategies	Healthier Possible Consequences
Example: Sometimes I feel scared when I'm alone.	I smoke pot. I go to the bar and drink. I cut myself. I spend money on my credit cards.	I feel sick after smoking or drinking too much. I get into fights at the bar. I bleed. I spend too much money for things I don't need.	Use mindful breathing. Remember my connection to the universe. Use safe-place visualization. Remember what I value.	I won't feel as anxious. I won't hurt myself. I'll have more money. I'll feel more relaxed.
1.				
2.				
3.				
4.				

On each worksheet, pick four distressing situations from the past and examine how you coped with them. Identify the unhealthy coping strategies you used and what the consequences were for you and anyone else who was involved. Then record which new distress tolerance skills could have been used to cope with those situations in a healthier way. Review chapters 1 and 2 and pick the distress tolerance skills that you found to be helpful. Consider these to be options for the "New Coping Strategies" column as you're completing the two worksheets. Most importantly, be specific. If you write, "Use a new coping thought," write what that thought is. Or if you write, "Take a time-out," include what you're going to do. Be specific so you don't forget in the future. Finally, record what the healthier consequences would have been if you had used your new distress tolerance skills.

Use the examples provided to guide you, and make photocopies of the worksheets if you need additional space.

CREATE AN EMERGENCY COPING PLAN

Hopefully, you've been practicing the new distress tolerance skills from chapters 1 and 2 and you now have a good idea about which ones work best for you. Or maybe using the New Coping Strategies worksheet in the last section helped you predict which ones are going to work best for you. Now you'll be ready for the next step, which will help you create a personally tailored plan for dealing with some common distressing situations, both when you're with other people and when you're alone.

For situations when you're with other people, list four coping strategies that you think will be the most effective for you. Again, be specific and include as many details about that strategy as you can. Begin with your most effective strategy, then the second most effective strategy, and so on. The plan is that you'll try the first strategy to see if it helps you cope with the distressing situation; then if it doesn't, you'll move on to the next strategy, and so on. Again, refer to any distress tolerance skills you found helpful in chapters 1 and 2, your New Coping Strategies worksheet in the last section, and any experience you have using the distress tolerance skills so far.

MY EMERGENCY COPING PLAN FOR DEALING WITH SITUATIONS

When I'm Upset and Dealing with Other People

First, I'll _____

_____

Next, I'll _____

_____

Then, I'll _____

_____

Finally, I'll _____

_____

MY EMERGENCY COPING PLAN FOR DEALING WITH SITUATIONS

When I'm Upset and Alone

First, I'll _____

_____

Next, I'll _____

_____

Then, I'll _____

_____

Finally, I'll _____

_____

Then, when you've finished making both plans, copy each of them on a single note card and keep the plans with you in your wallet or purse. This strategy will provide you with constant reminders about your new distress tolerance skills, and you'll no longer have to rely on your old, ineffective strategies. Plus you won't have to try to remember what to do the next time you're feeling angry, hurt, or upset. You can simply pull out your card and follow your own Emergency Coping Plan.

CONCLUSION

Remember to practice your new distress tolerance skills as often as possible, and don't get frustrated if you don't get them right on the first try. Learning new skills is hard, and it often feels awkward. But anyone can learn these distress tolerance skills, and they have already helped thousands of people just like you. Good luck.

CHAPTER 3

Basic Mindfulness Skills

An operational working definition of mindfulness is: the awareness that emerges through paying attention on purpose, in the present moment, and nonjudgmentally to the unfolding of experience moment by moment.

—Jon Kabat-Zinn (2003)

MINDFULNESS SKILLS: WHAT ARE THEY?

Mindfulness, also known as meditation, is a valuable skill that has been taught for thousands of years in many of the world's religions, including Christianity (Merton, 1960), Judaism (Pinson, 2004), Buddhism (Rahula, 1974), and Islam (Inayat Khan, 2000). Beginning in the 1980s, Jon Kabat-Zinn began using nonreligious mindfulness skills to help hospital patients cope with chronic pain problems (Kabat-Zinn, 1982; Kabat-Zinn, Lipworth, & Burney, 1985; Kabat-Zinn, Lipworth, Burney, & Sellers, 1987). More recently, similar mindfulness techniques were also integrated into other forms of psychotherapy (Segal, Williams, & Teasdale, 2002), including dialectical behavior therapy (Linehan, 1993a). Studies have shown mindfulness skills to be effective at reducing the odds of having another major depressive episode (Teasdale et al., 2000); reducing symptoms of anxiety (Kabat-Zinn et al., 1992); reducing chronic pain (Kabat-Zinn et al., 1985; Kabat-Zinn et al., 1987); decreasing binge eating (Kristeller & Hallett, 1999); increasing tolerance of distressing situations; increasing relaxation; and increasing skills to cope with difficult situations (Baer, 2003). As a result of findings like these, mindfulness is considered one of the most important *core skills* in dialectical behavior therapy (Linehan, 1993a).

So what exactly is mindfulness? One definition is offered above by mindfulness researcher Jon Kabat-Zinn. But for the purposes of this book, mindfulness is *the ability to be aware of your thoughts, emotions, physical sensations, and actions—in the present moment—without judging or criticizing yourself or your experience.*

Have you ever heard the expressions "be in the moment" or "be here now"? These are both different ways of saying: "be mindful of what's happening to you." But this isn't always an easy task. At any moment in time, you might be thinking, feeling, sensing, and doing many different things. For example, consider what's happening to you right now. You're probably sitting somewhere, reading these words. But at the same time, you're also breathing, listening to the sounds around you, noticing what the book feels like, noticing the weight of your body resting in the chair, and maybe you're even thinking about something else. It's also possible that you're aware of your emotional and physical states of being happy, sad, tired, or excited. Maybe you're even aware of bodily sensations, such as your heart beating or the rising and falling of your chest as you breathe. You might even be doing something that you're completely unaware of, like shaking your leg, humming, or resting your head in your hand. That's a lot to be aware of, and right now, you're just reading a book. Imagine what's happening to you when you're doing other things in your life, like talking with someone or dealing with people at work. The truth is, no one is 100 percent mindful all the time. But the more mindful you learn to be, the more control you will gain over your life.

But remember, time never stands still and each second of your life is different. Because of this, it's important that you learn to be aware "in each present moment." For example, by the time you finish reading this sentence, the moment that you started reading it is gone and your present moment is now different. In fact, *you* are now different. The cells in your body are constantly dying and being replaced, so physically you're different. Equally important, your thoughts, feelings, sensations, and actions are never exactly the same in every situation, so they're different too. For these reasons, it's important that you learn to be mindful of how your experience changes in each individual moment of your life.

And lastly, in order to be fully aware of your experiences in the present moment, it's necessary that you do so without criticizing yourself, your situation, or other people. In dialectical behavior therapy this is called radical acceptance (Linehan, 1993a). As described in chapter 2, radical acceptance means tolerating something without judging it or trying to change it. This is important because if you're judging yourself, your experience, or someone else in the present moment, then you're not really paying attention to what's happening in that moment. For example, many people spend a lot of time worrying about mistakes they've made in the past or worrying about mistakes that they might make in the future. But while they're doing this, their focus is no longer on what's happening to them *now*; their thoughts are somewhere else. As a result, they live in a painful past or future, and life feels very difficult.

So to review, mindfulness is the ability to be aware of your thoughts, emotions, physical sensations, and actions—in the present moment—without judging or criticizing yourself or your experience.

A "MINDLESS" EXERCISE

Obviously, mindfulness is a skill that requires practice. Most people get distracted, "zone out," or spend most of their daily lives being unmindful or running on autopilot. As a result, they then get lost, anxious, and frustrated when a situation doesn't happen as they expect it to. Here are some common ways in which all of us have experienced being unmindful. Check (✓) the ones that you've done:

_____ While driving or traveling, you don't remember the experience or which roads you took.

_____ While having a conversation, you suddenly realize that you don't know what the other person is talking about.

_____ While having a conversation, you're already thinking about what you're going to say next before the other person has even stopped speaking.

_____ While reading, you suddenly realize that you've been thinking about something else and have no idea what you just read.

_____ While walking into a room, you suddenly forget what you came to get.

_____ After putting something down, you can't remember where you just put it.

_____ While taking a shower, you're already planning what you have to do later and then you forget if you've already washed your hair or some other body part.

_____ While having sex, you're thinking about other things or other people.

All of these examples are fairly harmless. But for people with overwhelming emotions, being unmindful can often have a devastating effect on their lives. Consider the example of Lee. Lee thought that everyone at work hated him. One day, a new employee whom Lee found attractive approached him in the cafeteria and asked to sit down. The woman tried to be friendly and make conversation, but Lee was more engaged in the conversation in his own head than he was in the one with the woman.

"She's probably just stuck up like the rest of them," he thought. "Why would someone like her be interested in me anyway? Why would she want to sit with me? It's probably just a joke someone else put her up to." From the moment the woman sat down and tried to talk with him, Lee just became angrier and more suspicious.

The woman did her best to make small talk. She asked Lee how he liked working at the company, how long he'd been there, and she even asked him about the weather, but Lee never noticed. He was so wrapped up in his own conversation, and in paying attention to his own self-critical thoughts, that he never even recognized that the woman was trying to be friendly.

After five minutes of unsuccessfully trying, the woman finally stopped talking to Lee. Then a few minutes later, she moved to a different table, and when she did, Lee congratulated himself. "I knew it," he thought, "I knew she wasn't really interested in me." But at the expense of being right, Lee's unmindfulness and self-criticism had cost him another opportunity to meet a potential friend.

WHY ARE MINDFULNESS SKILLS IMPORTANT?

Now that you have a better idea of what mindfulness is—and isn't—it's probably easy to see why this skill is so important. But for the purposes of this workbook, let's be very clear about why you need to learn mindfulness skills. There are three reasons:

1. Mindfulness skills will help you focus on one thing at a time in the present moment, and by doing this you can better control and soothe your overwhelming emotions.

2. Mindfulness will help you learn to identify and separate judgmental thoughts from your experiences. These judgmental thoughts often fuel your overwhelming emotions.

3. Mindfulness will help you develop a skill that's very important in dialectical behavior therapy called *wise mind* (Linehan, 1993a).

Wise mind is the ability to make healthy decisions about your life based on both your rational thoughts and your emotions. For example, you've probably noticed that it's often difficult—or impossible—to make good decisions when your *emotions* are intense, out of control, or contradict what's rational. Similarly, it's often difficult to make informed decisions when your *thoughts* are intense, irrational, or contradict how you feel. Wise mind is a decision-making process that balances the reasoning of your thoughts with the needs of your emotions, and it is a skill that will be discussed further in chapter 4.

ABOUT THIS CHAPTER

Throughout this chapter and the next, you'll be presented with exercises to help you become more mindful of your moment-to-moment experiences. This chapter will introduce you to beginning mindfulness exercises to help you observe and describe your thoughts and emotions more carefully. In dialectical behavior therapy, these are called "what" skills (Linehan, 1993b), meaning they'll help you become mindful of *what* you're focusing on. Then in the next chapter, you'll be taught more advanced mindfulness skills. In dialectical behavior therapy, these are called "how" skills (Linehan, 1993b), meaning they'll help you learn *how* to be both mindful and nonjudgmental in your daily experiences.

The exercises in this chapter will teach you four "what" skills:

1. To focus more fully on the present moment

2. To recognize and focus on your thoughts, emotions, and physical sensations

3. To focus on your moment-to-moment stream of awareness

4. To separate your thoughts from your emotions and physical sensations

As you read the following exercises, it's important that you practice them in the order in which they're presented. The exercises in this chapter are grouped according to the four "what" skills, and each exercise builds on the previous exercise.

Exercise: Focus on a Single Minute

This is the first exercise that will help you focus more fully on the present moment. It's simple to do, but it often has an amazing effect. Its purpose is to help you become more mindful of your own sense of time. For this exercise, you'll need a watch with a second hand or, preferably, a stopwatch.

Many people feel that time goes by very quickly. As a result, they're always in a rush to do things and they're always thinking about the next thing they have to do or the next thing that could go wrong. Unfortunately, this just makes them more unmindful of what they're doing in the present moment. Other people feel that time goes by very slowly. As a result, they feel like they have more time than they actually do and they frequently find themselves running late. This simple exercise will help you become more mindful of how quickly or slowly time actually does go by.

Instructions

To begin this exercise, find a comfortable place to sit in a room where you won't be disturbed for a few minutes and turn off any distracting sounds. Begin timing yourself with your watch or stopwatch. Then, without counting the seconds or looking at the watch, simply sit wherever you are. When you think that one minute has passed, check the watch again, or stop the timer. Note how much time really has passed.

Did you allow less than a full minute to pass? If so, how long was it—a few seconds, twenty seconds, forty seconds? If it wasn't a full minute, consider how this affects you. Are you always in a rush to do things because you don't think you have enough time? If so, what does the result of this exercise mean for you?

Or did you allow more than a minute to pass? If so, how long was it—one-and-a-half minutes, two minutes? If so, consider how this affects you. Are you frequently late for appointments because you think that you have more time than you really do? If so, what does the result of this exercise mean for you?

Whatever your results were, one of the purposes of learning mindfulness skills is to help you develop a more accurate awareness of all your moment-to-moment experiences, including your perception of time. If you'd like, return to this exercise in a few weeks after you've been practicing your mindfulness skills and see if your perception of time has changed.

Exercise: Focus on a Single Object

Focusing on a single object is the second mindfulness skill that will help you concentrate more fully on the present moment. Remember, one of the biggest traps of being unmindful is that your attention wanders from one thing to the next or from one thought to the next. And as a result, you often get lost, distracted, and frustrated. This exercise will help you focus your attention on a single object. The purpose of this exercise is to help you train your "mental muscle." This means you will learn to maintain your focus on whatever it is you're observing. And with practice, you'll get better at focusing your attention, just like an athlete who exercises certain muscles to become stronger.

During this exercise, you will eventually become distracted by your thoughts, memories, or other sensations. That's okay; this happens to everyone who does this exercise. Do your best not to criticize yourself or stop the exercise. Just notice when your mind wanders and return your focus to whatever object you're observing.

Pick a small object to focus on. Choose something that can rest on a table, is safe to touch, and is emotionally neutral. It can be anything, such as a pen, a flower, a watch, a ring, a cup, or something similar. Don't choose to focus on something that could hurt you or on a picture of someone you don't like. These will stir up too many emotions for you right now.

Find a comfortable place to sit in a room where you won't be disturbed for a few minutes, and put the object on a table in front of you. Turn off any distracting sounds. If you have a stopwatch or an alarm clock, set the timer for five minutes. Do this exercise once or twice a day for two weeks, choosing a different object to focus on each time.

You can photocopy the instructions if you want extra copies to refer to, or you can record the instructions in a slow, even voice on an audio-recording device and play them while you're exploring the object.

Instructions

To begin, sit comfortably and take a few slow, deep breaths. Then, without touching the object, begin looking at it and exploring its different surfaces with your eyes. Take your time exploring what it looks like. Then try to imagine the different qualities that the object possesses.

- *What does the surface of the object look like?*

- *Is it shiny or dull?*

- *Does it look smooth or rough?*

- *Does it look soft or hard?*

- *Does it have multiple colors or just one color?*

- *What else is unique about the way the object looks?*

Take your time observing the object. Now hold the object in your hand or reach out and touch the object. Begin noticing the different ways it feels.

- *Is it smooth or is it rough?*

- *Does it have ridges or is it flat?*

- *Is it soft or is it hard?*

- *Is it bendable or is it rigid?*

- *Does the object have areas that feel different from each other?*

- *What does the temperature of the object feel like?*

- *If you can hold it in your hand, notice how much it weighs.*

- *What else do you notice about the way it feels?*

Continue exploring the object with both your sight and your sense of touch. Continue to breathe comfortably. When your attention begins to wander, return your focus to the object. Keep on exploring the object until your alarm goes off or until you have fully explored all the qualities of the object.

Exercise: Band of Light

This is the third exercise that will help you focus more fully on the present moment. It will help you become more mindful of the physical sensations in your body. Read the instructions before beginning the exercise to familiarize yourself with the process. Then you can either keep these instructions near you if you need to refer to them while you're doing the exercise, or you can record them in a slow, even voice on an audio-recording device and play them while you're observing the sensations in your body.

As with the other exercises in this chapter, most likely your focus will begin to wander while you're doing this exercise. That's okay. When you recognize that your focus is drifting, gently return your attention to the exercise and do your best not to criticize or judge yourself.

Instructions

To begin, find a comfortable place to sit in a room where you won't be disturbed for ten minutes. Turn off any distracting sounds. Take a few slow, long breaths and then close your eyes. Using your imagination, envision a narrow band of white light circling the top of your head like a halo. As this exercise progresses, the band of light will slowly move down your body, and as it does, you will become aware of the different physical sensations you're feeling beneath the band of light.

As you continue to breathe with your eyes closed, continue to see the band of white light encircling the top of your head and notice any physical sensations you feel on that part of your body. Perhaps you will notice your scalp tingling or itching. Whatever sensations you notice are okay.

- Slowly the band of light begins to descend around your head, passing over the tops of your ears, your eyes, and the top of your nose. As it does, become aware of any sensations you feel there, even small sensations.

- Notice any muscle tension you may be feeling on the top of your head.

- As the band of light slowly descends over your nose, mouth, and chin, continue to focus on any physical sensations you might be feeling there.

- Pay attention to the back of your head where you may be having sensations.

- Notice any sensations you may be feeling in your mouth, on your tongue, or on your teeth.

- Continue to watch the band of light in your imagination descend around your neck, and notice any feelings in your throat or any muscle tension on the back of your neck.

- Now the band widens and begins to move down your torso, across the width of your shoulders.

- Notice any sensations, muscle tension, or tingling you might be feeling in your shoulders, upper back, upper arms, and upper chest area.

- As the band of light continues to descend down around your arms, notice any feelings you're aware of in your upper arms, elbows, forearms, wrists, hands, and fingers. Become aware of any tingling, itching, or tension you might be holding in those places.

- Now become aware of your chest, the middle of your back, the side of your torso, your lower back, and stomach. Again, notice any tension or sensations, no matter how small they might be.

- As the band continues to move down your lower body, become aware of any sensations in your pelvic region, buttocks, and upper legs.

- Be sure to pay attention to the backs of your legs and notice any feelings there.

- Continue to watch the band of light descend around your lower legs, around your calves, shins, feet, and toes. Notice any feelings or tension you're experiencing.

Then as the band of light disappears after completing its descent, take a few more slow, long breaths, and when you feel comfortable, slowly open your eyes and return your focus to the room.

Exercise: Inner-Outer Experience

Now that you've practiced being mindful of both an object outside of yourself and your internal physical sensations, the next step is to combine the two experiences. This is the first exercise that will teach you how to recognize and focus on your thoughts, emotions, and physical sensations. This will be done by teaching you to shift your attention back and forth in a mindful, focused way between what you are experiencing internally, such as your physical sensations and thoughts, and what you are experiencing externally, such as what you notice using your eyes, ears, nose, and sense of touch.

Read the instructions before beginning the exercise to familiarize yourself with the experience. Then you can either keep these instructions near you if you need to refer to them while you're doing the exercise, or you can record them in a slow, even voice on an audio-recording device so that you can listen to them while you practice shifting your focus between your internal and external awareness.

Instructions

To begin, find a comfortable place to sit in a room where you won't be disturbed for ten minutes. Turn off any distracting sounds. Take a few slow, long breaths and relax.

Now, keeping your eyes open, focus your attention on an object in the room. Notice what the object looks like. Notice its shape and color. Imagine what that object would feel like if you could hold it. Imagine what the object must weigh. Describe the object silently to yourself, being as descriptive as possible. Take a minute to do this. Keep breathing. If your focus begins to drift, simply return your attention to the exercise without criticizing yourself. [Pause here for one minute if you are recording the instructions.]

When you have finished describing the object, return your focus to your body. Notice any physical sensations that you might be experiencing. Scan your body from your head to your feet. Notice any muscle tension you might be holding, any tingling you might be experiencing, or any other sensations of which you are aware. Take a minute to do this, and keep breathing slow, deep breaths. [Pause here for one minute if you are recording the instructions.]

Now redirect your attention to your sense of hearing. Notice any sounds that you can hear. Notice sounds you hear coming from outside your room and note to yourself what they are. Now become aware of any sounds you hear coming from inside the room and note to yourself what they are. Try to notice even small sounds, such as the ticking of a clock, the sound of the wind, or the beating of your heart. If you become distracted by any thoughts, return your focus to your sense of hearing. Take a minute to do this, and keep breathing. [Pause here for one minute if you are recording the instructions.]

When you have finished listening to the sounds that you can notice, return your focus to your body. Again, notice any physical sensations. Become aware of the weight of your body resting in the chair. Notice the weight of your feet resting on the floor. Notice the weight of your head resting on top of your neck. Notice in general how your body feels. If you become distracted by your thoughts, just notice what they are and refocus your attention as best you can on your physical sensations. Take a minute to do this, and keep breathing slow, deep breaths. [Pause here for one minute if you are recording the instructions.]

Once again, redirect your attention. This time, put your focus on your sense of smell. Notice any smells that are in the room, pleasant or otherwise. If you don't notice any smells, just become aware of the flow of air moving into your nostrils as you breathe in through your nose. Try your best to maintain your focus on your sense of smell. If you become distracted by any thoughts, return your focus to your nose. Take a minute to do this, and keep breathing. [Pause here for one minute if you are recording the instructions.]

When you have finished using your sense of smell, once again return your focus to your physical sensations. Notice any sensations that you might be feeling. Once again, scan your body from your head to your feet and become aware of any muscle tension, tingling, or other physical feelings. If your thoughts distract you, do your best to return your focus to your physical sensations. Take a minute to do this, and keep breathing slow, deep breaths. [Pause here for one minute if you are recording the instructions.]

Now, finally, redirect your attention to your sense of touch. Reach out with one of your hands to touch an object that is within reach. Or, if there is no object within reach, touch the chair you're sitting on or touch your leg. Notice what the object feels like. Notice if it's smooth or rough. Notice if it's pliable or rigid. Notice if it's soft or solid. Notice what the sensations feel like on the skin of your fingertips. If your thoughts begin to distract you, simply return your focus to the object that you're touching. Take a minute to do this, and keep breathing slow, deep breaths. [Pause here for one minute if you are recording the instructions.]

When you've finished, take three to five slow, long breaths and return your focus to the room.

Exercise: Record Three Minutes of Thoughts

This is the second exercise that will help you recognize and focus on your thoughts, emotions, and physical sensations. In this exercise, you will identify the number of thoughts you have in a three-minute period. This will allow you to become more mindful of just how quickly your mind really works. This exercise will also help you prepare for the next exercise, Thought Defusion.

The instructions for this exercise are simple: set a timer for three minutes and begin writing down every thought you have on a piece of paper. But don't try to record the thought word for word. Just write down a word or two that represents the thought. For example, if you were thinking about a project you have to complete at work by next week, simply write "project" or "work project." Then record your next thought.

See how many of your thoughts you can catch in three minutes, no matter how small the thoughts are. Even if you start thinking about this exercise, write "exercise." Or if you start thinking about the paper you're writing on, write "paper." No one else ever has to see this record, so be honest with yourself.

When you've finished, count the number of thoughts you had in three minutes and multiply that number by twenty to get an idea of how many thoughts you might have in an hour.

Exercise: Thought Defusion

This is the third exercise that will help you recognize and focus on your thoughts, emotions, and physical sensations. *Thought defusion* is a technique borrowed from acceptance and commitment therapy (Hayes, Strosahl, & Wilson, 1999), which has proven to be a very successful treatment for emotional distress.

When distressing thoughts keep repeating, it's often easy to get "hooked" on them, like a fish biting on a bait hook (Chodron, 2003). In contrast, thought defusion will help you mindfully observe your thoughts without getting stuck on them. With practice, this skill will give you more freedom to choose which thoughts you want to focus on and which thoughts you want to let go of instead of getting stuck on all of them.

Thought defusion requires the use of your imagination. The object of this skill is to visualize your thoughts, either as pictures or words, harmlessly floating away from you without obsessing about them or analyzing them. Whichever way you choose to do this is okay. Here are some suggestions that other people have found helpful:

- Imagine sitting in a field watching your thoughts float away on clouds.

- Picture yourself sitting near a stream watching your thoughts float past on leaves.

- See your thoughts written in the sand and then watch the waves wash them away.

- Envision yourself driving a car and see your thoughts pass by on billboards.

- See your thoughts leave your head and watch them sizzle in the flame of a candle.

- Imagine sitting beside a tree and watch your thoughts float down on leaves.

- Picture yourself standing in a room with two doors; then watch your thoughts enter through one door and leave through the other.

If one of these ideas works for you, that's great. If not, feel free to create your own. Just be sure that your idea captures the purpose of this exercise, which is to visually watch your thoughts come and go without holding on to them and without analyzing them. Remember to use the concept of radical acceptance while doing this exercise. Let your thoughts be whatever they are and don't get distracted fighting them or criticizing yourself for having them. Just let the thoughts come and go.

Read the instructions before beginning the exercise to familiarize yourself with the experience. If you feel more comfortable listening to the instructions, use an audio-recording device to record the instructions in a slow, even voice so you can listen to them while practicing this technique. When you are first using thought defusion, set a kitchen timer or an alarm clock for three to five minutes and practice letting go of your thoughts until the alarm goes off. Then as you get more accustomed to using this technique, you can set the alarm for longer periods of time, like eight or ten minutes. But don't expect to be able to sit still that long when you first start. In the beginning, three to five minutes is a long time to use thought defusion.

Instructions

To begin, find a comfortable place to sit in a room where you won't be disturbed for as long as you've set your timer. Turn off any distracting sounds. Take a few slow, long breaths, relax, and close your eyes.

Now, in your imagination, picture yourself in the scenario that you chose, watching your thoughts come and go, whether it's by the beach, near a stream, in a field, in a room, or wherever. Do your best to imagine yourself in that scene. After you do, start to become aware of the thoughts that you're having. Start to observe the thoughts that are coming up, whatever they are. Don't try to stop your thoughts, and do your best not to criticize yourself for any of the thoughts. Just watch the thoughts arise, and then, using whatever technique you've chosen, watch the thoughts disappear. Whatever the thought is, big or small, important or unimportant, watch the thought arise in your mind and then let it float away or disappear by whichever means you've chosen.

Just continue to watch the thoughts arise and disappear. Use pictures to represent the thoughts or words, whatever works best for you. Do your best to watch the thoughts arise and disappear without getting hooked into them and without criticizing yourself.

If more than one thought comes up at the same time, see them both arise and disappear. If the thoughts come very quickly, do your best to watch them all disappear without getting hooked on any of them. Continue to breathe and watch the thoughts come and go until your timer goes off.

When you've finished, take a few more slow, long breaths and then slowly open your eyes and return your focus to the room.

Exercise: Describe Your Emotion

This is the fourth exercise that will help you recognize and focus on your thoughts, emotions, and physical sensations. So far, the exercises in this chapter have helped you learn to be more mindful of your physical sensations and thoughts. This next exercise will help you become more mindful of your emotions. As with some of the other exercises, the instructions for this exercise might sound simple, but the results can be powerful. This exercise will ask you to choose an emotion and then to describe that emotion by drawing it and exploring it.

So, to begin, pick an emotion. It can be either a pleasant or an unpleasant emotion. Ideally, you should choose an emotion that you're feeling right now, *unless that emotion is overwhelmingly sad or self-destructive.* If it is, you should wait until you feel more in control of your emotions before beginning this exercise. On the other hand, if you can't identify what you're feeling now, choose an emotion that you were feeling recently, something that you can easily remember. But, whichever you choose, try to be specific about what the emotion is. For example, if you got into a fight with your spouse or partner recently because he or she did something to you, that's the situation, not the emotion. Maybe this situation made you feel angry, hurt, sad, stupid, or something else. Be specific about how you feel. Here's another example. Maybe someone recently gave you a gift. That's the situation. Your emotion would depend on how you felt about the gift. If it was something you've always wanted, you might feel elated. If the gift came from someone you don't know very well, you might feel anxious about its purpose. Be specific about how you feel.

To help you choose an emotion, use this list of some commonly felt emotions.

LIST OF COMMONLY FELT EMOTIONS

Adored	Empty	Irritated
Afraid	Energetic	Jealous
Angry	Enlightened	Joyful
Annoyed	Enlivened	Lively
Anxious	Enraged	Lonely
Apologetic	Enthusiastic	Loved
Ashamed	Envious	Loving
Blessed	Excited	Mad
Blissful	Exhausted	Nervous
Bored	Flirtatious	Obsessed
Bothered	Foolish	Pleased
Broken	Fragile	Proud
Bubbly	Frightened	Regretful
Cautious	Frustrated	Relieved
Cheerful	Glad	Respected
Confident	Guilty	Restless
Content	Happy	Sad
Curious	Hopeful	Satisfied
Delighted	Hopeless	Scared
Depressed	Horrified	Scattered
Determined	Hurt	Secure
Disappointed	Hysterical	Shy
Disgusted	Indifferent	Smart
Disturbed	Infatuated	Sorry
Embarrassed	Interested	Strong

Surprised	Tired	Vulnerable
Suspicious	Unsure	Worried
Terrified	Upset	Worthless
Thrilled	Vivacious	Worthy

When you finish identifying the emotion you want to explore, write it down at the top of the Describe Your Emotion form (on the next page) or use a blank piece of paper.

Then, using your imagination, draw a picture of what your emotion might look like. This might sound hard to do, but just do the best you can. For example, if you are feeling happy, maybe a picture of the sun expresses how you feel or maybe a picture of an ice-cream cone would do better. The picture doesn't have to make sense to anyone else but you. Just give it a try.

Next, try to think of a sound that would further describe the emotion. For example, if you are feeling sad, maybe the sound of a groan would describe how you feel, such as "ugh." Or maybe a certain song expresses your emotion better. Describe the sound as best you can, and write it near your drawing.

Then describe an action that "fits" your emotion. For example, if you are feeling bored, maybe the action would be to take a nap. Or if you are feeling shy, maybe the action would be to run away and hide. Do your best to describe the action, and write it near your drawing.

The next step of this exercise is to describe the intensity of the emotion on which you're focusing. This will require some thought. Do your best to describe the strength of this emotion. Feel free to be creative and use metaphors if you need to. For example, if you are feeling very nervous, you might write that the feeling is so strong that your "heart feels like a drum at a rock concert." Or if you are only feeling a little angry, you might write that the intensity is like a "mosquito bite."

After describing the intensity of the emotion, briefly describe the overall quality of what the emotion feels like. Again, feel free to be as creative as you need to be in your description. If you are nervous, maybe it makes you feel like your "knees are made of jelly." Or if you are getting angry, it might make you feel like "water that's about to boil." Be as accurate as you can in your description and be as creative as you need to be in order to convey your feelings.

Finally, add any thoughts that arise due to your emotion. But be clear that what you describe is a thought and not another emotion. For example, don't choose any of the words in the list above to describe your thoughts. Those are emotions, not thoughts. Your thoughts should be able to finish the following sentences: "My emotion makes me think that..." or "My emotion makes me think about..." It's important that you begin separating your thoughts and your emotions because this will give you better control over both of them in the future. Here are some examples of thoughts that can arise from emotions. If you are feeling confident, a related thought might be that you think you can ask your boss for a raise, or it makes you remember other times in your life when you felt confident and were successful. Or if you are feeling fragile, a related thought could be that you think you can't handle any more stress in your life, or it makes you think about how you're going to struggle with future problems if you don't get stronger.

DESCRIBE YOUR EMOTION

Name the emotion: _____

Draw a picture of your emotion

Describe a related action: _____

_____

Describe a related sound: _____

_____

Describe the intensity of the emotion: _____

_____

Describe the quality of the emotion: _____

_____

Describe thoughts related to the emotion: _____

_____

Exercise: Focus Shifting

This next exercise will teach you the third "what" skill, which is learning to identify what you are focusing on in your moment-to-moment stream of awareness. Now that you've practiced being mindful of both your emotions and your sense experiences (seeing, hearing, touching), it's time to put the two experiences together. This exercise is similar to the Inner-Outer Experience exercise because it will also help you shift your attention back and forth in a mindful, focused way. However, this Focus Shifting exercise will address the shift between your emotions and your senses and help you differentiate between the two.

At some point in our lives, we all get caught in our emotions. For example, when someone says something insulting to you, maybe you feel upset all day, think poorly of yourself, get angry at someone else, or look at the world in a much gloomier way. This "emotional trap" is a common experience for everyone. But for someone struggling with overwhelming emotions, these experiences happen more frequently and intensely. Mindfulness skills will help you separate your present-moment experience from what's happening inside you emotionally, thereby giving you a choice as to which one you'll focus on.

Before starting this exercise, you'll also need to identify how you are currently feeling. If you need to refer to the list of emotions in the previous exercise, go ahead. Do your best to be as accurate as possible about how you feel. Even if you think that you're not feeling anything, you probably are. A person is never completely without emotion. Maybe you're just feeling bored or content. Do your best to identify what it is.

Read the instructions before beginning this exercise to familiarize yourself with the experience. Then you can either keep these instructions near you if you need to refer to them while you're doing the exercise, or you can record them in a slow, even voice on an audio-recording device so that you can listen to them while you practice shifting your focus between your emotions and your senses.

If you need to, set a timer for five to ten minutes for this exercise.

Instructions

To begin, find a comfortable place to sit in a room where you won't be disturbed for ten minutes. Turn off any distracting sounds. Take a few slow, long breaths, and relax.

Now close your eyes and focus your attention on how you are feeling. Name the emotion silently to yourself. Use your imagination to envision what your emotion might look like if it had a shape. The image doesn't have to make sense to anyone but you. Just allow your imagination to give your emotion a form or shape. Take a minute to do this, and keep breathing slow breaths. [Pause here for one minute if you are recording the instructions.]

Now open your eyes and put your focus on an object in the room where you're sitting. Notice what the object looks like. Notice its shape and color. Imagine what that object might feel like if you could hold it. *Imagine what the object must weigh. Describe the object silently to yourself, being as descriptive as possible. Take a minute to do this. Keep breathing. If your focus begins to drift, simply return your attention to the exercise without criticizing yourself.* [Pause here for one minute if you are recording the instructions.]

When you've finished describing the object, close your eyes and return your focus to your emotion. Think of a sound that might be related to your emotion. The sound can be anything that you think describes your emotion. It can be a noise, a song, or whatever. When you're done describing the sound to yourself, think of an action related to your emotion. Again, it can be anything that further enhances your understanding of your emotion. Take a minute to do this, and keep breathing slow, deep breaths. [Pause here for one minute if you are recording the instructions.]

Now, keeping your eyes closed, redirect your attention to your sense of hearing. Notice any sounds that you can hear. Notice sounds you hear coming from outside your room and note to yourself what they are. Now become aware of any sounds you hear coming from inside the room and note to yourself what they are. Try to notice even small sounds, such as the ticking of a clock, the sound of the wind, or the beating of your heart. If you become distracted by any thoughts, return your focus to your sense of hearing. Take a minute to do this, and keep breathing. [Pause here for one minute if you are recording the instructions.]

When you have finished listening to the sounds that you can notice, return your focus to your emotion. Keeping your eyes closed, silently describe the intensity and quality of your emotion to yourself. Again, feel free to be creative and use comparisons if you need to. Take a minute to do this, and keep breathing slow, deep breaths. [Pause here for one minute if you are recording the instructions.]

Once again, redirect your attention. This time, put your focus on your sense of smell. Notice any smells that are in the room, pleasant or otherwise. If you don't notice any smells, just become aware of the flow of air moving into your nostrils as you breathe in through your nose. Try your best to maintain your focus on your sense of smell. If you become distracted by any thoughts, return your focus to your nose. Take a minute to do this, and keep breathing. [Pause here for one minute if you are recording the instructions.]

When you have finished using your sense of smell, once again return your focus to your emotions. Notice any thoughts you might be having that are related to your emotion. Be as specific about the thought as you can, and make sure your thought isn't really another emotion. Take a minute to do this, and keep breathing slow, deep breaths. [Pause here for one minute if you are recording the instructions.]

Now, finally, redirect your attention to your sense of touch. Reach out with one of your hands to touch an object that is within reach. Or if there is no object within reach, touch the chair you're sitting in or touch your leg. Notice what the object feels like. Notice if it's smooth or rough. Notice if it's pliable or rigid. Notice if it's soft or solid. Notice what the sensations feel like on the skin of your fingertips. If your thoughts begin to distract you, simply return your focus to the object that you're touching. Take a minute to do this, and keep breathing slow, deep breaths. [Pause here for one minute if you are recording the instructions.]

When you've finished, take three to five slow, long breaths and return your focus to the room.

Exercise: Mindful Breathing

This Mindful Breathing exercise will help you learn the fourth "what" skill, which is learning to separate your thoughts from your emotions and physical sensations. (You already learned the basics of mindful breathing in chapter 2, Advanced Distress Tolerance Skills, but this exercise will give you an additional understanding of the skill.) Very often, when you're distracted by your thoughts and other stimuli, one of the easiest and most effective things you can do is to focus your attention on the rising and falling of your breath. This type of breathing also causes you to take fuller, deeper breaths, which can help you relax.

In order to breathe mindfully, you need to focus on three parts of the experience. First, you must count your breaths. This will help you focus your attention, and it will also help you calm your mind when you're distracted by thoughts. Second, you need to focus on the physical experience of breathing. This is accomplished by observing the rising and falling of your chest and stomach as you inhale and exhale. And third, you need to be aware of any distracting thoughts that arise while you're breathing. Then you need to let the thoughts go without getting stuck on them, as in the previous Thought Defusion exercise. Letting go of the distracting thoughts will allow you to refocus your attention on your breathing and help you further calm yourself.

Read the instructions before beginning the exercise to familiarize yourself with the experience. If you feel more comfortable listening to the instructions, use an audio-recording device to record the directions in a slow, even voice so that you can listen to them while practicing this technique. When you first start this technique, set a timer or an alarm clock for three to five minutes, and practice breathing until the alarm goes off. Then as you get more accustomed to using this technique to help you relax, you can set the alarm for longer periods of time, like ten or fifteen minutes. But don't expect to be able to sit still that long when you first start. In the beginning, three to five minutes is a long time to focus and breathe. Later, when you become more accustomed to using this style of breathing, you can also begin using it while you're doing other daily activities, like walking, doing the dishes, watching television, or having a conversation.

When using mindful breathing, many people feel as if they become "one" with their breathing, meaning that they feel a deep connection to the experience. If that happens for you, that's great. If not, that's okay, too. Just keep practicing. Also, some people feel light-headed when they first begin practicing this technique. This may be caused by breathing too fast, too deeply, or too slowly. Don't be alarmed. If you begin to feel light-headed, stop if you need to, or return your breathing to a normal rate and begin counting your breaths.

This is such a simple and powerful skill that, ideally, you should practice it every day.

Instructions

To begin, find a comfortable place to sit in a room where you won't be disturbed for as long as you've set your timer. Turn off any distracting sounds. If you feel comfortable closing your eyes, do so to help you relax.

To begin, take a few slow, long breaths, and relax. Place one hand on your stomach. Now slowly breathe in through your nose and then slowly exhale through your mouth. Feel your stomach rise and fall as you breathe. Imagine your belly filling up with air like a balloon as you breathe in, and then feel it deflate as you breathe out. Feel the breath moving in across your nostrils, and then feel your breath blowing out across your lips. As you breathe, notice the sensations in your body. Feel your lungs fill up with air. Notice the weight of your body resting on whatever you're sitting on. With each breath, notice how your body feels more and more relaxed.

Now, as you continue to breathe, begin counting your breaths each time you exhale. You can count either silently to yourself or aloud. Count each exhalation until you reach "4" and then begin counting at "1" again. To begin, breathe in slowly through your nose, and then exhale slowly through your mouth. Count "1." Again, breathe in slowly through your nose and slowly out through your mouth. Count "2." Repeat, breathing in slowly through your nose, and then slowly exhale. Count "3." Last time—breathe in through your nose and out through your mouth. Count "4." Now begin counting at "1" again.

This time, though, as you continue to count, occasionally shift your focus to how you're breathing. Notice the rising and falling of your chest and stomach as you inhale and exhale. Again, feel the breath moving in through your nose and slowly out through your mouth. If you want to, place one hand on your stomach and feel your breath rise and fall. Continue counting as you take slow, long breaths. Feel your stomach expand like a balloon as you breathe in, and then feel it deflate as you breathe out. Continue to shift your focus back and forth between counting and the physical experience of breathing.

Now, lastly, begin to notice any thoughts or other distractions that remove your focus from your breathing. These distractions might be memories, sounds, physical sensations, or emotions. When your mind begins to wander and you catch yourself thinking of something else, return your focus to counting your breath. Or return your focus to the physical sensation of breathing. Try not to criticize yourself for getting distracted. Just keep taking slow, long breaths into your belly, in and out. Imagine filling up your belly with air like a balloon. Feel it rising with each inhalation and falling with each exhalation. Keep counting each breath, and with each exhalation, feel your body relaxing, more and more deeply.

Keep breathing until your alarm goes off. Continue counting your breaths, noticing the physical sensation of your breathing and letting go of any distracting thoughts or other stimuli. Then, when your alarm goes off, slowly open your eyes and return your focus to the room.

Exercise: Mindful Awareness of Emotions

This is the second exercise that will help you learn to separate your thoughts, emotions, and physical sensations. Mindful awareness of your emotions starts with focusing on your breathing—just noticing the air moving in through your nose and out through your mouth, filling and emptying your lungs. Then, after four or five slow, long breaths, shift your attention to how you feel emotionally in the present moment. Start by simply noticing if you feel good or bad. Is your basic internal sense that you are happy or not happy?

Then see if you can observe your emotion more closely. What word best describes the feeling? Consult the list of emotions from the Describe Your Emotion exercise if you're having trouble finding the most accurate description. Keep watching the feeling, and while you do, continue describing to yourself what you observe. Notice the nuances of the feeling or perhaps the threads of other emotions woven into it. For example, sometimes sadness has veins of anxiety or even anger. Sometimes shame is intertwined with loss or resentment. Also notice the strength of your emotion and check to see how it changes while you watch it.

Emotions invariably come as a wave. They escalate, then they reach a crest, and finally they diminish. You can observe this, describing to yourself each point in the wave as the feeling grows and passes.

If you have difficulty finding an emotion that you're feeling in the present moment, you can still do this exercise by locating a feeling that you had in the recent past. Think back to a situation during the last several weeks when you had a strong emotion. Visualize the event—where you were, what was happening, what you said, how you felt. Keep recalling details of the scene until the emotion you had *then* is being felt again by you *right now*.

However you choose to observe an emotion, once the emotion is clearly recognized, stay with it. Keep describing to yourself the changes in quality, intensity, or type of emotion you are feeling.

Ideally, you should observe the feeling until it has significantly changed—in quality or strength—and you have some sense of the wave effect of your emotion. While watching your feeling, you'll also notice thoughts, sensations, and other distractions that try to pull your attention away. This is normal. Just do your best to bring your focus back to your emotion whenever your attention wanders. Just stay with it until you've watched long enough to observe your emotion grow, change, and diminish.

As you learn to mindfully observe a feeling, two important realizations can emerge. One is the awareness that all feelings have a natural life span. If you keep watching your emotions, they will peak and gradually subside. The second awareness is that the mere act of describing your feelings can give you a degree of control over them. Describing your emotions often has the effect of building a container around them, which keeps them from overwhelming you.

Read the instructions before beginning the exercise to familiarize yourself with the experience. If you feel more comfortable listening to the instructions, use an audio-recording device to record the directions in a slow, even voice so that you can listen to them while practicing this technique. If you record the directions, pause between each paragraph so you can leave time to fully experience the process.

Instructions

Take a long, slow breath and notice the feeling of the air moving in through your nose, going down the back of your throat, and into your lungs. Take another breath and watch what happens in your body as you inhale and let go. Keep breathing and watching. Keep noticing the sensations in your body as you breathe. [Pause here for one minute if you are recording the instructions.]

Now turn your attention to what you feel emotionally. Look inside and find the emotion you are experiencing right now. Or find an emotion that you felt recently. Notice whether the emotion is a good or a bad feeling. Notice whether it is pleasant or unpleasant. Just keep your attention on the feeling until you have a sense of it. [Pause here for one minute if you are recording the instructions.]

Now look for words to describe the emotion. For example, is it elation, contentment, or excitement? Or is it sadness, anxiety, shame, or loss? Whatever it is, keep watching and describing the emotion in your mind. Notice any change in the feeling and describe what's different. If any distractions or thoughts come to mind, do your best to let them go without getting stuck on them. Notice if your feeling is intensifying or diminishing, and describe what that's like. [Pause here for one minute if you are recording the instructions.]

Keep observing your emotion and letting go of distractions. Keep looking for words to describe the slightest change in the quality or intensity of your feeling. If other emotions begin to weave in, continue to describe them. If your emotion changes into an altogether new emotion, just keep observing it and finding the words to describe it. [Pause here for one minute if you are recording the instructions.]

Thoughts, physical sensations, and other distractions will try to grab your attention. Notice them, let them go, and return your focus to your emotion. Stay with it. Continue observing it. Keep going until you've observed your emotion change or diminish.

CONCLUSION

You've now learned some basic mindfulness skills. Hopefully, you have a better understanding of how your mind works and why these skills are important to learn. You should continue using them on a daily basis. In the next chapter, you will build on these skills and learn more advanced mindfulness skills.

CHAPTER 4

Advanced Mindfulness Skills

In the previous chapter, you learned what mindfulness is and you also learned the basic "what" skills of dialectical behavior therapy. This means that you learned to become more mindful of *what* you are focusing on by using these methods:

■ Focusing more fully on the present moment

■ Recognizing and focusing on your thoughts, emotions, and physical sensations

■ Focusing on your moment-to-moment stream of awareness

■ Separating your thoughts from your emotions and physical sensations

---

WHAT YOU'LL LEARN IN THIS CHAPTER

Now, in this chapter, you'll be introduced to the more advanced "how" skills of mindfulness (Linehan, 1993a). These skills will help you learn *how* to be both mindful and nonjudgmental in your daily experiences. In this chapter, you will learn five "how" skills:

1. How to use wise mind

2. How to use radical acceptance to acknowledge your daily experiences without judging them

3. How to do what's effective

4. How to create a mindfulness regimen for yourself in order to live your life in a more aware, focused way

5. How to overcome the hindrances of your mindfulness practice

As in the last chapter, it is important that you do the exercises in this chapter in the order that they're presented. Each of these exercises builds on the one before it.

WISE MIND

As stated in the last chapter, wise mind is the ability to make healthy decisions about your life based on both your rational thoughts and your emotions. This sounds easy to do, but let's consider the traps that many people often fall into.

For example, Leo was a successful salesman with a new company. He had a happy family and a fairly good future ahead of himself. However, Leo frequently became upset when he couldn't close a deal, and so he often felt depressed and thought of himself as a person who would never be able to fully succeed in his life. Despite the positive feedback he received from his supervisors, Leo couldn't shake the feelings of failure that came from deals he couldn't close. As a result, a few months after starting his job, Leo quit, just like he had quit similar jobs in the past. He went on to take a new job, but similar feelings of failure followed him wherever he went, and he never felt fully satisfied with himself.

Similarly, Takeesha was a popular college professor who always received high ratings from her students and other faculty members. But after a few unsuccessful personal relationships, Takeesha felt very lonely. She eventually stopped trying to meet new people because she anticipated that those relationships would just end in failure too. As a result, she felt unworthy of anyone's love and resigned herself to spend the rest of her life living alone.

Unfortunately, both Leo and Takeesha were overcome by what dialectical behavior therapy calls *emotion mind* (Linehan, 1993a). Emotion mind occurs when you make judgments or decisions based solely on how you feel. But keep in mind that emotions themselves are not bad or problematic. We all need emotions to live healthy lives. (You'll learn more about the role of emotions in chapters 6 and 7.) The problems associated with emotion mind develop when your emotions *control* your life. This trap is especially dangerous for people with overwhelming emotions because emotion mind distorts your thoughts and judgments and then these distortions make it hard to formulate healthy decisions about your life. Consider what happened to Leo and Takeesha: despite their successes, their emotions overwhelmed their lives and led them to make unhealthy decisions.

The balancing counterpart to emotion mind is *reasonable mind* (Linehan, 1993a). Reasonable mind is the part of your decision-making process that analyses the facts of a situation, thinks clearly about what is happening, considers the details, and then makes rational decisions. Obviously, rational thinking helps us solve problems and make decisions every day. But again, as with emotions, too much rational thinking can also be a problem. We all know the story of the very intelligent person who didn't know how to express his or her emotions and, as a result, lived a very lonely life. So here too a balance is needed in order to live a fulfilling, healthy life. But for people with overwhelming emotions, balancing feelings and rational thought is often hard to do.

The solution is to use wise mind to make healthy decisions about your life. Wise mind results from using both emotion mind and reasonable mind together (Linehan, 1993a). Wise mind is a balance between feelings and rational thoughts. Again, let's consider the examples of Leo and Takeesha. Both of them were being controlled by their emotion minds. If Leo had been making decisions with wise mind, before quitting his job he would have balanced his decision with reasonable mind. He should have reminded himself of the facts of the situation: he was already a successful salesman, and he only became upset when he couldn't close a deal. Therefore, was it reasonable that he should quit? Definitely not. What about Takeesha? She received great feedback from both her students and fellow faculty members. So was it reasonable to stop meeting new people after a few failed relationships? Definitely not. This is why using wise mind is so important.

You can develop wise mind by using the mindfulness skills you have already been practicing in chapter 3. Remember that part of what these exercises did was to help you recognize and separate your thoughts from your emotions. So you've already been using both your emotion mind and reasonable mind. And by practicing those mindfulness skills even more, it will become easier to make healthy decisions based on a balance of what your emotions and your rational thoughts tell you.

WISE MIND AND INTUITION

According to dialectical behavior therapy, wise mind is similar to intuition (Linehan, 1993b). Often, both intuition and wise mind are described as "feelings" that come from "the gut" or the stomach area. The exercise that follows will help you get more in touch with your gut feelings, both physically and mentally. This exercise will help you locate the center of wise mind in your body. This is the spot from which many people report making sensible, wise-mind decisions about their lives.

Interestingly, this phenomenon of gut feelings might be supported by scientific evidence. Researchers have discovered that a vast web of nerves covers the area of the stomach. This web of nerves is second in complexity only to the human brain, so some researchers have referred to this area as the *enteric brain*, meaning the brain in the stomach.

Exercise: Wise-Mind Meditation

When you begin using this technique, set a kitchen timer or an alarm clock for three to five minutes and practice this exercise until the alarm goes off. Then, as you get more accustomed to using this technique, you can set the alarm for longer periods of time, like ten or fifteen minutes. If you feel more comfortable listening to the instructions, use an audio-recording device to record the directions in a slow, even voice so that you can listen to them while practicing this technique.

Instructions

To begin, find a comfortable place to sit in a room where you won't be disturbed for as long as you've set your timer. Turn off any distracting sounds. If you feel comfortable closing your eyes, do so to help you relax.

Now locate the bottom of your sternum on your rib cage. You can do this by touching the bone at the center of your chest and then following it down toward your abdomen until the bone ends. Now place one hand on your abdomen between the bottom of your sternum and your belly button. This is the center of wise mind.

Take a few slow, long breaths and relax. Now slowly breathe in through your nose and then slowly exhale through your mouth. Feel your abdomen rise and fall as you breathe. Imagine your belly filling up with air like a balloon as you breathe in, and then feel it deflate as you breathe out. Feel the breath moving in across your nostrils and then feel your breath blowing out across your lips. As you breathe, notice any sensations in your body. Feel your lungs fill up with air. Notice the weight of your body as it rests on the seat in which you're sitting. With each breath, notice how your body feels, and allow your body to become more and more relaxed.

Now, as you continue to breathe, let your attention focus on the spot underneath your hand. Let your attention focus on the center of wise mind. Continue to take slow, long breaths. If you have any distracting thoughts, just allow those thoughts to leave you without fighting them and without getting stuck on them. Continue to breathe and focus on the center of wise mind. Feel your hand resting on your stomach.

As you focus your attention on your center of wise mind, notice what appears. If you've had any troubling thoughts, problems, or decisions that you have to make in your life, think about them for a few seconds. Then ask your center of wise mind what you should do about these problems or decisions. Ask your inner intuitive self for guidance, and then notice what thoughts or solutions arise out of your center of wise mind. Don't judge whatever answers you receive. Just note them to yourself and keep breathing. Continue to focus your attention on your center of wise mind. If no thoughts or answers come to your questions, just continue breathing.

Now continue to notice your breath rising and falling. Keep breathing and returning your focus to the center of wise mind until the timer goes off. Then when you've finished, slowly open your eyes and return your focus to the room.

HOW TO MAKE WISE-MIND DECISIONS

Now that you've had practice locating your wise-mind center, you can "check in" with that area of your body before you make decisions. This can help you determine if a decision is a good one. To do this, simply think about the action you are about to take and focus your attention on your center of wise mind. Then consider what your wise mind tells you. Does your decision feel like a good one? If so, then maybe you should do it. If it doesn't feel like a good decision, then maybe you should consider some other options.

Learning to make reliably good decisions about your life is a process that evolves as long as you are alive, and there is no single way to do this. Checking in with your center of wise mind is simply *one* way that often works for some people. However, some words of caution are needed here. When you first use wise mind to make decisions about your life, it will probably be difficult to tell the difference between an intuitive gut feeling and a decision made the old way with emotion mind. The difference can be determined in three ways:

1. *When you made your decision were you being mindful of both your emotions and the facts of the situation?* In other words, did you make the decision based on both emotion mind and reasonable mind? If you haven't considered the facts of the situation and are being controlled by your emotions, you're not using wise mind. Sometimes we need to let our emotions settle and "cool off" before we can make a good decision. If you've recently been involved in a very emotional situation, either good or bad, give yourself enough time for your hot emotions to cool down so that you can use reasonable mind.

2. *Did the decision "feel" right to you?* Before you make a decision, check in with your center of wise mind and notice how it feels. If you check in with your center of wise mind and you feel nervous, maybe the decision you're about to make isn't a good one or a safe one. However, maybe you feel nervous because you're excited about doing something new, which can be a good thing. Sometimes it's hard to tell the difference, and that's why using reasonable mind to make your decision is also important. Later, when you have more experience making healthy decisions for your life, it will be easier to tell the difference between a good nervous feeling and a bad nervous feeling.

3. *You can sometimes tell if you've used wise mind by examining the results of your decision.* If your decision leads to beneficial results for your life, chances are you used wise mind to make that decision. When you start using wise mind, keep track of your decisions and the results in order to determine if you're *really* using wise mind. Remember, wise mind should help you make healthy decisions about your life.

RADICAL ACCEPTANCE

Another very important part of wise mind, and mindfulness in general, is a skill called radical acceptance (Linehan, 1993a). (You already explored radical acceptance in chapter 2, Advanced Distress Tolerance Skills, but the following description will help you understand how it relates to mindfulness skills.) Radical acceptance means tolerating something without judging it or trying to change it. Remember the definition of mindfulness that we gave you in the last chapter? Mindfulness is the ability to be aware of your thoughts, emotions, physical sensations, and actions—in the present moment—*without judging or criticizing yourself or your experience*. Radical acceptance is a very important piece of being mindful because if you're judging yourself, your experience, or someone else in the present moment, then you're not really paying attention to what's happening in that moment. In many ways, judgment is the royal road to suffering, because when you judge others you get angry and when you judge yourself you get depressed. So in order to be truly mindful in the present moment, and in order to be fully centered in wise mind, you must practice being nonjudgmental.

Radical acceptance might sound like a difficult skill to master, but it's definitely worth the effort. Consider this example. Thomas struggled with a problem that's very common for people with overwhelming emotions. He divided everyone and everything into two categories: they were either all good or all bad. There was no in-between for him. When people treated him nicely, they were good, but when someone disagreed with him, he considered them to be bad, even if the person had just been on his good side a few minutes before. This quick fluctuation between good and bad led Thomas to make a lot of judgments and critical remarks about himself and others. Over the years, the accumulation of fluctuations and judgments made Thomas very sensitive to situations that could go wrong. He always expected that other people would make mistakes, insult him, or betray him in some way. One time his sister said that she couldn't help him take his car to the repair shop, and Thomas blew up at her. He criticized her for being ungrateful and selfish. However, the truth was that she had to take her own daughter to the doctor, but Thomas never heard her reasoning. He was too wrapped up in his own judgmental thinking to really listen to anyone else. In truth, Thomas had created a pattern in his life where all of his judgments and critical thinking became realities, and this led to a very lonely and distressing life.

When Thomas was finally introduced to the skill of radical acceptance, he was critical of it too. "This is ridiculous," he thought, "This stupid idea isn't going to help me. I don't need this. How can anyone not be critical?" But with the urging of his family, Thomas decided to try using radical acceptance. At first, it was very difficult for him to not make judgments about himself and other people, but he continued using the exercises in this workbook, and, with practice, radical acceptance became easier. Slowly his thinking began to change. Thomas spent less time obsessing over judgmental thoughts and critical remarks, and he spent less time anticipating that other people would insult or betray him. He also no longer thought of people as either just good or bad. He began to recognize that everyone makes mistakes, and that's okay. He also became more mindful of his thoughts, feelings, sensations, and actions in the present moment, which helped him focus better on his daily experiences and make healthier choices for his life.

As you can see from this example, one of the hardest parts of using radical acceptance is recognizing when you're being judgmental of yourself or others. This takes practice, and the skills in the workbook will help. But recognizing when you're being judgmental also takes time. You're going to make mistakes. When you're first learning to be nonjudgmental, there will be times when you *will* be judgmental. Then you'll recognize what you're doing, and you'll be further critical of yourself for being judgmental. But that's okay too. That's part of the learning process. Learning how to use radical acceptance is a lot like the story of a man who's walking down a city street and falls through an open manhole to the sewer. He climbs out, looks in the hole, and says, "I better not do that again." But the next day, walking down the same street, he steps into the same open manhole, climbs out, and says, "I can't believe I did it again." Then on the third day, he's about to step into the same open manhole when he suddenly remembers what happened on the two previous days, so he avoids the fall. On the fourth day, the man remembers to walk around the open manhole as soon as he starts walking down that street. And on the fifth day, he chooses to walk down a different street in order to avoid the problem completely. Obviously, learning how to use radical acceptance will take you longer than five days, but the process of falling into the same judgmental traps will happen in a very similar way.

Below are several exercises to help you develop a nonjudgmental attitude and to use the skill of radical acceptance. But before you start, let's clarify radical acceptance a little more, because it can often be a confusing concept for many people. To use radical acceptance *does not* mean that you silently put up with potentially harmful or dangerous situations in your life. For example, if you are in a violent or abusive relationship and you need to get out, then get out. Don't put yourself in harm's way and simply tolerate whatever happens to you. Radical acceptance is a skill that is supposed to help you live a healthier life; it is not a tool to fill your life with more suffering.

However, there's no doubt that it will be tough to start using radical acceptance because it will require you to think about yourself, your life, and other people in a new way. But once you start using radical acceptance, you'll find that it actually gives you more freedom. You'll no longer spend as much time judging yourself and others, and so you'll be free to do many other things instead. Radical acceptance is one of the most important tools to learn in dialectical behavior therapy, and it's definitely worth the effort.

Exercise: Negative Judgments

The first step to changing a problem is to recognize when that problem occurs. So to begin changing your judgmental thinking, the first step is to recognize when you're being judgmental and critical. On page 87 is a Negative Judgments Record. For the next week, do your best to keep track of all the negative judgments and criticisms that you make. This includes those you make about things you read in the newspaper or see on television, judgments you make about yourself and other people, and so on. Make photocopies of the Negative Judgments Record if you need to, and keep one folded in your pocket so that you can record your judgments as soon as you recognize that you're making them. If you decide that you're only going to write down your negative judgments once a day, such as before you go to sleep, the process of learning radical acceptance will take longer. At the end of the day, you might forget many of the negative judgments that you've made.

In order to remind yourself to write down your negative judgments, it might help to give yourself visual reminders. Some people have found that wearing something special to remind them, like a new ring or a bracelet, prods their memories to write down their judgments. Other people put up sticky notes around their home and office with the word "judgments" written on them. Use whatever works best for you. Do this exercise for at least one week, or until you recognize that you're starting to catch yourself in the moment when you're making negative judgments. Keep track of *when* you made the judgment, *where* you were, and *what* the negative judgment was. Use the following example to help you.

(NOTE: *When you have completed a Negative Judgments Record, keep it to use in the Judgment Defusion exercise later in this chapter.*)

EXAMPLE: NEGATIVE JUDGMENTS RECORD

When?	Where?	What?
Sunday, 2 P.M.	Home	I thought: "I hate Sundays; they're always so boring."
Sunday, 6:30 P.M.	Home	I told my girlfriend I didn't like the shirt she was wearing.
Monday, 8:30 A.M.	In the car pool on the way to work	I thought about how much I hate the people on the road who always drive like idiots.
Monday, 11 A.M.	Work	I thought about how stupid my coworkers are for asking me the same questions every day.
Monday, 12:30 P.M.	Work	I thought about how much I hate my boss for buying me a computer that's not fast enough to do my work.
Monday, 1:45 P.M.	Work	I got mad at myself for making a mistake and called myself an "idiot."
Monday, 2:30 P.M.	Work	I got mad at the president after reading about his views on foreign policy in the newspaper.
Monday, 4:15 P.M.	Work	I thought about the ugly color they painted the room I'm sitting in.
Monday, 5:15 P.M.	In the car pool on the way home	I told Sandra she was being rude for keeping her car radio turned up too loud.
Monday, 11:30 P.M.	Home	I got upset with myself for staying up so late and not getting enough sleep.

NEGATIVE JUDGMENTS RECORD

When?	Where?	What?

RADICAL ACCEPTANCE AND BEGINNER'S MIND

Now that you've recognized many of your negative judgments, you're closer to using full radical acceptance. Remember, radical acceptance means that you observe situations in your life without judging or criticizing yourself or others. In the previous exercise, you focused on recognizing your *negative* judgments because they are usually the easiest ones to spot. But positive judgments can also be problematic.

Remember the example of Thomas we recently gave you? He divided everyone into two categories: either all good or all bad. He liked people when they were good, but when they did something to upset him, he got angry and labeled them "bad." So do you see how making even positive judgments about people or things can be problematic? When you think of someone (or something) with a rigid and predetermined idea of how that person is going to treat you, then it's easy to become disappointed, because no one (and nothing) is perfect. Presidents sometimes lie, religious people sometimes gamble, things that we like sometimes break, and people we trust sometimes hurt us. As a result, when you put someone into a category of being 100 percent good, trustworthy, saintly, wholesome, or honest, it's very easy to get disappointed.

But this doesn't mean that you should never trust anyone. What radical acceptance says is that you should approach people and situations in your life without judging them to be good or bad, positive or negative. In some forms of meditation, this is called *beginner's mind* (Suzuki, 2001). This means that you should enter every situation and every relationship as if you were seeing it for the very first time. This reoccurring newness prevents you from bringing any old judgments (good or bad) into the present moment, which allows you to stay more mindful. Plus, by keeping the situation fresh, it also helps you stay in better control of your emotions. As a result, it's easy to see why one of the goals of dialectical behavior therapy is to help you stop making any judgments at all, either positive or negative (Linehan, 1993b).

Exercise: Beginner's Mind

In the following exercise, you'll practice using radical acceptance and beginner's mind. This exercise is similar to the last one, but now you will need to be aware of both the positive and negative judgments that you make. Again, if you need to use visual reminders to help you remember to write down your judgments, use whatever works for you: a bracelet, a ring, a sticky note with the word "judgment" on it, and so on.

Do this exercise for at least one week or until you recognize that you're starting to catch yourself in the moments when you're making both positive and negative judgments. Keep track of *when* you made the judgment, *where* you were, and *what* the positive or negative judgment was.

As with the last exercise, make photocopies of the Beginner's Mind Record if you need to, and keep one folded in your pocket so that you can record your judgments as soon as you recognize that you're making them. The more quickly you record them after they occur, the sooner radical acceptance will become a regular part of your life. Use the example of the Beginner's Mind Record on the following page to help you. The blank Beginner's Mind Record for your use is on the page after that.

(*NOTE: When you have completed a Beginner's Mind Record, keep it to use in the Judgment Defusion exercise later in this chapter.*)

JUDGMENTS AND LABELS

Hopefully, after the last exercise, it's easy to see how putting labels on people, thoughts, and objects—making them either good or bad—can later lead to disappointment. In order to move closer to using radical acceptance, the next exercise will continue to help you monitor the judgments that you make and then it will help you let go of those judgments.

So far in this chapter, you've already recognized many of the problems associated with making judgments:

- Judgments can trigger overwhelming emotions.

- Judgments can often lead to disappointment and suffering.

- Judgments prevent you from being truly mindful in the present moment.

Obviously, one of the problems with judgments and criticisms is that they occupy your thoughts. In many cases, it can become very easy to start obsessing on a single judgment. Perhaps you've even had the experience of a single judgment occupying your thoughts all day. Maybe it was something bad about yourself or someone else. Or maybe it was something good about yourself or someone else. We've all had this experience. So when your thoughts are occupied by something that happened in the past or by something that might happen in the future, how mindful are you being about the present moment? Probably you're not being very mindful. And when those obsessive thoughts are judgments about yourself or someone else, how easy is it for your emotions to get triggered? Probably it's very easy, especially if you struggle with overwhelming emotions.

EXAMPLE: BEGINNER'S MIND RECORD

When?	Where?	What?
Friday, 12 P.M.	Lunch with Laura	I thought: "Laura is an incredibly talented person who never makes any mistakes."
Friday, 2:30 P.M.	Work	I called myself "incompetent," since I'm not going to be able to finish all my paperwork before five o'clock.
Friday, 2:45 P.M.	Work	After talking with my mother on the phone, I thought about what a lousy job she did raising me.
Friday, 5:30 P.M.	At the bar, after work	I was thinking that the bartender looked really nice and was probably the type of person who would make a really good husband.
Friday, 7:30 P.M.	Home	At first I told my boyfriend that he was sweet for making dinner, but when he put too much salt on my food, I told him he was an idiot.
Saturday, 2:30 P.M.	Shopping mall	I found the "perfect" pair of jeans that are going to make me look fantastic.
Saturday, 3:00 P.M.	Shopping mall	I was thinking about how ugly one of the guys in the store looked.
Saturday, 4:15 P.M.	Home	I got upset and called myself an idiot when I realized that the jeans didn't fit.
Saturday, 9 P.M.	Home	I got mad at my boyfriend for not helping me get all my chores completed today.
Saturday, 10:30 P.M.	Home	I was thinking about what a perfect day tomorrow is going to be.

BEGINNER'S MIND RECORD

When?	Where?	What?

Exercise: Judgment Defusion

The following Judgment Defusion exercise is designed to help you release or "let go" of your judgments and other obsessive thoughts. In the last chapter, you practiced using the thought defusion technique as a basic mindfulness exercise. This exercise is very similar. Again, the object is to watch your judgments arise and then to let go of them without getting stuck on them.

Like thought defusion, judgment defusion also requires the use of your imagination. The object of this exercise is to visualize your judgments, either as pictures or words, harmlessly floating away from you without obsessing about them or analyzing them. Whichever way you choose to do this is okay. If you used a technique in the last chapter that worked, use it again here. If you need a new visualization technique, here are just a few suggestions that other people have found helpful:

- Imagine sitting in a field watching your judgments float away on clouds.

- Picture yourself sitting beside a stream watching your judgments float past on leaves.

- Picture yourself standing in a room with two doors; then watch your judgments enter through one door and leave through the other.

If one of these ideas works for you, that's great. If not, feel free to create your own. Just be sure that your idea captures the purpose of this exercise, which is to visually watch your judgments come and go without holding on to them and without analyzing them.

Before you begin this exercise, review the records you filled out for the Negative Judgments exercise and the Beginner's Mind exercise, in order to refamiliarize yourself with some of the judgments you've made over the last few weeks. You can even keep these records near you so you can refer to them if you have trouble remembering any of your recent judgments. During the exercise, you will close your eyes and imagine whichever visualization technique you've chosen. Then you'll watch your past judgments (and any new judgments) come into your thoughts and float away, without you getting stuck on them.

Read the instructions before beginning the exercise to familiarize yourself with the experience. If you feel more comfortable listening to the instructions, use an audio-recording device to record the instructions in a slow, even voice so you can listen to them while practicing this technique. When you are first using judgment defusion, set a kitchen timer or an alarm clock for three to five minutes and practice letting go of your thoughts until the alarm goes off. Then, as you get more accustomed to using this technique, you can set the alarm for longer periods of time, like eight to ten minutes.

Instructions

To begin, find a comfortable place to sit in a room where you won't be disturbed for as long as you've set your timer. Turn off any distracting sounds. Take a few slow, long breaths, relax, and close your eyes.

Now, in your imagination, picture yourself in the scenario that you chose in order to watch your judgments come and go, whether it's by a stream, in a field, in a room, or somewhere else. Do your best to imagine yourself in that scene. After you do, start to become aware of the judgments that you're having, just like in the last exercises in which you wrote down your judgments. Start to observe the judgments that are coming up, whatever they are. Don't try to stop your thoughts, and do your best not to criticize yourself for any of the judgments. Just watch the judgments arise, and then, using whatever technique you've chosen, watch the judgments disappear. If you need to refer to any of the records from the past exercises to remind yourself of recent judgments, feel free to do that. But then close your eyes and watch those judgments float away.

Whatever the judgment is, big or small, important or unimportant, watch the judgment arise in your mind and then let it float away or disappear by whichever means you've chosen. Just continue to watch the judgments arise and disappear. Use pictures to represent the thoughts or words, whatever works best for you. Do your best to watch the judgments arise and disappear without getting hooked into them and without criticizing yourself. If more than one judgment comes up at the same time, see them both arise and disappear. If the judgments come very quickly, do your best to watch them all disappear without getting hooked on any of them. Continue to breathe and watch the judgments come and go until your timer goes off.

When you've finished, take a few more slow, long breaths, and then slowly open your eyes and return your focus to the room.

NONJUDGMENT AND YOUR DAILY EXPERIENCES

The purpose of the previous exercise is to help you let go of your judgments, and the more you practice it, the easier it will get. Then, after you've been practicing it regularly for at least a few weeks, it will become easy for you to let go of your judgments in the present moment. Hopefully, there will come a day, very soon, when a judgment will arise in your thoughts, either positive or negative, and you'll simply let it go. Maybe you'll need to close your eyes for a few seconds, if you're in a place where that's safe, and visualize the thought floating away. Or maybe you'll be in a conversation with someone when a judgment arises in your thoughts, and you'll simply be able to let it go. That is when you will truly be using radical acceptance.

Exercise: Judgments vs. the Present Moment

Now that you've practiced being mindful of your thoughts, feelings, and senses in the previous chapter, and you've practiced being mindful of your judgments in this chapter, the next step is to combine the two experiences. In this exercise you will learn to shift your attention back and forth in a mindful, focused way between your judgments and your physical sensations.

When you spend a lot of time obsessing over your thoughts and judgments, it's easy to get lost in your own fantasies about how the world *should* be. But again, these fantasies often lead to disappointment and suffering. As you continue to practice your mindfulness skills in your life, it will continue to be important to recognize and separate your judgments and fantasies from what's really happening in the moment. One of the easiest ways to do this is to become mindful of your physical senses—what you notice using your eyes, ears, nose, and senses of touch and taste. Often, people refer to this as *grounding* themselves. Grounding yourself in your physical sensations can stop you from obsessing over your judgments, and by doing so it will also help you become more mindful of what's happening in the present moment.

Read the following instructions before beginning the exercise to familiarize yourself with the experience. Then you can either keep these instructions near you if you need to refer to them while you're doing the exercise, or you can record them in a slow, even voice on an audio-recording device so that you can listen to them while you practice shifting your focus between your judgments and your present-moment awareness.

Instructions

To begin, find a comfortable place to sit in a room where you won't be disturbed for ten minutes. Turn off any distracting sounds. Take a few slow, long breaths, close your eyes, and relax.

Now, keeping your eyes closed, focus your attention on the weight of your body as it rests on the seat in which you're sitting. Notice the weight of your feet and legs resting on the ground. Notice the weight of your hands and arms resting. Notice the weight of your head resting on top of your neck. Mentally scan your body from head to toe and notice any sensations that you feel. Take your time. [Pause here for one minute if you are recording the instructions.]

Now notice any tension you might be feeling anywhere in your body, and imagine the tension melting away like wax in the hot sun. Again, take your time to scan your body for any tension, and keep taking slow, deep breaths. [Pause here for one minute if you are recording the instructions.]

When you are finished scanning your body, move your focus to your thoughts and judgments. Just notice any thoughts or judgments that arise in your mind, and when they do, allow them to float away by whichever means you found successful in the last exercises. Allow the thoughts and judgments to leave you without getting stuck on them. Take a minute to do this, and keep breathing slow, long breaths. [Pause here for one minute if you are recording the instructions.]

Now redirect your attention to your sense of hearing. Notice any sounds that you can hear coming from outside your room, and note to yourself what they are. Now become aware of any sounds you hear coming from inside the room, and note to yourself what they are. Try to notice even small sounds, such as the ticking of a clock, the sound of the wind, or the beating of your heart. If you become distracted by any thoughts, return your focus to your sense of hearing. Take a minute to do this, and keep breathing. [Pause here for one minute if you are recording the instructions.]

When you are finished noticing any sounds, once again redirect your focus to your thoughts and judgments. Notice any thoughts or judgments that arise in your mind, and when they do, allow them to float away by whichever means you found successful in the last exercises. Allow the thoughts and judgments to leave you without getting stuck on them. Take a minute to do this, and keep breathing slow, deep breaths. [Pause here for one minute if you are recording the instructions.]

Now, once again, redirect your attention. This time, put your focus on your sense of smell. Notice any smells that are in the room, pleasant or otherwise. If you don't notice any smells, just become aware of the flow of air moving into your nostrils as you breathe in through your nose. Try your best to maintain your focus on your sense of smell. If you become distracted by any thoughts, return your focus to your nose. Take a minute to do this, and keep breathing slow, deep breaths. [Pause here for one minute if you are recording the instructions.]

When you are finished noticing any smells, once again redirect your focus to your thoughts and judgments. Notice any thoughts or judgments that arise in your mind, and when they do, allow them to float away by whichever means you found successful in the last exercises. Allow the thoughts and judgments to leave you without getting stuck on them. Take a minute to do this, and keep breathing slow, long breaths. [Pause here for one minute if you are recording the instructions.]

Now redirect your attention to your sense of touch. Notice the sensation of whatever your hands are resting on. Or, keeping your eyes closed, reach out with one of your hands to touch an object that is within reach. Or, if there is no object within reach, touch the chair you're sitting in or touch your leg. Notice what the object feels like. Notice if it's smooth or rough. Notice if it's pliable or rigid. Notice if it's soft or solid. Notice what the sensations feel like on the skin of your fingertips. If your thoughts begin to distract you, simply return your focus to the object that you're touching. Take a minute to do this, and keep breathing slow, long breaths. [Pause here for one minute if you are recording the instructions.]

When you are finished noticing any touch sensations, once again redirect your focus to your thoughts and judgments. Notice any thoughts or judgments that arise in your mind, and when they do, allow them to float away by whichever means you found successful in the last exercises. Allow the thoughts and judgments to leave you without getting stuck on them. Take a minute to do this, and keep breathing slow, long breaths. [Pause here for one minute if you are recording the instructions.]

Now, slowly, open your eyes. Keep breathing slow, deep breaths. Take a few minutes to focus your visual attention on the room you're sitting in. Notice the objects that are in the room. Notice how light or dark the room is. Notice the different colors that are in the room. Notice where you are in the room. Move your head to look around. Take in all the visual information that you can. If your thoughts begin to distract you, simply return your focus to the room you're looking at. Take a minute to do this, and keep breathing slow, long breaths. [Pause here for one minute if you are recording the instructions.]

When you have finished noticing any visual sensations, once again redirect your focus to your thoughts and judgments. But this time, keep your eyes open. Pick a few objects in the room to focus on. But in your mind, continue to notice any thoughts and judgments that arise, and when they do, allow them to float away. Allow the thoughts and judgments to leave you without getting stuck on them. If you need to close your eyes to do this, that's okay. But open your eyes once the thoughts have floated away, and return your focus to the room you're in. Continue to monitor your thoughts and judgments and continue to let them go without getting stuck on them. Take a minute to do this, and keep breathing slow, long breaths. [Pause here for one minute if you are recording the instructions.]

When you've finished, if you still have time left, continue to switch your focus between your thoughts and judgments and what you notice visually. Then, when your timer goes off, take three to five slow, long breaths and return your focus to the room.

MINDFUL COMMUNICATION WITH OTHERS

As you continue to practice mindfulness skills by yourself, it's also very important that you begin to incorporate these skills into your interactions with others. Mindful communication is often the key to a successful relationship. If you're constantly making judgmental statements to someone, the chances are good that you'll lose that relationship. In the chapters on interpersonal effectiveness skills, you will learn how to ask others for what you need in a healthy way. But for now, let's look at how to be more mindful of the messages you send to other people.

Consider the following statements:

- "You make me mad."

- "You're such a jerk, I could scream."

- "Sometimes you make me so upset I just want to end it all."

- "I know that you did that to me on purpose just to hurt me."

What do all of these statements have in common? It's true that they all express some kind of emotion, such as anger, distress, and sadness. But more importantly, they're all judgments of the other person. Each of the statements blames the other person for the way the speaker feels. Now consider how you would feel if someone said one of these statements to you. What would you do? Maybe you would say something just as angry back to the person, which would lead to a big fight. The result would be that nothing gets resolved. Or maybe you would just shut down emotionally, stop listening, or walk away. Again, nothing would get resolved. Judgmental statements like these stop any form of effective communication. So what can you do instead?

One of the solutions is to turn "you" statements into mindful "I" statements.

- Mindful "I" statements are based on your own mindful awareness of how you feel.

- Mindful "I" statements are a more accurate description of how you feel.

- Mindful "I" statements let a person know how you feel in a nonjudgmental way.

- Mindful "I" statements evoke greater empathy and understanding from the other person, which allows the person to meet your needs.

Let's look at the four previous examples and turn them from "you" statements into mindful "I" statements.

Instead of saying "You make me mad," say "Right now, I feel very mad." Doesn't that sound less judgmental and blaming? If someone said the alternative statement to you ("I feel very mad"), wouldn't you be more willing to discuss the situation? Wouldn't you feel less angry?

Look at the second sentence. Instead of saying "You're such a jerk, I could scream," say "I feel so angry right now I could scream." Do you hear the difference it makes to change a "you" statement into an "I" statement? The other person no longer feels blamed and will be more willing to listen.

Let's look at the third sentence. Instead of saying "Sometimes you make me so upset I just want to end it all," say "I feel so upset and hopeless sometimes that I get very depressed."

And finally, look at the last sentence. Instead of saying "I know that you did that to me on purpose just to hurt me," say "I felt very hurt when you did that."

Again, mindful "I" statements are more accurate about how you feel, they are less judgmental, the other person will probably be more willing and able to listen to you if you use them, and most importantly, you are more likely to get your needs met if you use them.

Exercise: Mindful "I" Statements

Now let's look at some more judgmental "you" statements and have you practice turning them into mindful "I" statements. Write your alternative mindful "I" statement in the space to the right of the judgmental statement.

1.   "You make me feel horrible." _____

2.   "I know you're doing this on purpose to make me go crazy." _____

3.   "Why do you keep making me feel so angry?" _____

4.   "You're being insulting." _____

5.   "Stop fooling around; you're getting on my nerves." _____

6.   "If you don't listen to what I'm telling you, I'm not going to talk to you anymore."
     _____

7.   "You're being a jerk, stop it." _____

8.   "You're such a @%&!*#!, I can't believe it." _____

9.   "Why do you keep doing that to me?" _____

10. "Sometimes I feel like you're being too inflexible." _____

How did you do? Did it get harder to think of mindful "I" statements as the exercise progressed? Some of the later sentences probably required extra thinking. Let's look at some possible answers.

The first sentence was easy. The message is that the speaker feels horrible. So an alternative mindful "I" statement could be "I feel horrible" or "I feel horrible sometimes, when you (say that, do that, and so on)."

In the second sentence, the speaker feels crazy, anxious, or upset. So an alternative mindful "I" statement could be "I feel crazy/anxious/upset when you do that."

In the third sentence, the speaker feels angry. So an alternative mindful "I" statement could be "I feel angry right now."

In the fourth sentence, the speaker feels insulted or foolish. So an alternative mindful "I" statement could be "I feel like an idiot when you do that."

In the fifth sentence, the speaker feels anxious, tired, or angry. So an alternative mindful "I" statement could be "I feel anxious/tired/angry when you tease me like that."

In the sixth sentence, the speaker feels insulted, unheard, and ignored. But he or she also probably feels upset about being ignored. So an alternative mindful "I" statement could be "I feel upset when you ignore me."

In the seventh sentence, the speaker might feel many things. Usually, when you ask someone to stop doing something, it's because the action hurts. So maybe the speaker feels hurt, and an alternative mindful "I" statement could be "I feel hurt when you do that."

The eighth sentence is trickier. The speaker calls the other person some insulting expletive. This also usually indicates that the speaker's feelings have been hurt. So an alternative mindful "I" statement could be similar to the last sentence: "I feel very hurt when you do that."

The ninth sentence is phrased as a question, but it's really a statement about how the speaker feels. Again, the implication is that the speaker feels hurt, insulted, belittled, or something similar. So an alternative mindful "I" statement could be any version of these: "I feel very hurt (or insulted, or whatever) when you do that to me."

And lastly, the tenth sentence is the trickiest because the speaker uses the word "feel." Maybe you were tricked into thinking that this sentence didn't need to be changed. But this sentence is really a hidden judgment about the other person. What the speaker really means is "I *think* you're too inflexible." But people often exchange the word "think" for "feel" in order to hide their criticism or make their judgment sound less harsh. However, now you know better, so don't fall into the same trap. In this case, something about the other person's inflexible actions make the speaker feel uncomfortable or trapped. Maybe the other person never considers other points of view before he or she makes decisions. So an alternative mindful "I" statement could be "I feel uncomfortable when you don't consider my point of view."

Mindful "I" statements are clearly a more effective way of communicating how you feel and what you need, but they depend on your mindful awareness of your own feelings. Hopefully, after practicing the exercises in the last two chapters, you've become more skilled at recognizing your own emotions and you can start using mindful "I" statements to let others know how you feel.

DOING WHAT'S EFFECTIVE

Using successful communication skills, such as mindful "I" statements, is a part of what dialectical behavior therapy calls "doing what's effective" (Linehan, 1993b). This means that you do what's appropriate and necessary in the present moment—to resolve a problem, cope with a situation, or reach your goal—even if what you do feels unnatural, uncomfortable, or it goes against what you are experiencing emotionally. For example, you're probably not comfortable making statements like the ones you made in the last exercise, where you speak directly to the other person about how you feel. But sometimes in order to get what you want, you have to modify what you feel like doing, especially if you struggle with overwhelming emotions. Here are some other examples of doing what's effective:

- You're in the grocery store shopping for your weekly supply of food, but unfortunately, so are many other people. After shopping for an hour and waiting in line for fifteen minutes, you feel exhausted. You're so tired and annoyed that you think about leaving your shopping cart and just walking out. But if you did walk out, then you'd be without groceries for a week or you'd just have to start all over again at some other supermarket. So you stay in line and just get it over with.

- You're driving down the freeway and the car in front of you is driving below the speed limit in the left-hand lane. You feel so angry that you think about smashing into the car to push it out of the way. But if you did, you and the other driver would be seriously injured, and chances are you'd also get arrested. So you patiently wait for a chance to pass the driver, or you wait for your exit and then get off the freeway.

- You and your romantic partner get into a big argument. Both of you are yelling. You feel so hurt and upset that you think about walking out the door and ending the relationship. But in the back of your mind, you also recognize that this is the best relationship you've had in a long time, and you wish that it would work out. So, instead of leaving, you take a deep breath and use mindful "I" statements to let your partner know how you're feeling.

- Your boss gives you a new task even though you're already burdened with more work than you have time for. You feel insulted, angry, and taken advantage of. You're so mad that you think about screaming at your boss, telling him off, quitting, and walking out the door. But if you did, then you'd be without a paycheck for a long time. So you decide to bite your tongue for now until you can speak to your boss more calmly at some point in the near future, and you do the best you can.

- You ask your friend to take you shopping because she has a car and you don't. But your friend says she can't because she's busy doing something else. You feel annoyed and angry because you help her all the time when she asks you. You want to yell at her and tell her what a lousy friend she is. But if you did, you might lose her friendship completely. So instead of yelling, you call a different friend to ask for a ride.

As you can see, doing what's effective sometimes means *not* doing what you feel like doing or *not* doing what you've been habitually doing for many years. This is why mindfulness is such an important part of doing what's effective. If you're going to change the way you behave in the present moment, you have to be aware of what you're thinking, feeling, and doing in the present moment so that you can choose to do what's effective.

Doing what's effective also depends on not making judgments. You already know that making both positive and negative judgments can lead to disappointment and suffering. But making judgments about situations and your actions can also prevent you from doing what's effective. Here's an example: Judith had a math teacher who assigned homework that Judith thought was too hard. "This is ridiculous," she thought to herself. "How unfair of him to give us these assignments. This is wrong; he shouldn't be allowed to do this. I'm not going to do the homework." So she didn't. But as a result, she failed the class. Judith's judgments about what was "right" and "wrong" prevented her from doing what was effective. Clearly, it would have been more beneficial to her if she had remained mindful of her thoughts and feelings, avoided judging the assignments, and just done the best that she could.

Doing what's effective *is* doing what is necessary in a given situation in order to get a resolution to a problem. Doing what's effective *isn't* "selling out," "giving up," or "caving in."

Doing what's effective is a skill, just like acting. Sometimes in order to get what you want, you have to behave in a certain way. Sometimes you have to act as if you are competent, skilled, or satisfied in order to reach your goal, even if you don't feel that way. And that's what effective actions are designed to do—help you reach your goals. In the example above, Judith's goal was to get a satisfactory grade in her math class. But she allowed her judgments and feelings to prevent her from reaching that goal.

Remember, in order to do what's effective, you have to do the following:

- Be mindful of your thoughts and feelings.

- Avoid judging the situation or your actions.

- Choose actions that are appropriate and necessary to reach your goal.

- Do the best you can.

BEING MINDFUL IN YOUR DAILY LIFE

Now that you've almost completed these two chapters on mindfulness skills, you probably recognize the benefits of being mindful in your daily life. But to be realistic, no one is mindful all the time. There will certainly be moments in your life when you'll forget to be mindful. So what should you do?

In his book *Living the Mindful Life: A Handbook for Living in the Present Moment*, psychologist Charles Tart (1994, p. 13) remarks: "It does not take a really strenuous effort to make yourself become mindful and more present. The effort is very small. The problem is remembering to do it! We forget all the time. It is not hard, but we just do not remember to do it." So how should you remember to be mindful? Throughout his book, Dr. Tart uses a bell that rings at random times to remind the reader to be mindful of how he or she is thinking and feeling. But if you don't want to use a random bell, there are other ways to remind yourself. In some of the exercises in this chapter, you might have used a special ring or bracelet to remind yourself. Or maybe you used sticky notes. If those tools helped you, continue to use them to remind yourself to stay mindful.

However, the best way to continue to stay mindful in your daily life is to practice being mindful. The more you practice, the more you will remember to stay mindful. As part of the last exercise in this section, we have designed a simple daily mindfulness regimen to help you continue practicing your skills. It's very important that you continue to use these skills, and to practice other mindfulness exercises that you think are necessary, even as you move on to learning other dialectical behavior skills in this workbook. Mindfulness skills are so important to the overall effectiveness of dialectical behavior therapy that they have been labeled "core" skills (Linehan, 1993a).

DAILY MINDFULNESS REGIMEN

Your daily mindfulness regimen will consist of three skills that you've already learned:

1. Mindful breathing

2. Wise-mind meditation

3. Doing tasks mindfully

Mindful breathing is a skill you learned in chapter 3, Basic Mindfulness Skills. Remember, to breathe mindfully, you need to focus on three parts of the experience:

1. You must count your breaths. This will help you focus your attention, and it will also help you calm your mind when you're distracted by thoughts.

2. You need to focus on the physical experience of breathing. This is accomplished by observing the rising and falling of your breath as you slowly inhale and exhale.

3. You need to be aware of any distracting thoughts that arise while you are breathing. Then you need to let the thoughts float past without getting stuck on them, as you did in the Thought Defusion exercise. Letting go of the distracting thoughts will allow you to refocus your attention on your breathing and help you further calm yourself.

Practice breathing mindfully for three to five minutes a day at a minimum. But if you want to practice it longer, do it for as long as you can. Remember, the more frequently you practice mindfulness skills, the calmer you will feel and the more control you will have over your present-moment experiences. Refer to the Mindful Breathing exercise in chapter 3 if you need to review the instructions.

The wise-mind meditation is a skill you learned earlier in this chapter. It will help you focus your attention on your center of wise mind, which is also sometimes called your center of intuition or "gut feelings." Remember, wise mind is just one decision-making process that many people find helpful. It incorporates using both your emotion mind and your reasonable mind, meaning that wise-mind decisions require you to reflect on how you feel as well as the facts of a situation. This skill also helps you make intuitive decisions that "feel" right to you. Wise-mind meditation will help you make decisions based on the way your body reacts to a decision and your own inner knowledge (what you know to be "true" for you). Again, practice the wise-mind meditation for at least three to five minutes a day, or longer if you want to.

And finally, your daily mindfulness regimen will include doing tasks mindfully. This might sound like a new skill to you, but you've already practiced doing all the steps that are necessary. Doing tasks mindfully means doing all the things you normally do in your life, like talking, walking, eating, and washing, while also staying focused on your thoughts, emotions, physical sensations, and actions in the present moment, and without judging what is happening. In effect, this is the exercise where all the skills you've learned in the last two chapters finally come together.

To do tasks mindfully, you need to do the following:

■ Focus and shift your attention between your thoughts, feelings, physical sensations, and actions in order to be mindful of your present-moment experience.

■ Let go of distracting thoughts and judgments by allowing them to float past without getting stuck on them so that you don't get distracted from what's happening in the present moment.

■ Use radical acceptance to remain nonjudgmental.

■ Use wise mind to make healthy decisions about your life.

■ Do what's effective in order to accomplish your goals.

Some people find it helpful to use the following memory device to remind themselves to do tasks mindfully:

"Mindfulness is like a FLAME."

Focus and shift your attention to be mindful of the present moment.

Let go of distracting thoughts and judgments.

Use radical Acceptance to remain nonjudgmental.

Use wise Mind to make healthy decisions.

Do what's Effective to accomplish your goals.

Let's look at some examples of doing tasks mindfully, using all the skills you've learned in chapters 3 and 4.

After reading these two chapters, Loretta began approaching many of her tasks mindfully. At night, she would even brush her teeth mindfully. First, she focused her attention on how the toothbrush felt in her hand and how the tube felt as she squeezed out the paste. She was also aware of how her body felt, standing in front of the bathroom mirror, and how the weight of her body felt as she stood in front of the sink. Then, as she began to brush, she became aware of the taste in her mouth, the feel of the bristles on her gums, and the movement of her arm as she brushed. When distracting thoughts arose, such as things she did earlier in the day, she imagined the thoughts floating down a river on a leaf. If judgments arose about people she knew, she did the same thing and watched the judgments float away. Then she continued to shift her focus every few moments to her breathing, feeling it rise and fall. Loretta did a good job being as aware as possible of simply brushing her teeth in that moment. At other times throughout the day, she had similar experiences with other activities. When she washed the dishes, she paid attention to how the water felt and to the smell of the dish soap. While she was cooking, she was very aware of the heat from the stove, the sensation of hunger in her stomach, the sound of the water boiling, and her distracting judgments, which usually concerned whether or not her husband would like the meal. She did her best to let those judgments go and to be as fully present in the moment of cooking as she could be.

Similarly, Scott did his best to be mindful throughout the day. As he walked, he focused his attention on how his feet felt as they touched the pavement. Sometimes, he was even aware of how his feet felt moving in his socks. Then he would shift his focus to what he was seeing. He visually scanned what was around him as he walked, and he made mental notes to himself: "Right now, I'm seeing a woman, a tree, a building," and so on. When distracting thoughts arose, he imagined the thoughts coming in one door and leaving through another. If he saw someone on the street whom he didn't like and judgments arose, he would also let those judgments go. Similarly, if positive judgments arose about people or places he liked, he did his best to let those go too. For example, once he caught himself thinking "Oh look, there's Mike. He's the guy that loaned me twenty dollars that time. He's the greatest guy in the world. I wish I could be more like him." Scott knew that he couldn't stop those judgments from arising, but instead of getting stuck on them, he would let them go. And if the judgments came back, he would let them go again.

But clearly, the greatest challenge to using mindfulness skills is when you are interacting with someone else. Talking or arguing with someone and being mindful at the same time is often difficult. But it is also the most important time to be mindful, especially for someone struggling with overwhelming emotions. Here's an example.

Claire had been practicing her mindfulness skills for a few weeks when she went shopping for a new dress with her friend Laura. Sometimes, Claire worried that Laura really didn't like her. As a result, when Laura made suggestions, Claire did whatever Laura wanted because she was afraid of losing Laura's friendship. However, Claire didn't like the fact that Laura pushed her into doing things.

On the way to the store, Claire drove and she did her best to remain mindful of what she was doing. She felt the steering wheel in her hands. She felt the weight of her body resting in the seat. She felt her breath rising and falling as she breathed. She was also very aware of what she was seeing, especially the other cars. But she was also very aware of Laura talking to her as she drove. Naturally, judgments about Laura came up while Claire was driving, and she did her best to just let them go. However, some judgments were easier to let go of than others.

When they got to the shopping mall, Claire also had opportunities to use radical acceptance. There were certain stores she liked and certain stores she didn't like. At first, she was positive that she would find the "perfect" dress in the store she really liked because they always had the "best" clothes. But quickly, Claire recognized the positive judgments she was making, and she let them go. That was lucky too, because none of the stores she liked had the dress she was looking for. In the past, she would have been crushed and gotten upset. But because of radical acceptance, her neutrality and her nonjudgmental attitude allowed her to cope with the situation in a healthier way.

Later, the two women found themselves in a higher-end store looking at dresses that were more expensive than what Claire could afford. However, both she and Laura found a dress that they loved. Immediately, Laura began pressuring Claire to buy it. "Don't worry about how much it costs," Laura said. Claire looked at herself in the mirror and fell in love with the dress, regardless of the price tag. Claire was about to buy the dress when she remembered to use wise mind to help her make her decision. Her emotion mind loved the dress, but her reasonable mind reminded her that she already had a hefty credit card bill and this dress was far too expensive. In the dressing room, Claire took a few slow, deep breaths and put her hand on her center of wise mind. Her abdomen felt very nervous, not happy and excited. Instantly, she knew it was a very bad idea to buy the expensive dress, so she gave it back to the salesclerk and left the store.

Claire was proud of herself for making the right decision, but the drama didn't end there. Laura began making fun of Claire for being "too cheap" to buy the dress. Again, Claire's mind began to fill with judgments about Laura. She did her best to let them go, but as Laura continued to ridicule her, Claire's only goal became leaving the mall and dropping Laura at home. Internally, Claire wanted to scream at Laura, but she knew that would end up in a big fight. Claire thought about doing what was effective in that moment. She knew that she just had to get home as quickly and safely as possible without getting into a fight that she might later regret.

Claire drove home silently, listening to Laura's criticisms. She was relieved when she finally let Laura off at her house. Later, when Claire was feeling less angry, she even found the courage to call Laura to discuss what happened. Claire did a great job using mindful "I" statements such as "I felt hurt when you teased me." Laura understood and said she was sorry. Claire was proud of herself for handling the situation in a new, healthier way.

BE MINDFUL OF YOUR MINDFULNESS ACTIVITIES

Obviously, it will take lots of practice to become as mindful as Claire was in that situation. But hopefully, you see the benefits of using mindfulness in all of your daily tasks.

In the beginning of chapter 3, Basic Mindfulness Skills, you learned that there were three main reasons why you should learn mindfulness skills:

1. They will help you focus on one thing at a time in the present moment, and by doing this you can better control and soothe your overwhelming emotions.

2. They will help you learn to identify and separate judgmental thoughts from your experiences.

3. They will help you develop wise mind.

Unfortunately, there is no shortcut to becoming instantaneously and permanently mindful. But as Dr. Charles Tart said, learning how to be mindful isn't a strenuous activity; you simply have to remember to do it. So, however you need to remember to be mindful, we hope it works for you. One way is to use the Weekly Mindfulness Activities Record on page 112. This will help you remember to follow your daily mindfulness regimen. Make photocopies of this page for each week to record how often you use mindful breathing, wise-mind meditation, and do tasks mindfully.

Under the headings of "Mindful Breathing" and "Wise-Mind Meditation," record the length of time you spend doing each exercise. This will help you keep track of your improvement doing these exercises. Under the headings of "Doing Tasks Mindfully," record what it was that you did mindfully and where you were when you did it.

Then, under the headings labeled "Other Mindful Exercise," record any further mindfulness exercises that you do during the week.

Remember, these mindfulness skills are "core" skills in dialectical behavior therapy (Linehan, 1993a). So continue to use them even as you move on to using the other skills in this workbook.

RESISTANCES AND HINDRANCES TO MINDFULNESS PRACTICE

It is common to encounter inner resistance and difficulties as you practice mindfulness and develop skills. What many people do not know is that there are some hindrances to mindfulness that are so common that they have been recognized by meditation teachers and practitioners for thousands of years!

This final section of the chapter will help you identify five common hindrances to mindfulness meditation and suggest ways you can work skillfully with each one.

The Five Hindrances

Desire, aversion, sleepiness, restlessness, and *doubt* are the five hindrances long recognized as common obstacles to meditation (and mindfulness) practice.

These energies appear as obstacles when they take you out of the present moment or cause you to become lost in thoughts and feelings that interfere with your mindfulness practice of observing accurately and without judgment. However, they do not have to be obstacles. In truth, they can become your wisest teachers if you are willing to recognize, observe, and learn from them.

- *Desire* refers to the wish for things to be different—right now! This can be a wish for a different sense experience (to "feel better" or "feel happy or peaceful," for example) or to become someone or something different than what you experience yourself as now (become the "perfect person" or "perfect meditator," for example).

- *Aversion* means having anger for or ill will toward what is here. Aversion includes other forms of resistance to present-moment experience, such as feeling bored or afraid. Often, the very activity of judgment or judgmental thinking is an expression of aversion.

WEEKLY MINDFULNESS ACTIVITIES RECORD

For the week of _____

Day	Mindful Breathing	Wise-Mind Meditation	Doing Tasks Mindfully	Doing Tasks Mindfully	Other Mindful Exercise	Other Mindful Exercise
Monday	Time:	Time:	What: Where:	What: Where:		
Tuesday	Time:	Time:	What: Where:	What: Where:		
Wednesday	Time:	Time:	What: Where:	What: Where:		
Thursday	Time:	Time:	What: Where:	What: Where:		
Friday	Time:	Time:	What: Where:	What: Where:		
Saturday	Time:	Time:	What: Where:	What: Where:		
Sunday	Time:	Time:	What: Where:	What: Where:		

■ *Sleepiness* means just that—feeling sleepy, heavy, and dull. It is important to note that the causes of sleepiness can include physical fatigue, but, also, a second kind of sleepiness is actually a resistance to something happening in mind and body that may be frightening or painful. Learning to distinguish between these two is very helpful.

■ *Restlessness* is the opposite of sleepy. It can be very uncomfortable. It is a "storm" of thoughts, feelings, and sensations that demand movement and are quite distracting.

■ *Doubt* is that inner voice that says, "I can't handle this. I don't know how to do it. What good is this? This definitely is *not* for me." Doubt is often expressed as words in your mind and feelings of fear and resistance to what is happening.

Working Wisely with the Hindrances

The first and most potent way to handle any of the hindrances is to make the *experience* of the hindrance itself a focus for your mindfulness. Acknowledge what is happening without fighting it. Gently place attention on desire, aversion, sleepiness, restlessness, or doubt, and look deeply, allowing the energy to reveal itself in all of its forms. Patiently return your soft and curious attention time and again, as often as necessary, to the hindrance energy, naming it and learning what it has to teach you. The lessons can come in many ways, including thoughts, memories, feelings, and body sensations.

In addition, you may find benefits in the following specific suggestions for each hindrance:

■ *For desire, recall that no matter how many times you get what you desire, you always want more.* Let this wisdom empower you to resist the temptation of desire and learn from it instead. Keep noticing and naming desire without acting on it.

■ *For aversion, recognize anger and ill will as some of your strongest teachers.* Resolve to learn from them. At times, it also helps if you can work to balance them by developing thoughts of compassion, kindness, and forgiveness.

■ *For sleepiness, know it as a powerful condition that demands your full attention.* It can help to sit up straight, even stand. Splash water on your face. Take a break and do something active, walking mindfully, for example.

■ *For restlessness, besides making it the object of mindfulness, it can be very helpful to sharpen your concentration.* Take a more narrow or smaller focus, for example, placing attention at the tip of your nose for practicing mindful breathing, or relaxing and counting your breaths from one to ten and back to one until the restlessness subsides.

■ *For doubt, especially when your mind is racing everywhere, it can help to concentrate attention in the present moment with some resolve and steadiness.* Other remedies for doubt can be conversation with mindfulness teachers and others who follow this path, and inspirational readings related to how others handle doubt.

Finally, remember to take a kind and interested nonjudging attitude toward the hindrances when they appear. When you can treat them as teachers, not obstacles, they will cease to be hindrances!

CHAPTER 5

Exploring Mindfulness Further

MINDFULNESS AND MEDITATION

The mindfulness skills that are at the core of the dialectical behavior therapy approach are actually linked directly to a much larger and more ancient tradition of meditation. In that larger tradition is a significant body of experience and wisdom related to developing and practicing mindfulness. This experience and wisdom has much to offer anyone interested in mindfulness, whether they seek improved psychological or physical health, personal enrichment, or even spiritual growth.

This chapter invites you to explore mindfulness further by trying some additional practices adapted from the ancient tradition of meditation and now appearing in many clinical settings that teach mindfulness-based approaches for a variety of health-related conditions.

The intention and hope is that you will develop an even deeper appreciation for the power of mindfulness to support you, promote your happiness, and lead you increasingly to rest in wise mind.

Marsha Linehan, who developed dialectical behavior therapy, has noted this larger context for mindfulness in commenting that the mindfulness skills central to dialectical behavior therapy are "psychological and behavioral versions of meditation practices from Eastern spiritual training." Linehan goes on to say that in developing dialectical behavior therapy, "I have drawn most heavily from the practice of Zen, but the skills are compatible with most Western contemplative and Eastern meditation practices" (Linehan, 1993b, p. 63).

In the past twenty-five years or so, many health care professionals have become interested in mindfulness and its applications in treating a wide variety of health-related conditions ranging from stress to chronic pain to anxiety and depression to cancer. In bringing mindfulness forward in Western health care settings, the ancient teachings and wisdom of various contemplative and meditative traditions have provided much valuable insight.

Although many (like Linehan) have drawn upon these older traditions for guidance, the actual practices used for purposes of health and healing do not require adherence to any specific faith or religious beliefs, nor do they carry any specific cultural requirements. The practice of mindfulness is truly something for all human beings. The practices you will find in this chapter also apply equally to any interested person.

First, you will learn about the role of "heartful" qualities of kindness and compassion and how they are actually embedded attitudes in any activity of mindfulness.

Next, you will learn how mindfulness can deepen, breath by breath in the present moment, by attention to and the support of the dimensions of spaciousness and stillness.

Kindness, compassion, spaciousness, and *stillness*—this chapter invites you to bring attention more consciously to these qualities and discover their power to support and deepen your practice of mindfulness.

ENHANCING YOUR MINDFULNESS SKILLS USING KINDNESS AND COMPASSION

In dialectical behavior therapy, a core "how" skill is being nonjudgmental. In mindfulness-based stress reduction, a mindfulness approach to stress reduction developed by Jon Kabat-Zinn and others, *nonjudging* is the first of seven attitudes considered to be the foundation of mindfulness practice. The others are *patience, beginner's mind, trust, non-striving, acceptance,* and *letting go* (Kabat-Zinn, 1990, p. 33).

Yet you may have noticed that it is *not* always so easy to be nonjudging. In fact, the habits of judging and criticizing are deeply ingrained in nearly everyone, for a wide variety of reasons.

Because of this deep-habit energy of judging, meditation teachers have long taught the importance of building a foundation for mindfulness upon attitudes of kindness and compassion.

For example, the well-respected meditation teacher Christina Feldman has observed that "attention, awareness, understanding, and compassion form the basic skeleton of all systems of meditation." She goes on to say, "Compassion is a fundamental principle of meditation. Meditation is not a narcissistic, self-interested path. It provides the foundation for love, integrity, compassion, respect and sensitivity" (Feldman, 1998, p. 2).

In recent years, health psychologists have begun to look more deeply at "positive" emotions and attitudes and their role in promoting health. The rich tradition of positive mental health inquiry builds on the work of psychologists Gordon Allport and Abraham Maslow in the 1960s and continues strongly today. It is motivated in large part by an interest in developing an expanded vision of human capacity and potential. Of particular interest on this theme is that expanded human potential has been one of the primary goals of meditation training since ancient times.

Contemporary health psychologists and researchers Shauna L. Shapiro and Gary E. R. Schwartz have written about the positive aspects of meditation. They point out that mindfulness is about *how* one pays attention. In addition to the seven attitudinal qualities identified by Kabat-Zinn, Shapiro and Schwartz suggest that an additional five qualities be incorporated to address the affective (or "heart") dimension of mindfulness. The five "heart" qualities they name are: *gratitude, gentleness, generosity, empathy,* and *lovingkindness* (Shapiro & Schwartz, 2000, pp. 253–273).

Lovingkindness deserves special mention. It has been popularized by the meditation teacher Sharon Salzberg (1995; 1997; 2005). As health-care professionals learn more about lovingkindness, this form of meditation is gaining popularity in a variety of health-care settings as a meditation practice that supports mindfulness and also carries healing potential of its own.

Lovingkindness is variously described as deep friendliness and welcoming or as a quality embodying compassion and cherishing, filled with forgiveness and unconditional love. It is a deep human capacity, always present, at least potentially. It can be seen when one observes a mother tenderly caring for her child.

Lovingkindness can be a powerful aid to your mindfulness practice. All you need to do is to admit and allow feelings of kindness and compassion into your way of paying attention mindfully. Resting in kindness this way, *with compassion and affection embedded in your attention,* can protect you from the deep habits of judging and criticism and support you in the "how" dialectical behavior therapy skill of being truly nonjudgmental.

Exercise: Meditation Practice for the Lovingkindness of Yourself and Others

The following is a brief meditation practice to cultivate lovingkindness for yourself and for others. Practice it whenever and for as long as you like. Try it as a "lead-in" to any of your formal mindfulness practices.

Instructions

Take a comfortable position. Bring your focus mindfully to your breath or body for a few breaths. Open and soften as much as feels safe to you as you allow yourself to connect with your natural inner feelings of kindness and compassion for others.

Now shift your attention to yourself. It could be a sense of your whole self or some part that needs care and attention, such as a physical injury or the site of an illness or a feeling of emotional pain.

Imagine speaking gently and quietly to yourself, as a mother speaks to her frightened or injured child. Use a phrase like "May I be safe and protected" or "May I be happy" or "May I be healthy and well" or "May I live with ease" or make up one of your own. Let the phrase you pick be something anyone would want (safety, ease, joy, and so on). Pick one that works for you. It can be a single phrase. Then put all your heart into it each time you speak to yourself. Let kindness and compassion come through you.

Practice by repeating your phrase to yourself silently as if singing a lullaby to a baby. Practice for as long as you like. It may help to practice for just a few minutes at a time at first and later build up to a longer practice.

When you like, you can shift your attention and focus to a friend or someone you know who is troubled. You can also focus on groups of people, such as "all my friends" or "all my brothers and sisters."

When you wish, you can experiment with difficult people in your life. Try sending them kindness and your wish that they might be happy, and watch your inner response. In doing loving-kindness for a difficult person, you are *not* allowing them to abuse or hurt you but are making an attempt to see that they, too, are human beings who seek happiness. This can change your relationship to the situation and release you from resentment you may be holding.

Please note that in doing lovingkindness meditation, you are likely to experience many different feelings! Some may even be disturbing, such as sadness, grief, or anger. If this happens, you have *not* made a mistake. It is common for deeply held feelings to be released as one practices lovingkindness. This release is actually a kind of healing in itself. Just pay attention to all of your feelings, honoring each one, and continue your practice.

ATTENTION TO SPACIOUSNESS AND STILLNESS DEEPENS MINDFULNESS

The core dialectical behavior therapy skill of mindfulness includes the "what" skill of observing and the "how" skill of nonjudging. But old habits of attention can often make it difficult to observe fully or to really be nonjudging. When it seems especially difficult to be mindful, observe closely, or be nonjudging, you simply may not be relaxing enough or resting in your wholeness. Instead, you are very likely overly identified with some active and present smaller part or parts of yourself.

Meditation teachers often use the metaphor of an ocean when illustrating your wholeness compared to identification with a smaller part of yourself (your thoughts and judgments or your feelings of anger or fear, for example). In this metaphor, it is noted that the waves and the ocean are not separate. Although the waves are varied and can be intense and dramatic, they still are made of water and are part of the greater ocean, even down to the deepest depths. It is said that your wholeness (sometimes called *big mind* or some similar term) is like the ocean, while the parts (feelings, thoughts, stories in your mind) are like the waves—constantly rising and falling, appearing and disappearing, while their essence, the ocean, is always present.

The tendency to *identify* with the wave and to lose your feeling of connection with the larger ocean of who you are is very strong. Practicing mindfulness, learning to recognize the reasoning mind and the emotional mind when they arise, can offer freedom from rigid identification with your smaller parts, as you have discovered.

And by shifting your focus at times, on purpose, to experiences often not noticed or taken for granted, you can become much more flexible in your attention, more mindful, and more able to break the habitual identification with old habits of thinking and feeling.

Choosing *space* and *stillness* (or *silence*) as your objects of mindfulness can be a very potent practice for gaining this flexibility and freedom from the habits of identifying with the "waves" of your mind (thoughts or feelings that are deep and intense).

Exercise: Meditation Practice for Mindfulness of Space, Inside and Outside of You

The following two meditation practices offer you a means to cultivate awareness of space (inner and outer) and of stillness and silence.

Try these practices with a sense of curiosity and playfulness. You don't have to make anything special happen or become anyone or anything other than who you already are!

In fact, it is helpful to consider the possibility that *you actually already have vast spaciousness and stillness available to you (like the vast ocean depths) and all that is required is to allow space and stillness to reenter your awareness.* Let the spaciousness and stillness within you "come back in," so to speak. There is no work you have to do—none whatsoever! Just bring kind attention to what is already here.

Instructions

Take a comfortable position. Collect attention by focusing mindfully on your breath sensations for a few breaths.

When you feel steady and focused, widen the focus to include all sounds, letting them come to you without adding or subtracting anything. Focus on the direct experience of sound without being caught in the name or story about any sound.

Practice mindfulness of breath sensations and sounds for a few more breaths.

Now bring your attention to the spaces between the breaths, there between in-breath and out-breath, and there, at the end of the out-breath before the next in-breath. Let your attention rest there, in the spaces between each breath. Come back to the space whenever your attention wanders.

When you notice that sounds draw your attention, first notice the sound, then notice the spaces between the sounds. Notice how one sound is louder, another softer, one closer, one farther, and how all have space between and around them. Notice how all the sounds exist within a larger container of space. Let your attention rest in the space that holds all the sounds, allowing them to come and go.

When you wish, open your eyes. Look around at what is before you. What do you see? Objects, of course, but do you see the space between the objects? Look more closely. See the space and the shape of the space between objects near and far. Can you see the vast space that holds all the objects you are viewing? Relax and look deeply.

Whenever you like, practice noticing space, either as a formal meditation practice (as suggested above with breath sensations, sounds, or viewed objects) or more informally, just paying attention in different situations as you go about your day.

You may even want to experiment with noticing the space that contains your thoughts and feelings. Can you relax, observe, and allow thoughts and feelings to arise, change, and leave the space of the present moment?

Exercise: Meditation Practice to Turn Toward Stillness and Silence

Instructions

Take a comfortable position. Establish and steady your attention in the present moment by focusing mindfully on your breath sensations for a few breaths.

When you notice that your attention moves to something else, thoughts or sounds for example, you don't have to fight that and you don't have to follow it. Just let the breath sensations return to your awareness, with patience and kindness.

As you practice mindfulness of your breath, you may begin to notice that a sense of inner stillness arises. It may appear only in brief flashes at first, but don't be discouraged. Just let it come. Continue noticing any feelings of stillness you experience. Relax in them, and allow them to come to you. Initially, you may notice the stillness in your body as a feeling of calm and ease. Then, it will become easier to experience the stillness in your mind when your thoughts quiet down.

Sometimes the stillness appears more clearly as silence. When you notice any sense of silence, between sounds or between thoughts, for instance, let your attention rest there. Let it return there when it wanders.

Listen carefully to all sounds as they come and go. Don't focus on any one sound, but instead focus on the silence and space between the sounds. As your attention steadies, notice how the sounds arise from silence and return to silence. Let your attention rest in the silence as you listen for the next sound.

CONCLUSION

In practicing mindfulness, you are joining a vast and ancient tradition, cultivated by countless human beings for thousands of years. Many teachers have pointed out that practicing mindfulness includes the attitudes of kindness and compassion in the way you pay attention. As you become more mindful, a growing sense of wholeness, including spaciousness and stillness, becomes brighter and can help transform your experience of living. This chapter invites you to draw upon some valuable teachings from the tradition of mindfulness meditation—by focusing on kindness and compassion and spaciousness and stillness—in order to discover more about your own amazing and powerful resources for healing and enriching your life.

CHAPTER 6

Basic Emotion Regulation Skills

YOUR EMOTIONS: WHAT ARE THEY?

To put it simply, emotions are signals within your body that tell you what's happening. When something pleasurable is happening to you, you feel good; when something distressing is happening to you, you feel bad. In many ways, your emotions are like an instant news service that gives you constant updates about what you're doing and what you're experiencing.

Your initial reactions to what is happening to you are called *primary emotions*. These are strong feelings that come on quickly, that don't involve having to think about what's happening. For example, if you won a contest, you might instantaneously feel surprised. When someone you care about dies, you quickly feel sad. When someone does something that offends you, you might immediately feel angry.

But in addition to experiencing primary emotions, it's also possible to experience *secondary emotions*. These are emotional reactions to your primary emotions. Or to put it another way, secondary emotions are feelings about your feelings (Marra, 2005). Here's a simple example. Erik yelled at his sister because she did something that made him feel angry. His feeling of anger came on very quickly. But a little later he felt guilty about getting so angry with her. Anger was his primary emotion, and guilt was his secondary emotion.

However, it's also possible that you can experience numerous secondary emotions in response to a single primary emotion. Here's a more complicated example. Shauna became anxious when she was asked to make a future presentation at work. As the day drew closer, she became depressed as she thought about how anxious she was getting, and then she started to feel worthless that she couldn't make a simple presentation. Then, the day after the presentation, she started to feel guilty that she had made such a big deal about it in the first place. You can see how a person's emotions can get very complicated very quickly. Anxiety was Shauna's primary emotion, and depression, worthlessness, and guilt were all her secondary emotions in response to her anxiety.

It's possible that your primary emotional reaction to a situation can set off a limitless chain reaction of distressing secondary emotions that cause you much more pain than your original emotion does. For this reason, it's important that you try to identify what your original primary emotion is in a distressing situation so that you can learn to cope with that feeling before the avalanche of secondary emotions overwhelms you. This is where emotion regulation skills can be helpful. Emotion regulation skills are an important part of dialectical behavior therapy because they will help you cope with your distressing primary and secondary feelings in new and healthier ways (Dodge, 1989; Linehan, 1993a).

These skills are especially useful, because without them, people often choose to deal with their primary and secondary emotions in ways that only cause them more suffering. In Shauna's example, it's easy to imagine that she could have chosen to use alcohol or drugs to deal with her feelings of anxiety, cutting or self-mutilation to deal with her feelings of depression, and binge eating to deal with her feelings of guilt. These are all harmful coping strategies that are often used by people with overwhelming emotions. For this reason, it's extremely important that you learn the emotion regulation skills in this workbook so that you can cope with your primary and secondary emotions in healthier ways and avoid the prolonged suffering that often accompanies them.

Emotion regulation skills are also important for dealing with another problem called *ambivalence*. Ambivalence occurs when you have more than one emotional reaction to the same event and each emotion pulls you in a different direction or makes you want to do something different. For example, Tina had grown up without her father in her life. Then one day when she was twenty-five, her father contacted her and wanted to see her. Tina felt excited about the opportunity of forming a new relationship with him, but she was equally angry with him for abandoning her family. Clearly Tina's emotions were split, and they pulled her in two different directions about what to do.

If you've been dealing with overwhelming emotions for a long time, it's easy to understand that you might feel frustrated and hopeless about controlling your emotional reactions. But remember: although it might be difficult to control your primary emotional reaction, there's still hope that you can learn to control your secondary emotional responses as well as how you choose to cope with your emotions. And it could be that later on, when you start using all the skills in this workbook, especially the mindfulness skills, you might even gain some control over your primary emotional responses too.

HOW DO EMOTIONS WORK?

Emotions are electrical and chemical signals in your body that alert you to what is happening. These signals often begin with your senses of sight, touch, hearing, smell, and taste. Then the signals travel to your brain, where they are processed in an area called the *limbic system*, which specializes in observing and processing emotions so that you can respond to emotional situations. The limbic system is also connected to the rest of your brain and body so that it can tell your body what to do in response to an emotional situation.

Your emotions are extremely important for many reasons, especially your survival. Here's an example. Louise was walking down Main Street when suddenly a very large and angry dog began barking viciously and running toward her. In that instant, an emotional signal was sent from her eyes and ears to her brain. Her limbic system then processed the information without Louise having to think about what to do. This type of response is called *fight or flight,* and it determined if Louise was going to stay to fight the dog or run away. Wisely, she chose to run away, and she escaped without being harmed. Her emotions helped her survive and avoid any pain.

Now let's suppose that two weeks later she was once again walking through town when she started to turn down Main Street. Very quickly, she began to feel afraid. This is called a *conditioned response.* Louise's limbic system was trying to protect her by helping her remember the dangerous dog on Main Street. Sensibly, she chose to walk down a different street to avoid the dog. In this example, Louise's emotions initially helped her escape danger and pain, and later, they also helped her avoid potential harm.

Here's another example of how emotions work. Sheila was walking through town when she suddenly saw Courtney, a good friend from many years before. Immediately, Sheila felt happy. When Courtney saw Sheila, she smiled right away. Sheila noticed her smile and thought, "She must be happy to see me too." So Sheila smiled as well. The two women quickly reconnected and made plans to do something together in the near future. The encounter made both women feel happy that they'd met accidentally after so many years.

In this example, the smile was an act of communication for both women. It helped each person recognize how the other person was feeling. If Courtney had frowned and looked the other way when she saw Sheila, Sheila would have recognized the expression as one of disgust and would probably have avoided contact with her. Every person, no matter what their culture, has the ability to express emotions in the same way and to recognize emotional expressions in other people. A smile is a smile no matter where you were born.

These are just two very simple examples, but you can see that emotions serve many purposes. Emotions are signals that help you to do the following:

- Survive ("fight or flight").

- Remember people and situations.

- Cope with situations in your daily life.

- Communicate with others.

- Avoid pain.

- Seek pleasure.

WHAT ARE EMOTION REGULATION SKILLS?

As you've already learned, emotion regulation skills will help you cope with your reactions to your primary and secondary emotions in new and more effective ways. (Remember, you can't always control what you feel, but you can control how you react to those feelings.) These are some of the most important techniques to learn in dialectical behavior therapy, so you might not be surprised that you've already been practicing some of them in the chapters on distress tolerance and mindfulness skills. The four skill groups in dialectical behavior therapy (distress tolerance, mindfulness, emotion regulation, and interpersonal effectiveness) overlap and reinforce each other because this helps you learn the skills more easily and to remember them more quickly.

In dialectical behavior therapy, there are nine emotion regulation skills that will help you gain control of your emotions and the behaviors associated with them (Linehan, 1993b). These skills are as follows:

1. Recognizing your emotions

2. Overcoming the barriers to healthy emotions

3. Reducing your physical vulnerability

4. Reducing your cognitive vulnerability

5. Increasing your positive emotions

6. Being mindful of your emotions without judgment

7. Emotion exposure

8. Doing the opposite of your emotional urges

9. Problem solving

This chapter will cover the first five emotion regulation skills, and the next chapter will cover the last four skills. As in the previous chapters, the exercises in these two chapters will build on each other, so make sure that you do the exercises in order.

RECOGNIZING YOUR EMOTIONS

Learning how to recognize your emotions and their effect on your life is the first step to controlling your high-intensity emotional reactions. Very often, people spend their lives paying little attention to how they feel. As a result, there are a lot of important things happening inside them that they know little about. The same holds true for people struggling with overwhelming emotions, but it occurs in a different way. Very often, people struggling with this problem recognize the tidal wave of distressing emotions that overcomes them (such as sadness, anger, guilt, shame, and so on), but by the time they recognize the tidal wave, it's too late to do anything about it.

To control your overwhelming emotional reactions, it's first necessary to slow down the emotional process so that it can be examined. And then, after it's examined, you can make healthier decisions. This exercise will help you begin this process by examining an emotional situation that has already occurred in the past. It will require you to be as honest with yourself as possible. The purpose of this exercise is to discover what emotions you were feeling (both primary and secondary emotions) and then figure out how those emotions affected your actions and feelings later on.

Let's consider an example. Ling struggled with overwhelming emotions that often got out of control. One evening, she came home from work and found her husband drunk on the sofa again. He refused to go to psychotherapy and he didn't consider himself an alcoholic, so he wouldn't go to a meeting of Alcoholics Anonymous. Ling immediately felt angry, so she started screaming at her husband, calling him a "worthless drunk." But he just lay there without arguing or moving. She wanted to hit him, but she didn't. After a few minutes, Ling started to feel hopeless and ashamed too. She had tried everything to help her husband, but nothing seemed to work. She didn't feel like she could stay in her marriage any longer, but she also didn't believe in divorce. Ling went to the bathroom and locked herself in. She thought about killing herself, to end the pain she was feeling. But instead, she took out a razor and started cutting herself on her leg just enough to make herself bleed. That night she forgot to set her alarm because she was too upset, so she missed the first few hours of work and got reprimanded by her manager.

Ling's story is common for many people. Using this story, let's follow the six-step process that will help you recognize your emotions (Linehan, 1993b).

1. *What happened?* This is your opportunity to describe the situation that led to your emotions. In this example, Ling comes home and once again finds her husband drunk. He refuses to get help or to talk about his problem.

2. *Why do you think that situation happened?* This is an opportunity for you to identify the potential causes of your situation. This is a very important step because the meaning that you give to the event will often determine what your emotional reaction is to that event. For example, if you think someone hurt you on purpose, you will react very differently than if you think someone hurt you by accident. Here, Ling believes that her husband is an alcoholic who hates her and regrets marrying her in the first place, so he has just given up on his life to hurt her.

3. *How did the situation make you feel, both emotionally and physically?* Try to identify both primary and secondary emotions if you can. Learning how to identify your emotions will take practice, but it will be worth the effort that you make. If you need help finding words to describe how you feel, see the List of Commonly Felt Emotions in chapter 3. Also, try to identify how you were feeling physically. Emotions and physical sensations, especially muscle tension, are strongly related. In this example, Ling's primary emotion is anger (after seeing her husband drunk), and then she feels the secondary emotions of hopelessness and shame. Physically, she notices that all the muscles in her face and arms become very tense, and she feels sick to her stomach.

4. *What did you want to do as a result of how you felt?* This question is very important because it identifies your *urges*. Often, when a person is overwhelmed with emotions, he or she has the urge to say or do something that is drastic, painful, or extremely dangerous. However, the person doesn't always do these things; sometimes the urges are just thoughts and impulses. When you start to notice what you *want* to do and compare it

with what you *actually* do, the results can be cause for hope. If you can control some urges, chances are good that you can control other urges too. In this example, Ling had the urge to do two things that would have been very dangerous and deadly: hit her husband and kill herself to end her pain. Thankfully, she didn't do either one, which later gave her hope that she could control other urges as well.

5. *What did you do and say?* This is where you identify what you actually did as a result of your emotions. In this example, Ling locks herself in her bathroom and begins to mutilate herself. She also yells at her husband and calls him a "worthless drunk."

6. *How did your emotions and actions affect you later?* Here you can identify the longer-term consequences of what you felt and did. In Ling's example, she oversleeps for work the next morning since she forgets to set her alarm, and she is disciplined by her boss, which puts her job at risk.

Exercise: Recognizing Your Emotions

On the next page is an example of the Recognizing Your Emotions Worksheet with Ling's experience filled in. On the following page, there's a blank worksheet for you to fill in an example from your own life. Before you use the blank worksheet, make photocopies of it so that you can continue to use it in the future. Or simply write the headings on a clean sheet of paper to make your own worksheet.

For now, use the worksheet to examine an emotional incident from your recent past. Pick a situation that you can clearly remember. Do your best to identify your primary and secondary emotions. And remember, be as honest as you can with yourself. No one has to see this worksheet except for you.

Then, for at least the next two weeks, pick a situation that happens to you each day and examine it using the Recognizing Your Emotions Worksheet. Remember, you need to practice examining past situations so that you can later learn how to identify your emotions and their consequences *while they are happening.*

EXAMPLE: RECOGNIZING YOUR EMOTIONS WORKSHEET

Questions	Your Responses
When did the situation happen?	Last night.
What happened? (Describe the event.)	I came home and my husband was lying on the sofa drunk again. He still refuses to go to therapy or AA. I yelled at him and called him a "worthless drunk." But he just sat there, without saying anything. So I went in the bathroom and cut myself.
Why do you think that situation happened? (Identify the causes.)	My husband is an alcoholic who hates me and regrets marrying me. I also think he's given up on his own life and just does things like this to hurt me on purpose.
How did that situation make you feel, both emotionally and physically? (Try to identify both the *primary* and the *secondary* emotions.)	Primary emotions: Anger Secondary emotions: Hopelessness and shame Physical sensations: Face and arms became tense, sick to my stomach
What did you want to do as a result of how you felt? (What were your urges?)	I wanted to hit my husband, and I had the urge to kill myself to end my pain.
What did you do and say? (What actions or behaviors did you engage in as a result of how you felt?)	I locked myself in the bathroom and started cutting myself. Then I went to bed by myself because I was so angry. I yelled at my husband and called him a "worthless drunk."
How did your emotions and actions affect you later? (What short-term or long-term consequences were there as a result of your actions?)	I was so angry when I went to bed that I forgot to set my alarm. So I woke up late for work. When I got in, my boss yelled at me again. He said that if I'm late one more time, he'll have to fire me.

RECOGNIZING YOUR EMOTIONS WORKSHEET

Questions	Your Responses					
When did the situation happen?						
What happened? (Describe the event.)						
Why do you think that situation happened? (Identify the causes.)						
How did that situation make you feel, both emotionally and physically? (Try to identify both the *primary* and the *secondary* emotions.)	Primary emotions: Secondary emotions: Physical sensations:					
What did you want to do as a result of how you felt? (What were your urges?)						
What did you do and say? (What actions or behaviors did you engage in as a result of how you felt?)						
How did your emotions and actions affect you later? (What short-term or long-term consequences were there as a result of your actions?)						

Exercise: Emotional Record

To help you recognize your emotions, it's often helpful to say how you're feeling out loud. This method of labeling might sound silly at first, but the act of saying how you feel out loud will highlight your emotions for you and help you pay extra attention to what you're experiencing. Describing your emotions aloud, especially your overwhelming emotions, can also help deflate your distressing feelings. So the more you can talk about an emotion, the less urge you might have to do something about it. You do not have to scream how you feel; it might be enough to say your emotion quietly to yourself. Just find what works best for you. Say to yourself: "Right now I feel …" And remember to pay attention to your pleasant and joyful emotions too. The more you're able to recognize them and say them out loud, the more fully you'll be able to enjoy those feelings.

Then, in order to further reinforce the experience, record your emotions in your Emotional Record. Recording your feelings throughout the week will help you recognize, label, and describe your emotions.

EXAMPLE: EMOTIONAL RECORD

When Did It Happen and Where Were You?	How Did You Feel? ("Right now, I feel …")	Did You Say How You Felt Out Loud?	What Did You Do After You Recognized How You Felt?
Thursday night, at home	I feel angry.	Yes	I went to the kitchen and had a glass of wine.
Thursday night, at home	I feel sad.	No	I tried to go to sleep, but I kept thinking about how sad I was.
Friday morning, on the bus	I feel agitated.	Yes	I tried to calm down by distracting myself and reading the newspaper.
Friday morning, at work	I feel pissed off.	Yes	I went outside and had a cigarette.
Friday afternoon, at work	I feel jealous.	No	I continued to ignore my friend who's dating a woman that I like.
Friday night, at home	I feel lonely.	Yes	I decided to go to the movies by myself and have a good time.
Saturday afternoon, at the park	I feel happy.	Yes	I stayed at the park with my friends.
Saturday night, at Ben's house	I feel cheerful.	Yes	I didn't say much to anyone because I didn't want to mess up my feelings.

EMOTIONAL RECORD

When Did It Happen and Where Were You?	How Did You Feel? ("Right now, I feel …")	Did You Say How You Felt Out Loud?	What Did You Do After You Recognized How You Felt?

OVERCOMING THE BARRIERS TO HEALTHY EMOTIONS

Now that you've started to recognize your emotions more fully, hopefully you're also noticing how your emotions can influence your behaviors and thoughts. Please look carefully at the following diagram.

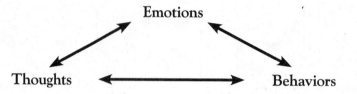

This diagram depicts how your emotions can *influence* your thoughts and behaviors and also how your emotions can be *affected by* your thoughts and behaviors. For example, Jim lost his favorite watch (a behavior). He felt sad (an emotion), and then he thought to himself, "I'm so absentminded; I'm an idiot" (a thought). But this thought just made him feel more depressed (an emotion), so he went home and got drunk (a behavior) and later felt ashamed (an emotion). Do you see how your emotions can be both the result and the cause of your thoughts and behaviors?

This can become a vicious cycle for your emotions if you get caught in self-destructive behaviors or self-critical thinking. But this cycle can also lead to more fulfilling emotional experiences if you engage in healthy behaviors and self-affirming thoughts. For example, maybe after Jim lost his watch (a behavior) and felt sad (an emotion), he could have used a coping thought like "Mistakes happen; nobody's perfect." Then he might have been able to forgive himself for his mistake (another thought) and continue his day, feeling at ease (an emotion). Or after feeling sad about losing his watch, maybe he could have gone for a long walk (a behavior), which would have made him feel refreshed (an emotion). There were many coping thoughts and behaviors Jim could have used to prevent getting caught in a cycle of distressing emotions.

EMOTIONS AND YOUR BEHAVIORS

Clearly, your emotions and your behaviors are strongly linked, and, not surprisingly, stronger emotions often lead to bigger behavioral reactions. As a result, many people with overwhelming feelings also struggle with out-of-control behaviors. People with overwhelming emotions often do many self-destructive things when they feel angry, depressed, or anxious. They cut or mutilate themselves, manipulate others (which often leads to fights and destructive relationships), overeat, undereat, drink alcohol excessively, and use street drugs. Obviously, these types of behaviors are harmful to everyone who's involved. Yet people who engage in these behaviors often do them repeatedly. So the question remains: why do people do these types of things? The answer lies in your emotions.

Let's start with the basics: many behaviors are repeated because they are rewarded. A person goes to work for the reward of a paycheck. A student goes to school for the reward of a degree. People play sports for the reward of competing. A musician plays an instrument for the reward of creating music. And a gardener plants flowers for the reward of seeing them blossom. All of these rewards *reinforce* these behaviors and make them more likely to be repeated in the future. If you didn't get a paycheck for going to work, you wouldn't go anymore. If your teachers told you that there was no chance for you to graduate, you'd probably drop out. And if you only got weeds every time you planted a garden, you'd probably stop doing that too.

In the same way, your emotions can serve as rewards that reinforce your behavior. Here's a simple example of how pleasurable emotions can reinforce a behavior: Phil helped his friend Stefan move into a new apartment (a behavior). Stefan was very grateful, which made Phil feel happy about helping him (an emotion). So the next time Stefan asked for a favor, Phil was happy to help him again (another behavior) because it would make him feel good again (another emotion).

However, emotions can reinforce self-destructive behaviors as well. Consider this example: Teresa, who struggled with overwhelming emotions, once said, "If I feel bad, I want my husband to feel bad too." Logically, this doesn't make sense, but thoughts, emotions, and behaviors aren't always logical. As a young girl, Teresa had never been taught how to cope with her distressing emotions. When she was in emotional or physical pain, she suffered alone without anyone's help. No one paid attention to how she felt.

Then, as an adult, she realized that someone would give her and her pain attention if she hurt the other person too, usually by making them feel upset. For example, when Teresa felt upset at work, she would go home and pick a fight with her husband about something unimportant (her behavior), and he would feel miserable as well. Then he would finally recognize how Teresa felt and talk to her about her feelings (which was her emotional reward). Teresa may not have been consciously aware that she was hurting her husband on purpose, but that didn't matter. At some point in her life, her thoughts had become automatic: "I feel bad, so I have to make someone else feel bad; then I'll feel better." And because her behavior was consistently rewarded with a positive (although illogical) emotional experience—validation from her husband—her behavior was reinforced and repeated in the future.

The Basics	Teresa's Experience
Emotion or thought	"I feel sad."
⇩	⇩
Behavior	She starts a fight with her husband.
⇩	⇩
Behavior is rewarded	Her husband recognizes how she feels.
⇩	⇩
Behavior is repeated	There are more fights in the future.

However, the way Teresa coped with her distressing feelings only made her feel better for a very limited amount of time. In the long term, her marriage suffered at the expense of her emotional validation. Teresa and her husband had frequent fights as a result of her behaviors, and these fights always made her feel even worse.

The emotional rewards that reinforce self-destructive behaviors are important to understand. Two types of self-destructive behaviors that people with overwhelming emotions often engage in are cutting/self-mutilation and manipulating others. Both of these behaviors offer short-term rewards that make them likely to be repeated, but both types of behaviors are also followed by long-term damage. (In the next section, Reducing Your Physical Vulnerability to Overwhelming Emotions, you'll learn about self-destructive eating and substance-use behaviors too.)

Cutting/Self-Mutilation

Many people who cut, burn, or scar themselves say that their actions make them feel better or that their actions relieve some of their pain. To a certain degree, they're right. Cutting and other types of self-mutilation can cause the body to release natural painkillers called *endorphins* that help heal the wound. These painkillers can make a person feel physically and emotionally better for a very short amount of time. Yet as temporary as these rewards are, these physical and emotional feelings reinforce self-mutilation in the future. But remember, these behaviors can be dangerous and possibly lead to death or infection. And while the pain relief is temporary, the scars, the memories, and the guilt that often accompany these actions still remain.

If you engage in any cutting or self-mutilating behaviors, identify what those behaviors are in the space below. Then identify what the temporary rewards might be. And finally, identify what the long-term cost and dangers are, due to those behaviors.

The cutting and self-mutilating behaviors that I engage in are _____

_____

_____

The temporary rewards for my behaviors are _____

_____

_____

The long-term costs and dangers of my behaviors are _____

_____

_____

Manipulating Others

In the earlier example, you saw why Teresa picked fights with her husband when she was feeling upset. Her actions, though damaging to her marriage, made her feel better for a short amount of time. Her behavior was rewarded with emotional validation, so it was repeated in the future. But, the frequent fights with her husband made her feel even worse in the long run.

Similarly, other forms of manipulation can have short-lived emotional rewards that lead to repetition. When you force someone into doing what you want, maybe you feel satisfied or in control. These can all be strong emotional rewards, especially considering that many people with overwhelming emotions feel like their own lives are out of control. But, again, even these emotional rewards are temporary.

Here are some examples. Whenever Brandy felt bored she liked to "mess with people," just to give herself pleasure. Often she would lie to her friends and tell them phony rumors she claimed to have heard about them. Then, when her friends would get upset, Brandy would pretend to comfort them. This made her feel powerful, until her friends discovered the truth and then stopped talking to her. Similarly, Jason was very controlling of his girlfriend Patricia. When they would go out for dinner, he would order for her, even if she wanted something different. He also wouldn't let her spend time with her friends; he was constantly calling her on her cell phone to see where she was; and he told her that if she ever left him, he'd kill himself. Patricia really cared about Jason, and she didn't want to see him get hurt, but eventually, Jason's manipulative behaviors wore her out. So, despite his suicidal threats, Patricia broke up with him.

Remember, no one likes to be manipulated. Eventually, the person who is being manipulated gets tired of being controlled and puts up resistance. Then the relationship becomes confrontational and unrewarding and often ends very painfully. This is usually the worst possible result for a person struggling with overwhelming emotions because he or she is often extremely afraid of being abandoned by others. In fact, all the manipulative behaviors are usually attempts to cope with this fear of being left alone and to force people to stay with them. But when the relationships fail, the fear of being abandoned becomes a reality, and this can set off even more incidents of self-destructive behaviors.

If you engage in any manipulative behaviors, identify what those behaviors are in the space below. Then identify what the temporary rewards might be. And finally, identify what the long-term cost and dangers are due to those behaviors.

The manipulative behaviors that I engage in are _____

_____

_____

The temporary rewards for my behaviors are _____

_____

_____

The long-term costs and dangers of my behaviors are _____

_____

_____

REDUCING YOUR PHYSICAL VULNERABILITY TO OVERWHELMING EMOTIONS

In addition to recognizing how your thoughts and behaviors can influence your emotions, it's also important that you recognize how other health-related issues influence how you feel. Here are some examples.

Food

Your body needs the nutrients it gets from food in order to keep functioning properly, just as a car depends on gasoline to keep running. As a result, the food you eat affects how you feel directly, both emotionally and physically.

Different foods can affect the way you feel as can the amount of food you eat. For example, foods with a lot of fat in them, like ice cream and pastries, can temporarily make you feel pleased and satisfied. But if you eat too much of them, you might start to feel heavy and sluggish. Over time, if you eat an excessive amount of food with high levels of fat or sugar, you'll also gain weight. This often makes people feel sad or unhappy about themselves, and it can also lead to health problems like diabetes and heart disease. Other foods with high sugar content, like candy and soda, can quickly make you feel energized. But as the effect wears off, these foods can leave you feeling very tired or even depressed.

Just as eating too much of certain foods can make you feel ill, eating too little food can also make you feel unhealthy. Getting too few nutrients in your diet can make you feel dizzy or light-headed since you're not getting the energy you need to keep functioning.

It's recommended that you eat a moderate amount of a wide variety of healthy foods every day, including fruits, vegetables, grains, and proteins. If you are curious about your diet or need help creating a healthy diet, contact a medical professional or a certified dietician for advice. Or visit a reputable nutrition Web site, such as the site for the United States Department of Agriculture at www.mypyramid.gov where you can find recommendations and guidelines for eating a healthy, well-balanced diet.

In the space below, record any thoughts you have about how your own eating habits affect how you feel, and then write at least two ways you can improve your eating habits in order to feel better.

My eating habits affect how I feel because _____

_____

_____

I can improve my eating habits by

1) _____

_____

2) _____

_____

Overeating and Undereating

Also, be aware that some people with overwhelming emotions use food in self-destructive ways, either by drastically overeating or undereating. Sometimes people overeat because the food makes them feel emotionally calm, or even numb, for a short amount of time. And, again, these feelings lead to the person's behavior being repeated in the future. Equally dangerous is the fact that some people try to control their overeating by engaging in purging activities like vomiting. Frequent purging can lead to a very dangerous eating disorder called *bulimia* that can have devastating effects on your body.

Drastic undereating can also make a person feel good for a short amount of time. Undereating can serve as a form of self-control. Many times, people with overwhelming emotions feel like their lives are out of their own control, and undereating gives them a sense of power over their lives that makes them feel better. However, this quest for control can be dangerous because excessive undereating can lead to *anorexia*, an extremely unhealthy and potentially life-threatening eating disorder characterized by a person's drastically reduced weight.

If you engage in any overeating or undereating, identify what those behaviors are in the space below. Then identify what the temporary rewards might be. And finally, identify what the long-term costs and dangers are due to those behaviors.

The overeating or undereating behaviors that I engage in are _____

_____

_____

The temporary rewards for my behaviors are _____

_____

_____

The long-term costs and dangers of my behaviors are _____

_____

_____

Drugs and Alcohol

Like food, anything else you put in your body will affect how you feel. Alcohol and drugs often make a person feel temporarily happy, numb, excited, or just different. Naturally, these feelings can lead to repeated use of these substances, especially after the temporary feelings have worn off. However, the excessive use of alcohol, street drugs, or abused prescription drugs can lead to many health complications, addiction problems, legal issues, financial difficulties, and relationship problems.

For example, alcohol is a depressant that makes you feel tired, sluggish, and sad. Many people don't believe this because they say alcohol makes them feel more energized and social. However, alcohol actually makes them feel less self-conscious, so they're more willing to do or say things that they normally wouldn't. But with enough alcohol in anyone's body, he or she will start to feel sad and tired, and the less you weigh, the quicker the alcohol will start to take effect on your body and feelings.

The use of street drugs and certain prescription drugs can have similar effects. Certain drugs, such as cocaine and crack, can initially make a person feel "good" or "energized." But after the effects of the drug wear off, the person may also start to feel depressed, anxious, or paranoid. The same is also true of many other street drugs, such as marijuana, methamphetamines, and heroin. Certain prescription drugs can also make you feel depressed and anxious, so be sure to check with the medical professional who prescribed them if you're feeling any distressing side effects.

Nicotine from tobacco products and caffeine are also considered to be drugs, although they are legal and very prominent in our society. Nicotine is a stimulant that activates a person's muscles, regardless of the fact that some people say that smoking makes them feel more relaxed. In these cases, what the person is actually experiencing is a temporary sense of relief from his or her body, which has been craving more nicotine. Nicotine is a highly addictive substance that makes people want to smoke more cigarettes, and that craving can make a person feel very irritated until he or she smokes again.

Caffeine is also a stimulant that is found in coffee, tea, many sodas, sports drinks, and some painkillers. If you drink too much caffeine, you will start to feel jittery, shaky, and irritated. You can also become addicted to caffeine, and if you don't get enough of it in your body after you're addicted, you can become irritated and possibly develop headaches and other physical symptoms.

With the regular use of alcohol, street drugs, and many prescription drugs, you may crave more of the substance just to feel the same effect it once gave you or to feel "normal." This is called *tolerance*. If you notice you are having this experience with any substance, including prescribed drugs, you should speak with a medical professional. You should also speak with a medical professional if you have a history of alcohol or drug abuse and you want to stop. Withdrawal from alcohol and some other drugs can be potentially dangerous.

In the space below, identify what the temporary rewards might be for your behavior and identify possible long-term costs and dangers. Then record any thoughts you have about how your own alcohol and drug use affects how you feel, and write at least two ways you can improve your habits in order to feel better.

The alcohol or drug-using behaviors that I engage in are _____

_____

_____

The temporary rewards for my behaviors are _____

_____

_____

The long-term costs and dangers of my behaviors are _____

_____

_____

My alcohol and drug use affects how I feel because _____

_____

_____

I can improve my alcohol and drug habits by

1) _____

_____

2) _____

_____

Physical Exercise

The human body is designed for motion and activity. Because of this, it's important that everyone engage in some amount of regular exercise in order to keep their bodies healthy and functioning properly. Without exercise, your body won't burn up the extra energy it stores from the food you eat. As a result, you might start to feel sluggish, you might start to gain weight, and you may even feel a little depressed. It's recommended that everyone engage in approximately thirty minutes of moderate or vigorous exercise most days of the week. This can include walking, jogging, swimming, biking, weight training, or any other activity that makes your body work harder than it usually does. Regular exercise is especially important to keep your heart healthy.

Even if your movement is limited or if you've never exercised before, there's always something that you can do that's within your safety limits. Be sure to check with a medical professional or a physical fitness trainer before engaging in any type of strenuous activity, like weight lifting. And talk with your medical professional if you experience any abnormal pain when you exercise.

In the space below, record any thoughts you have about how your own exercise habits (or lack of exercise) affect how you feel, and then write at least two ways you can improve your habits in order to feel better.

My exercise habits affect how I feel because _____

_____

_____

I can improve my exercise habits by

1) _____

_____

2) _____

_____

Sleep

Getting enough sleep is one of the most important things you can do to feel healthy. The average adult needs approximately seven or eight hours of sleep each night. Children and some adults need slightly more. If you're not getting enough sleep each night, you probably feel sluggish and tired all day and you probably also find it hard to think clearly. It's no wonder that a lack of sleep is often the cause of accidents and poor decision-making ability.

No amount of caffeine can make up for the sleep you missed the night before. In fact, caffeine, alcohol, and other drugs can all interfere with your ability to sleep at night. Your body needs a proper amount of rest because it uses the time when you are asleep to repair itself. If you're not sleeping, your body can't heal itself properly.

If you wake up many times throughout the night, if you snore excessively, or if you wake up gasping for breath, these can all be signs of sleep disorders, and you should talk to a medical professional.

Do your best to develop proper sleep habits in order to get the rest that you need. Refer to the Guide to Sleep Hygiene on page 142 to develop healthy sleep habits if you need help. Then, in the space below, record any thoughts you have about how your own sleep habits affect how you feel, and write at least two ways you can improve your sleep habits in order to feel better.

My sleep (or lack of sleep) affects how I feel because _____

_____

_____

I can improve my sleep habits by

1) _____

_____

2) _____

_____

Illness and Physical Pain

Obviously, if you're experiencing any illness or physical pain, this will affect how you feel emotionally. Your physical feelings and your emotional feelings are directly connected, and sometimes it's hard or impossible to feel emotionally healthy if you aren't also feeling physically healthy. Therefore, it's critical that you get medical help for any illness or physical pain you might be experiencing. Furthermore, it's also extremely important for you to follow the advice of the medical professional who is treating your illness and to follow the prescription plan for any medications you might be given.

To prevent possible illness and physical pain in the future, if you aren't already experiencing them now, use the guidelines in this section to create a healthier life based upon proper nutrition, plenty of exercise, avoidance of alcohol and nonprescribed drugs, and plenty of necessary sleep.

In the space below, record any thoughts you have about how your own illness or physical pain affects how you feel, and then write at least two ways you can treat any illness or pain in order to feel better.

My illness or pain affects how I feel because _____

_____

_____

I can treat my illness or pain by

1) _____

_____

2) _____

_____

GUIDE TO SLEEP HYGIENE

Proper sleep habits are essential for any healthy lifestyle. Use the following suggestions if you have trouble falling asleep or staying asleep.

- Avoid caffeine for at least six hours before going to sleep.

- Avoid alcohol, nicotine, and street drugs before going to sleep and throughout the night.

- Avoid bright lights, including television, before going to sleep because they are stimulating.

- Don't exercise or eat a heavy meal shortly before going to sleep.

- Avoid napping during the day because it will make you less tired at night.

- Make your bedroom as comfortable as possible. Keep the temperature at a cool, comfortable level, keep your room as dark as possible (use a sleep mask if you need one), and minimize as much noise as possible (use earplugs if you need them).

- Only use your bed for sleeping and sexual activity, not for working, reading, or watching television. This way, your body will associate your bed with sleep, not with activity.

- If you have trouble falling asleep or if you wake up in the middle of the night and can't fall back to sleep, get out of bed and do something soothing until you feel tired enough to go back to sleep. Don't lie in bed thinking about other things; this will just make you feel more aggravated and make it harder to get back to sleep.

- Go to bed at the same time every night and wake up at the same time every morning. Create a regular pattern of sleeping and waking that your body can predict.

- Use some kind of relaxation method before going to sleep in order to calm your body and mind: take a bath, meditate, pray, write down your thoughts, use relaxation skills, and so on.

- If your sleep problems persist, if you can't stay awake during the day, or if you're feeling depressed, contact a medical professional for advice.

Physical Tension and Stress

If you experience physical tension on a regular basis, you also probably feel emotionally stressed-out, anxious, drained, or irritated. Muscle tension, like an illness, directly affects your emotions. Similarly, if you feel anxious, your emotions can often lead to muscle tension, especially in the neck and shoulders, as well as stomach ailments and skin problems.

There are many situations in modern life that can make you feel physically tensed and stressed: long working hours, a job you don't like, commuting to work, difficult relationships, a demanding family schedule, what's happening in the world news, politics, and so on. As a result, it's very important that you find healthy ways to cope with tension and stress so that they don't lead to further illness.

Many good coping skills are found in this book in the mindfulness and distress tolerance chapters. The mindful breathing exercise is very effective for helping you relax, as are many of the self-soothing exercises. Go back to those chapters, if you need to, to find exercises that work for you.

In the space below, record any thoughts you have about how your physical tension and stress affect how you feel, and then write at least two ways you can cope with your stress and tension in order to feel better.

My tension and stress affect how I feel because _____

_____

_____

I can treat my tension and stress by

1) _____

_____

2) _____

_____

Exercise: Recognizing Your Self-Destructive Behaviors

Now that you've learned about different forms of self-destructive behaviors and physical vulnerabilities, make photocopies of the following Recognizing Your Self-Destructive Behaviors Worksheet to observe your own self-harming actions for the next two weeks. This worksheet is very similar to the Recognizing Your Emotions Worksheet found earlier in this chapter. However, this exercise asks you to observe your self-destructive behaviors and then to identify what the emotional rewards were for your behavior and why those rewards were only temporary. Use the following example worksheet to help you.

EXAMPLE: RECOGNIZING YOUR SELF-DESTRUCTIVE BEHAVIORS WORKSHEET

Questions	Your Responses
When did the situation happen?	Tonight
What happened? (Describe the event.)	My girlfriend and I got into a fight. I asked her to come over, but she said she was too busy. Then I told her I didn't know what I would do to myself if she didn't come over, so she did.
Why do you think that situation happened? (Identify the causes.)	She's selfish sometimes. But I also know she's tired when she gets home from work. She's also studying for some classes she's taking. We were both in bad moods.
How did that situation make you feel, both emotionally and physically? (Try to identify both the *primary* emotions and the *secondary* emotions.)	Primary emotions: Anger Secondary emotions: Hopeless, annoyed, afraid that she might leave me Physical sensations: My face became hot, my hands clenched.
What did you want to do as a result of how you felt? (What were your urges?)	I wanted to scream at her and tell her how selfish she is. I also thought about scarring my arm, like I've done in the past.
What did you do and say? (What self-destructive behaviors did you engage in as a result of how you felt?)	I told her she had to come over if she really loved me, or I didn't know what I would do. Then I hung up the phone without waiting for her reply. I went in the kitchen and ate a half-gallon of ice cream while I waited for her to come over. I didn't sleep all night.
What was the emotional reward for your self-destructive behavior? (Identify how the emotional reward was temporary.)	By manipulating her, I got her to come over, which made me feel good. But when she came over, we fought. The ice cream also made me feel good for a little while, but I've been putting on too much weight lately, which makes me feel guilty. Not sleeping another night just made me feel worse the next morning.

RECOGNIZING YOUR SELF-DESTRUCTIVE BEHAVIORS WORKSHEET

Questions	Your Responses
When did the situation happen?	
What happened? (Describe the event.)	
Why do you think that situation happened? (Identify the causes.)	
How did that situation make you feel, both emotionally and physically? (Try to identify both the *primary* emotions and the *secondary* emotions.)	Primary emotions: Secondary emotions: Physical sensations:
What did you want to do as a result of how you felt? (What were your urges?)	
What did you do and say? (What self-destructive behaviors did you engage in as a result of how you felt?)	
What was the emotional reward for your self-destructive behavior? (Identify how the emotional reward was temporary.)	

OBSERVING YOURSELF WITHOUT JUDGING YOURSELF

As you can see from the previous exercise, self-destructive behaviors can only offer you temporary relief. In the long term, they are all more damaging to yourself and others. For this reason, it's important that you begin to notice what the rewards are for all of your behaviors, but especially the self-destructive ones.

But at the same time, also remember that you shouldn't criticize or judge yourself if you discover unhealthy rewards reinforcing your behaviors. Remember that the principle on which dialectical behavior therapy is based states that two apparently contradictory things can both be true. The most important *dialectic* is accepting yourself without judgment while simultaneously changing destructive behaviors so you can live a healthier life (Linehan, 1993a). It's not wrong to admit that some of your behaviors need to be changed; you can still be a good, kind, and loving person. Your behaviors probably exist as they do because you were never taught how to deal with your overwhelming and distressing emotions in any other way. If you had been shown a healthier way to deal with your emotions, you'd probably do it, wouldn't you? That's what the skills in this workbook are all about—teaching you healthier ways to cope with your feelings.

REDUCING YOUR COGNITIVE VULNERABILITY

You've already learned how your thoughts influence how you feel. Remember Jim who lost his watch? He originally thought, "I'm so absentminded; I'm an idiot," which just made him feel worse about what he had done. This type of thought is called a *trigger thought* (McKay, Rogers, & McKay, 2003) because it triggers, or causes, emotional pain and suffering. If you frequently dwell on trigger thoughts, you probably experience overwhelming emotions more frequently than other people. However, we all have trigger thoughts that pop up from time to time. The goal of developing emotion regulation skills is to learn what to do with those thoughts when they do come up. Some of these thoughts are criticisms that we were told when we were children by our parents, guardians, teachers, and others. But other trigger thoughts are self-criticisms that we use to insult ourselves or make our lives more difficult.

Below are several trigger thoughts that often cause a person to feel emotionally distressed. Check (✓) any of them that you use, and then write any additional trigger thoughts in the space provided. If you have trouble remembering a trigger thought that you use, think of the last time you felt upset, angry, sad, depressed, worried, or anxious, and then remember the thoughts you had that made you feel worse. These are your trigger thoughts. Here are some examples:

_____ "I'm an idiot/jerk/moron/_____."

_____ "I can't do anything right."

_____ "I'm a failure."

_____ "I'm incompetent."

_____ "No one's ever going to love me."

_____ "I'm unlovable."

_____ "There's something wrong with me."

_____ "I'm broken."

_____ "No one cares about me."

_____ "Everyone always leaves me."

_____ "People always hurt me."

_____ "I can't trust anyone."

_____ "I'm going to be alone forever."

_____ "I can't make it in life without the help of _____."

_____ "I don't deserve to be happy/successful/loved/ _____."

_____ Other ideas: _____

_____

Obviously a trigger thought can be a powerful negative force in your life if it constantly comes to your attention and leads to distressing emotions. But remember, in addition to trigger thoughts, Jim also used a coping thought, "Mistakes happen; nobody's perfect," and then he was able to feel more at ease. Coping thoughts can be an equally powerful force if you know how to use them. In this section, you'll learn three cognitive skills to help you deal with trigger thoughts and overwhelming emotions: thought and emotion defusing, coping thoughts, and balancing your thoughts and feelings.

Exercise: Thought and Emotion Defusion

Thought defusion (Hayes et al., 1999) is a practice that was already taught in chapter 3, Basic Mindfulness Skills, but it's so important as an emotion regulation skill that it deserves to be repeated here too. Thought defusion is a skill that helps you "unhook" from your thoughts and overwhelming emotions. This is a skill that requires the use of your imagination. The purpose is to visualize your thoughts and emotions either as pictures or words, harmlessly floating away from you, and without obsessing about them, analyzing them, or getting stuck on them.

Typically, people find that imagining their thoughts and emotions floating away in one of the following ways is helpful. But if you've already been using a different means of visualization, or if you want to create something similar, do what works best for you. Here are some examples:

- Imagine sitting in a field watching your thoughts and emotions floating away on clouds.

- Picture yourself sitting near a stream watching your thoughts and emotions floating past on leaves.

- See your thoughts and emotions written in the sand, and then watch the waves wash them away.

Remember to continue using the concept of radical acceptance while doing this exercise. Let your thoughts and related emotions be whatever they are, and don't get distracted by fighting them or criticizing yourself for having them. Just let the thoughts and emotions come and go.

For the purposes of learning emotion regulation skills, you can use one of two variations of this thought- and emotion-defusion exercise. You can start the exercise without any preconceived thoughts and simply watch whatever thoughts and related emotions arise, and then let them come and go without getting stuck on any of them. Or you can begin this exercise by first focusing on one of your trigger thoughts. Recall a recent distressing memory in which your trigger thoughts arose. Notice how you feel emotionally and physically, and then begin the thought-defusion exercise. In this case, many memories from that event (and the trigger thought itself) will come to your thoughts automatically. As they do, continue as usual to watch those thoughts and emotions come and go without analyzing them or getting stuck on them.

Read the instructions before beginning the exercise to familiarize yourself with the experience. If you feel more comfortable listening to the instructions, use an audio-recording device to record the instructions in a slow, even voice so that you can listen to them while practicing this technique. When you are first using thought defusion, set a kitchen timer or an alarm clock for three to five minutes and practice letting go of your thoughts and related emotions until the alarm goes off. Then, as you get more accustomed to using this technique, you can set the alarm for longer periods of time like eight or ten minutes. But don't expect to be able to sit still that long when you first start.

Do this exercise as often as possible. Then, when you feel comfortable with the skill, you can begin letting go of trigger thoughts and distressing emotions in your daily life by briefly closing your eyes and imagining the thoughts and emotions floating past.

Instructions

To begin, find a comfortable place to sit in a room where you won't be disturbed for as long as you've set your timer. Turn off any distracting sounds. Take a few slow, long breaths, relax, and close your eyes.

Now, in your imagination, picture yourself in the scenario that you chose to watch your thoughts come and go, whether it's by the beach or a stream, in a field or a room, or wherever. Do your best to imagine yourself in that scene.

After you do, also start to become aware of the thoughts that you're having. Start to observe the thoughts that are coming up, whatever they are. Don't try to stop your thoughts, and do your best not to criticize yourself for any of the thoughts. Just watch the thoughts arise, and then, using whatever technique you've chosen, watch the thoughts disappear.

If any of your thoughts is a trigger thought, just note to yourself that you're having a trigger thought, observe any emotion that it brings up, and then let the thought and emotion go past, by whatever means you've chosen, without getting stuck on them and without analyzing them.

Whatever the thought or emotion is, big or small, important or unimportant, watch it arise in your mind and then let it float away or disappear by whichever means you've chosen.

Keep breathing slowly, in and out, as you watch your thoughts and emotions float away.

When you notice distressing emotions arising in you because of your thoughts, let them float past in your imagination.

Just continue to watch the thoughts and feelings arise and disappear. Use pictures or words to represent your thoughts and feelings, whatever works best for you. Do your best to watch the thoughts and related feelings arise and disappear without getting hooked into them and without criticizing yourself.

If more than one thought or feeling comes up at the same time, see them both arise and disappear. If the thoughts and feelings come very quickly, do your best to watch them all disappear without getting hooked onto any of them.

Continue to breathe and watch the thoughts and feelings come and go until your timer goes off.

When you've finished, take a few slow, long breaths, and then slowly open your eyes and return your focus to the room.

Using Coping Thoughts

Coping thoughts are designed to soothe your emotions when you're in a distressing situation. They are statements that remind you of your strength, your past successes, and some commonly held truths. Do you remember what happened to Jim when he lost his watch? Originally, he thought, "I'm so absentminded; I'm an idiot," which made him feel depressed. But then he used the coping thought "Mistakes happen; nobody's perfect," and he was able to feel more at ease. You already learned about using self-encouraging coping thoughts in chapter 2, Advanced Distress Tolerance Skills, but they're so important for helping you regulate your emotions that they need to be repeated here. In the following List of Coping Thoughts, you'll find many coping thoughts that you can use to remind yourself of your strength and your past successes when you find yourself in a distressing situation.

Find a few coping thoughts that you consider powerful and motivating, or create your own. Then write them on a note card and keep them with you in your wallet to remind yourself of them when you're in a distressing situation. Or put them on sticky notes and post them in spots where you can see them on a regular basis, like on your refrigerator or mirror. The more often you see these soothing and self-affirming thoughts, the quicker they'll become an automatic part of your thought process.

Here's a list of some coping thoughts that many people have found to be helpful (McKay et al., 1997). Check (✓) the ones that might be helpful for you and then create your own.

LIST OF COPING THOUGHTS

_____ "Mistakes happen; nobody's perfect."

_____ "This situation won't last forever."

_____ "I've already been through many other painful experiences, and I've survived."

_____ "This too shall pass."

_____ "My feelings are like a wave that comes and goes."

_____ "My feelings make me uncomfortable right now, but I can accept them."

_____ "I can be anxious and still deal with the situation."

_____ "I'm strong enough to handle what's happening to me right now."

_____ "This is an opportunity for me to learn how to cope with my fears."

_____ "I can ride this out and not let it get to me."

_____ "I can take all the time I need right now to let go and relax."

_____ "I've survived other situations like this before, and I'll survive this one too."

_____ "My anxiety/fear/sadness won't kill me; it just doesn't feel good right now."

_____ "These are just my feelings, and eventually they'll go away."

_____ "It's okay to feel sad/anxious/afraid sometimes."

_____ "My thoughts don't control my life; I do."

_____ "I can think different thoughts if I want to."

_____ "I'm not in danger right now."

_____ "So what?"

_____ "This situation sucks, but it's only temporary."

_____ "I'm strong and I can deal with this."

_____ Other ideas: _____

_____

_____

Balancing Your Thoughts and Feelings

As you've already learned, overwhelming emotions can be caused by many events. But you can also be overwhelmed by your emotions when you only pay attention to part of what's really happening. This type of thinking is called *filtering* (Beck, Rush, Shaw, & Emery, 1979). Here are some examples:

- Zeva was a straight-A student, she always made the honor roll, and she had already received a full scholarship to her first choice of colleges. But when she got a poor grade on her math test she broke down. "I'm such a loser," she thought to herself, and, very quickly, she felt overwhelmed, upset, and angry.

- Antonio asked his girlfriend if she could come over at three o'clock. She said that she was busy until seven, and she'd come over then. Antonio immediately got angry and accused her of abandoning him.

- Jennifer grew up in a typical middle-class family in a fairly good neighborhood. Most often, her parents were kind and supportive, and they always tried to do their best for her. However, one day when Jennifer was five, her father punished her for talking back to him, and she was grounded for a week. Later, as an adult, whenever Jennifer thought about her young life, she only remembered that incident, and she got upset whenever she thought about it.

Do you see the filtering in each person's thought process? Zeva was devastated by one less-than-perfect grade because she filtered out all of her past successes. Antonio filtered out the fact that his girlfriend said she would come over at a different, more convenient time. And Jennifer filtered out all of her positive childhood experiences and only focused on the one hardship she'd experienced.

Imagine living your life with dark sunglasses on all the time so that it's impossible to see the colors of the world. Think about what a limited, dreary life you might have. Similarly, when you filter your experience and only focus on the distressing elements of your life, you're also choosing to live a limited, unfulfilling life.

In order to begin balancing your thoughts—and therefore your emotions as well—it's necessary to examine the evidence that supports both sides of an emotion-stimulating event:

- Evidence supporting your self-criticisms versus evidence that you're a good person

- Evidence that only bad things happen to you versus evidence that good things happen too

- Evidence that no one cares about you versus evidence that people do care about you

- Evidence that you never do anything right versus evidence of your past successes

- Evidence that the current situation is awful versus evidence that it's not as bad as you think

■   In general, evidence for the bad versus evidence for the good

Seeing the "big picture" is the opposite of filtering. This can be hard to do if you've spent your life narrowly focusing on just the negative evidence in your life. But you can learn to see the big picture by examining the evidence that goes against your distressing thoughts and feelings. These facts, which are often ignored by people with overwhelming emotions, fill out the rest of the big picture and can often change how you feel about a situation. Then, with practice, you'll filter less of your experiences and become less overwhelmed by your emotions.

In order to see the big picture, use the following guidelines. Whenever you find yourself in a situation in which you feel overwhelmed by your emotions, ask yourself these questions:

1.   What happened?

2.   As a result, what did you think and feel? (Be specific.)

3.   What evidence *supports* how you think and feel?

4.   What evidence *contradicts* how you think and feel?

5.   What's a more accurate and fair way to think and feel about this situation?

6.   What can you do to cope with this situation in a healthy way?

Naturally, when you start to feel overwhelmed by a situation, first ask yourself what happened. This is the best place to start. Identify what it is that's making you feel upset. Using Zeva as an example, she would have noted that she got a poor grade on her math test.

Second, identify your thoughts and feelings. Remember, your thoughts greatly influence how you feel. But if your thoughts about a situation are being filtered and you're not seeing the big picture, your thoughts are more likely to cause overwhelming, distressing emotions. In Zeva's example, she thought, "I'm such a loser," and then she felt overwhelmed, upset, and angry.

Third, ask yourself what evidence supports how you're thinking and feeling about the situation. This is usually an easy question to answer. If you've spent your life filtering your experiences so that you only see the negative, distressing facts, it's easy to think of lots of reasons why you feel so distressed and overwhelmed. After all, this is what you usually do. Zeva could easily identify why she was feeling so upset: she had studied hard, as she always did, but had gotten a poor grade on her test, which was her lowest score all year.

The fourth question, however, is usually new and challenging for people struggling with overwhelming emotions. Asking yourself to identify the evidence that contradicts how you think and feel about a situation requires that you view the situation in a new and deeper way. For instance, imagine how much different the world must look to a person standing on the street when compared to a person flying above in an airplane. They're both looking at the same landscape, but the person in the plane has a better view of the whole landscape—the big picture.

Similarly, you need to examine more of the facts and evidence that affect your situation and make up your big picture. As you saw earlier in the examples, people often filter out the positive elements of their lives and ignore the facts that might change the way they feel about a situation. If you really want to stop being overwhelmed by your emotions, you'll have to look at all those facts.

Remember what Zeva filtered out? She's a straight-A student, she's on the honor roll, and she got a full scholarship to her first choice of colleges. Now consider how that information contradicts what she thought ("I'm a loser") and how she felt (overwhelmed, upset, and angry). Obviously, Zeva filtered out some very important pieces of her big picture.

Remember, since this question is new for you, it often takes some time to think of an answer. So give yourself a few minutes to think about the possible facts before saying, "There is no contradictory evidence." Be fair and kind to yourself. There's always evidence for and against any topic. And even if the contradictory evidence is minor, it still adds to your big picture. Consider Zeva's example. Even if her example was different and she was a B student or a hardworking student, these facts still could have changed the way she felt about the poor grade. No fact or contradictory piece of evidence is too small to be overlooked.

Next, keeping in mind the new evidence that contradicts the trigger thought, ask yourself if there is a more accurate and fair way to think and feel about this situation. This is a good time to be mindful of your emotions and to use radical acceptance. Remember, this exercise is designed to help you look at your emotional reactions in a new way; it is not designed to criticize you. Therefore, don't be critical of yourself. Try to be accepting of yourself and your emotions as you continue to see your emotions in a new way. In this step, add the new evidence to your big picture and try to create a more accurate and fair way to think and feel about this situation. In reality, this might not change how you feel right now, but it will help you to notice how you could feel about this situation in the future. Using these skills, Zeva's answer could have been something like, "It's okay to feel disappointed because I studied a lot and I didn't do well. But this is just one bad grade. I mostly get A's, and I'm doing well in general."

Finally, Zeva would have asked, "What can I do to cope with this situation in a healthy way?" Here is where you should draw from all the skills and techniques you've learned in this workbook to help you distract, relax, and cope. For example, Zeva could have used some of the distress tolerance and self-soothing skills to calm her emotions, like talking to a friend or listening to some relaxing music. She could also have used her mindfulness skills, like mindful breathing or thought defusion. Or she could have used a coping thought, like "Nobody's perfect; everyone makes mistakes."

Obviously, using the questions in this exercise isn't going to magically change the way you feel right away. But asking yourself these questions will help you recognize the facts that you've been filtering out, and it will also show you the possibilities of how you might react to a similar situation in the future. Then, with practice, you'll start reacting to those similar situations in a new, healthier way.

Seeing the big picture will also give you hope for your future. Many people who filter their experiences feel hopeless and desperate because they're only seeing the problems and the difficulties in their lives. But looking for contrary evidence opens up their perspectives and lets them see that their lives do include some positive experiences. Looking for evidence against overwhelming emotions is like taking off those dark sunglasses so that you can see the variety of colors in your life, and that's a hopeful experience.

Use the following evidence log to help you recognize the evidence for and against the ways you think and feel. Make photocopies of the log and keep one with you. Then, when you're in a situation in which you feel overwhelmed, use the log to help you see the big picture. Use the following example of Zeva's experience to help you.

EXAMPLE: BIG-PICTURE EVIDENCE LOG

Questions	Your Responses
What happened?	I got a poor grade on my math test.
As a result, what did you think and feel? (Be specific.)	Thought: "I'm such a loser." Feelings: Overwhelmed, upset, and angry
What evidence supports how you're thinking and feeling?	I studied as hard as I could, like I usually do, and I still only got a poor grade. That's my lowest grade in class all year.
What evidence contradicts how you're thinking and feeling?	I'm a straight-A student. I'm on the honor roll. And I got a full scholarship to my first choice of colleges.
Considering all the evidence, what's a more accurate and fair way to think and feel about this situation?	It's okay to feel disappointed because I studied a lot and still didn't do well. But this is just one bad grade. I mostly get A's, and I'm doing well in general.
What can you do to cope with this situation in a healthier way?	Talk to my friends. Listen to music I like. Use thought defusion. Use mindful breathing. Use my coping thought: "Nobody's perfect; everybody makes mistakes."

BIG-PICTURE EVIDENCE LOG

Questions	Your Responses
What happened?	
As a result, what did you think and feel? (Be specific.)	Thoughts: Feelings:
What evidence *supports* how you're thinking and feeling?	
What evidence *contradicts* how you're thinking and feeling?	
Considering all the evidence, what's a more *accurate and fair* way to think and feel about this situation?	
What can you do to cope with this situation in a healthier way?	

INCREASING YOUR POSITIVE EMOTIONS

Before you picked up this workbook for the first time, you were probably an expert on distressing emotions and you understood what a life filled with them could feel like. Now, however, you understand that many people with overwhelming emotions discount their pleasurable emotions, filter them out, or never take the opportunity to experience them in the first place. As a result, they focus only on their distressing emotions, such as anger, fear, and sadness, and they rarely notice their pleasurable emotions, such as happiness, surprise, and love.

Maybe that's what you did before, but now you know that it's very important for you to begin noticing your pleasurable emotions. As you continue to use dialectical behavior therapy to improve your life, you'll want to find more ways of experiencing pleasurable emotions, if you don't have enough of them in your life already. This doesn't mean that you'll never experience another distressing feeling. That's impossible. We all have distressing emotions at different points in our lives. But your life doesn't have to be dominated by them.

One very reliable way of focusing on pleasurable emotions is to create pleasurable experiences for yourself. Again, this is a skill that you've already learned in chapter 1, Basic Distress Tolerance Skills, but it deserves to be repeated here. To begin building a more balanced, healthier life for yourself, take some time out of each day to create a pleasurable experience for yourself, and make note of how you felt and what you thought as a result of that experience.

If you need help thinking of pleasurable experiences, use the Big List of Pleasurable Activities found in chapter 1 on pages 15-16. Then use the following Pleasurable Activities Log and the example to record what you did, how you felt, and what you thought about the experience. Remember, try to do something pleasurable for yourself every day. You deserve it.

EXAMPLE: PLEASURABLE ACTIVITIES LOG

When?	What Did You Do?	How Did You Feel?	What Did You Think?
Wednesday night	I took a hot bath.	Very relaxed and calm	"I should do this more often."
Thursday afternoon	I treated myself to a delicious lunch at work.	Satisfied and happy	"I enjoy good food even if I can't always afford it."
Thursday night	I turned off my phone and watched a movie.	Very good; laughed a lot	"I don't watch enough comedies."
Friday night	I went to dinner with my boyfriend.	Excited, nervous, happy	"I wish we went out like that more often."
Saturday morning	I went to temple for religious services	Holy, special, calm	"I should come more often."
Saturday afternoon	I went for a walk at the lake.	Calm and peaceful	"The lake was beautiful."
Saturday afternoon	I went out for ice cream after the walk.	Happy, like I used to when I was younger	"I miss being this happy."
Saturday night	I stayed at home and read.	Relaxed and quiet	"Sometimes it's nice to do quiet things."
Sunday morning	I slept late.	Very rested	"I don't get enough sleep during the week."
Sunday night	I took another bubble bath.	Very relaxed	"I should do this every night."

PLEASURABLE ACTIVITIES LOG

When?	What Did You Do?	How Did You Feel?	What Did You Think?

CHAPTER 7

Advanced Emotion Regulation Skills

In this chapter you will learn four advanced emotion regulation skills:

1. Being mindful of your emotions without judgment

2. Emotion exposure

3. Doing the opposite of your emotional urges

4. Problem solving

In chapter 3, Basic Mindfulness Skills, you learned how to recognize and describe your emotions. Now, in this chapter, emotion exposure will further help you practice two very important things. First, you will learn to observe the natural life cycle of your emotions, watching them rise and fall, shift and change as new emotions replace old ones. Second, you'll learn that you can endure—without avoidance or resistance—your strong feelings. You'll get practice staying "in" the emotion even though you want to run or turn the feeling into action (shouting, hitting, or breaking things). Emotion exposure is a crucial process for learning *not to fear your feelings*. And it will strengthen your emotion regulation skills. The more you practice this exposure work, the more confident you'll become as you face tough emotional challenges.

In addition to being mindful of your emotions without judgment and emotion exposure, you'll learn a behavioral technique called *doing the opposite of your emotional urges*. When you have a strong emotion, it affects behavior in two ways. First, you change your facial expression and body language to reflect your feeling. If you're angry, you may begin to scowl and tighten your fists. On the other hand, if you're scared, your eyes may open wide while you hunch your shoulders. The second behavioral change comes from action urges that accompany every emotion. Anger, for example, may produce urges to shout or hit, while fear might push you to cower or back away.

"Doing the opposite of your emotional urges" is a strategy that blocks ineffective, emotion-driven responses while often helping you to soften the feeling itself.

The next step will be learning key behavior analysis and problem-solving skills to deal more effectively with high-emotion situations. You'll identify what prompts the emotion and learn how to develop alternative strategies to cope with emotion-triggering events.

The last thing we'll do in this chapter is introduce you to an exercise regime called the Weekly Regulator. It will help you to keep practicing the key emotion regulation skills you've learned here. Learning to be mindful of your emotions with9out judging them decreases the chance that they will grow in intensity and become even more painful.

BEING MINDFUL OF YOUR EMOTIONS WITHOUT JUDGMENT

Learning to be mindful of your emotions without judging them decreases the chance that they will grow in intensity and become even more overwhelming or painful.

Exercise: Being Mindful of Your Emotions Without Judgment

This technique begins with the mindful awareness of your breath. Focus on the feeling of the air moving across your throat, how your ribs expand and contract, and the sense of your diaphragm stretching and releasing. After four or five slow, deep breaths, you can do one of two things: (1) observe whatever current emotion you may be feeling, or if you can't identify an emotion, (2) visualize a recent scene where you experienced an emotional reaction. If you visualize a scene, notice as many details as possible. Try to remember what was said and how you and others acted.

Read the instructions before beginning the exercise to familiarize yourself with the experience. If you feel more comfortable listening to the instructions, use an audio-recording device to record the directions in a slow, even voice, so that you can listen to them while practicing this technique.

Instructions

While breathing slowly and evenly, bring your attention to where you are feeling the emotion in your body. Is it a feeling in your chest or stomach, in your shoulders, or in your face or head? Are you feeling it in your arms or legs? Notice any physical sensations connected with the emotion. Now be aware of the strength of the feeling. Is it growing or diminishing? Is the emotion pleasant or painful? Try to name the emotion or describe some of its qualities.

Now try to notice your thoughts. Do you have thoughts about the emotion? Does the emotion trigger judgments about others or about yourself? Just keep watching your emotion and keep observing your judgments.

Now imagine that each judgment is one of the following:

- *A leaf floating down a stream, around a bend, and out of sight*

- *A computer pop-up ad that briefly flashes on the screen and disappears*

- *One of a long string of boxcars passing in front of you at a railroad crossing*

- *A cloud cutting across a windy sky*

- *A message written on a billboard that you approach and pass at high speed*

- *One of a procession of trucks or cars approaching and passing you on a desert highway*

Choose the image that works best for you. The key is to notice the judgment, place it on a billboard or leaf or boxcar, and let it go.

Just keep observing your emotion. When a judgment about yourself or others begins to manifest, turn it into a visualization (leaf, cloud, billboard, and so on) and watch while it moves away and out of sight.

Now it's time to remind yourself of the right to feel whatever you feel. Emotions come and go, like waves on the sea. They rise up and then recede. Whatever you feel, no matter how strong or painful, is legitimate and necessary. Take a slow breath and accept the emotion as something that lives in you for a little while—and then passes.

Notice your judgmental thoughts. Visualize them and then let them pass. Let your emotions be what they are, like waves on the sea that rise and fall. You ride your emotions for a little while, and then they leave. This is natural and normal. It's what it means to be human.

Finish the exercise with three minutes of mindful breathing, counting your out-breaths (1, 2, 3, 4 and then repeating 1, 2, 3, 4) and focusing on the experience of each moment as you breathe.

Looking back on this exercise, you may have found it to be hard work. Watching and letting go of judgments may feel very foreign, very strange. But you are doing something important—you are learning to observe rather than be controlled by judgmental thoughts. We encourage you to do this exercise three or four times before going on to the next step.

Remember, the key steps to the practice of observing your emotions without judging them are as follows:

- Focus on breath.

- Focus on emotion (current or past).

- Notice physical sensations connected to emotion.

- Name the emotion.

- Notice judgments (about self, others, or the emotion itself) and let them go. Use "leaves on a stream" or other image.

- Watch the emotion; emotions are like waves on the sea.

- Remind yourself that you have a right to your feelings.

- Continue to notice and let go of judgments.

- Finish with three minutes of mindful breathing.

EMOTION EXPOSURE

Facing your emotions instead of avoiding them is a major goal of dialectical behavior therapy. Emotion exposure helps you develop the capacity to accept feelings and be less afraid of them.

Step 1 is to begin keeping an Emotion Log so you can become more aware of specific emotional events and how you cope with them. For the next week, keep a record in your Emotion Log for every significant emotion you experience. Under "Event," write down what precipitated your feeling. Triggering events could be internal—a thought, memory, or another feeling—or they could be external, something you or someone else said or did. Under "Emotion," write a word or phrase that sums up your feeling. Under "Coping or Blocking Response," write what you did to try to push the emotion away. Did you try to suppress or hide it? Did you act on it by picking a fight or avoiding something scary? This record of your coping or blocking response will help you identify emotions for doing emotion exposure later in this chapter.

Example: Emotion Log

Linda, who had been struggling with anger and feelings of rejection, kept the following Emotion Log during the week before Christmas. Neither of her divorced parents had invited her for the holiday.

LINDA'S EMOTION LOG

Date	Event	Emotion	Coping or Blocking Response
12/18	My brother calls, wants to know if I'm going to Dad's house for Christmas. But I wasn't invited.	Hurt, rejected, angry	Said "No" in a very leave me alone voice. Changed the subject. Criticized him for being stupid and still trying to be part of the family. Told him Dad doesn't even like him.
12/18	Stuff I said to my brother.	Guilty	Turned it into anger. Sent my father an e-mail, telling him he was a jerk for not inviting me.
12/19	Called my mother, but she was too busy to talk.	Rejected, angry	Thought about what a lousy mother she was. Sent an e-mail not to bother "taking time from her busy schedule" to call me back.
12/20	Saw a beautiful castle in a toy store window. Remembered the crappy after-thought Christmas presents I used to get.	Rejected, sad	Got an ice cream and watched all the "stupid ants" running around, doing their Christmas shopping, slaves to the season.
12/21	Bought my father a leather briefcase.	Angry, guilty	Hoping he opens it at his party and feels crappy he didn't invite me. Wrote a phony note saying "Thanks for being a great dad," and apologizing for my e-mail.
12/22	My mother called back.	Rejected, angry	Very cold to her. Told her I was busy when she invited me for a pre-Christmas dinner.

EMOTION LOG

Date	Event	Emotion	Coping or Blocking Response

As you look back over your Emotion Log, we'd like you to pay attention to two things. First, identify the emotions that seem chronic, that show up over and over. Second, notice what coping or blocking mechanisms you typically use and their outcome. Do they work? Do you feel better or worse a few hours after you use them?

Emotions that show up repeatedly or have blocking strategies that create more pain than they relieve will be good targets for emotion exposure. Emotions with ineffective or destructive blocking strategies require exposure because you need practice facing and feeling them—without your traditional methods of avoidance. Those don't work and often just get you in more trouble.

Linda, after reviewing her log, realized that the things she did to cope with feelings of rejection (attacking or criticizing people, being cold and rejecting) were only digging her into a deeper emotional pit. She ended up with overwhelming feelings of guilt and self-hate and seemed even more alienated from her family.

Linda needed to learn how to *be* with her feelings and how to observe them without the traditional avoidance strategies. Emotion exposure would prove to be a tremendously important skill for her. Here's how it works.

Exercise: Emotion Exposure

As soon as you start feeling the emotion you've chosen to work on, do the following procedure. You can either read the instructions to yourself or record and listen to them.

Instructions

Take three or four deep diaphragmatic breaths. Notice how the breath feels in your throat, as it fills your lungs, and as it stretches your diaphragm. While breathing slowly, notice how you feel inside your body, particularly your stomach and chest. Notice your neck and shoulders and face. [Pause here for a few seconds if you are recording the instructions.]

Now notice how you feel emotionally. Just keep your attention on the feeling till you have a sense of it. Describe that feeling to yourself. Label it. Notice the strength of the feeling. Find words to describe the intensity. Notice if the emotion is growing or diminishing. If the emotion were a wave, at what point of the wave are you now—ascending on the leading edge, on the crest, beginning to slide down the far side? [Pause here for a few seconds if you are recording the instructions.]

Now notice any changes in the feeling. Are there other emotions beginning to weave into the first one? Describe to yourself any new emotions that have appeared. Just keep watching and looking for words to describe the slightest change in the quality or intensity of your feelings. [Pause here for a few seconds if you are recording the instructions.]

As you continue to watch, you may notice a need to block the emotion, to push it away. That's normal, but try to keep watching your emotions for just a little while longer. Just keep describing to yourself what you feel and noticing any changes. [Pause here for a few seconds if you are recording the instructions.]

Notice what it's like not to act on your feelings, not to blow up or avoid, not to hurt yourself. Just be aware of the feeling without action, watching but not doing.

Remind yourself that this is a wave that passes, like countless other emotional waves in your life. Waves come and go. There are many times when you've felt good. Soon this wave will pass, and you will feel, again, a period of calm. Watch the wave and let it slowly pass.

If judgment—about yourself or another—arises, notice it and let it go. If you have a judgment about feeling this emotion, notice it and let it go. As best you can, try to accept this feeling. It is just one of life's struggles.

Stay aware of your emotions just a little longer. If they are changing, let them change. Describe to yourself what you feel. Keep watching until the emotion either changes or diminishes. [Pause here for a few seconds if you are recording the instructions.]

Finish the exercise with a few minutes of mindful breathing—counting your breaths and focusing on the experience of each breath.

We encourage you to do emotion exposure for brief periods at first—perhaps as little as five minutes. As you become more used to focusing on feelings, you will be able to tolerate emotion exposure for longer periods. Always be sure to end exposure with mindful breathing because it will soften high-intensity feelings and help to relax you. It will also strengthen mindfulness skills and increase your confidence in your effectiveness.

Remember, the key steps to doing the Emotion Exposure exercise are:

- Focus on your breathing.

- Notice how you feel inside your body.

- Notice and describe your emotion.

- Notice if the feeling is growing or diminishing; see it like a wave.

- Describe any new emotions or changes in quality.

- Notice any need to block the emotion, but keep watching.

- Notice impulses to *act* on your emotion, but keep watching without acting.

- Notice judgments (about self, others, or the emotion itself), and let them go.

- Keep watching until the emotion either changes or diminishes.

- Finish with a few minutes of mindful breathing.

Example: Using Mindfulness of Your Emotions and Emotion Exposure

Adam had struggled for more than five years with feelings of hurt and anger regarding his ex-wife. They were now co-parenting Adam's seven- and ten-year-old children, with the kids spending half the week at each parent's home. Virtually every time they had contact, Adam's ex said something that enraged him. And it didn't end there. He seethed for days afterwards, plotting what he might say or do to get revenge.

The Being Mindful of Your Emotions Without Judgment exercise seemed daunting to Adam, but he was exhausted with the constant emotional upheaval. And his doctor had recently warned him about borderline hypertension. He started by focusing on current emotions—nothing to do with his ex-wife. To his surprise, he tended often to feel sad rather than angry.

As Adam observed his sadness, he became conscious of a heavy feeling in his abdomen and shoulders. He had a sudden image of himself carrying a great weight. Judgments came up—he should be stronger, he wasn't a good father, he had screwed up his life. He noticed these thoughts and let them go, imagining them as a string of boxcars passing before him.

Adam didn't fight the sadness—he watched it swell and recede like an ocean wave. He gave himself the right to be sad. Noticing the judgments and letting them go became easier after a few experiences with the exercise. And Adam gained confidence in his ability to calm himself with mindful breathing.

Emotion exposure was more challenging. For this exercise, Adam chose to work on feelings that came up around his ex-wife. His first emotion exposure incident followed a phone call where she accused him of being "cheap and never voluntarily spending anything on the kids."

Adam began by noticing the effect of these words on his body. He felt hot, with a disturbing sense of pressure in the chest and neck. (He wondered if it was his blood pressure.) Now he described the anger to himself. It felt hard and sharp, surging up with deep disgust. There was something else too—a sense of helplessness that seemed, he noticed, almost like despair. It was a feeling that things would never be better, never be different.

As the despair got stronger, Adam noticed an impulse to turn it off, to block it. He wanted a beer, and he started planning the retorts he would make to his ex-wife. With an effort, Adam continued to observe his emotions, not trying to hold on to any particular feeling but keeping his attention on *whatever* he felt.

Adam was also aware of impulses to act on the despair. He wanted to get angry instead, to call his ex and shout that she was poisoning his relationship with his kids. Then he had images of getting in his car and driving into a tree—half for revenge and half to end all the pain he was feeling.

While Adam observed his feelings, judgments kept coming up. His ex was evil, he had been stupid to marry her, she had destroyed his life, and it was too messed up to go on living. It took effort, but he put every thought on a boxcar and let it roll away.

After a time, Adam noticed something that surprised him. The despair feeling, if he didn't hold on to judgments, began to fade. It softened to a feeling closer to regret.

Adam now returned the focus to his breathing, counting and observing each breath. Three minutes later he felt a dark sort of calm—not the greatest feeling in the world but something he could live with.

DOING THE OPPOSITE OF YOUR EMOTIONAL URGES

There are good reasons for feeling whatever it is you feel. Even when they are painful, your emotions are legitimate and valid. The larger problem is emotion-driven behavior, because acting on emotions often creates destructive outcomes. Letting anger drive you to attack with words can disrupt your relationships. Letting fear drive you to avoid critical tasks and challenges can paralyze you at work.

A second problem with acting on emotion-driven impulses is that they *intensify* your original feeling. Instead of getting relief, you may get even more consumed with the emotion. This is where *opposite action* comes in. Rather than fueling your emotion, opposite action helps to regulate and change it. Here are some examples of opposite action.

EXAMPLE: OPPOSITE ACTION

Emotion	Emotion-Driven Behavior	Opposite Action
Anger	Attack, criticize, hurt, shout.	Validate, avoid or distract, use soft voice.
Fear	Avoid, hunch shoulders.	Approach what you fear, do what you've been avoiding, stand tall.
Sadness	Shut down, avoid, be passive, slump, hang your head.	Be active, get involved, set goals, stand straight.
Guilt/shame	Punish yourself, confess, avoid, shut down.	If unfounded guilt, continue doing whatever is triggering guilt; if guilt is justified, atone and make amends.

Notice that opposite action changes both body language (posture, facial expression) and actual behavior. Opposite action isn't about denying or pretending an emotion isn't happening. Rather, it is about *regulation*. You acknowledge the emotion but use the opposite behavior to reduce it or encourage a new emotion.

There are six steps to creating opposite action:

1. Start by acknowledging what you feel. Describe the emotion in words.

2. Ask yourself if there's a good reason to regulate or reduce the intensity of this emotion. Is it overpowering you? Does it drive you to do dangerous or destructive things?

3. Notice the specific body language and behavior (see the "Emotion-Driven Behavior" column in the table on page 171) that accompanies the emotion. What's your facial expression, your posture? What are you saying and how are you saying it? What, specifically, do you do in response to the emotion?

4. Identify opposite action. How can you relax your face and body so it doesn't scream "I'm angry" or "I'm scared"? How can you change your posture to convey confidence and vitality rather than depression? How can you move toward, not away from, what scares you? When you are angry, how can you acknowledge or ignore rather than attack? Make a plan for opposite action that includes a *specific* description of your new behavior.

5. Fully commit to opposite action, and set a time frame to work at it. How long will you maintain the opposite behavior? As you think about making a commitment, keep in mind why you want to regulate your emotions. What's happened in the past when you gave in to emotion-driven behavior? Were there serious costs to you, to others?

6. Monitor your emotions. As you do opposite action, notice how the original emotion may change or evolve. Opposite action literally sends a message to the brain that the old emotion is no longer appropriate—and it helps you shift to a less painful emotion.

Now it's time to do some advanced planning. You're going to identify some "frequent flyer" emotions and commit to opposite-action strategies that can help you with regulation.

Filling out the Opposite-Action Planning Worksheet is simple but potentially very important. In it you'll identify emotions you can expect to feel in the future and prepare a radically different response than you've had in the past.

Here's an example. Remember Linda and the Emotion Log she filled out just before Christmas? When she began working on her Opposite-Action Planning Worksheet, she identified several opposite actions that she thought might help with her anger, feelings of rejection, and guilt. Here's what she decided.

EXAMPLE: LINDA'S OPPOSITE-ACTION PLANNING WORKSHEET

Emotion	Emotion-Driven Behavior	Opposite Action	Time Period	Outcomes
Feeling rejected, angry	1. Withdrawing 2. Attacking 3. Little revenges	Say what hurt me in a soft, nonattacking voice. Be civil; end the conversation quickly. Do something for myself rather than planning revenge.	As long as the conversation lasts	My conversations were calmer, they didn't escalate into fights. I expressed how I felt in a civil way.
Guilt	1. Being "phony nice" 2. Attacking	Apologize straight up, but let people know I don't like how I was treated.	As long as the conversation lasts	People appreciated my honesty. I expressed how I felt in an honest way.

Over several weeks, Linda monitored her opposite-action outcomes to see how the new behavior worked. What she found was that her anger passed more quickly when she followed her opposite-action plan. Using a quiet voice and saying out loud what hurt her seemed to soften the upset. At first, she had been afraid to acknowledge her feelings of rejection because it made her more vulnerable. But after trying it several times (for example, telling her father she was sad not to be with him on Christmas day), Linda found that her anger often shifted to something less sharp, less painful. And she spent less time ruminating about ways she felt victimized.

Opposite action isn't easy. We won't pretend that it is. But opposite action quickly dulls the razor edge of overwhelming emotions. Fear often turns to empowerment, sadness to engagement, anger to detachment, and shame and avoidance to willingness. Planning opposite-action strategies can give you an incredibly effective tool for emotion regulation.

OPPOSITE-ACTION PLANNING WORKSHEET

Emotion	Emotion-Driven Behavior	Opposite Action	Time Period	Outcomes

PROBLEM SOLVING

Sometimes emotion regulation has to start *before* the overwhelming feelings begin. Problem solving focuses on the triggering event and finds new, more effective ways to respond.

Behavior Analysis

Problem solving begins with something called *behavior analysis*. Basically, this amounts to tracing the sequence of events that led up to a problematic emotion. The Behavior Analysis Worksheet will take you step by step through the process.

EXAMPLE: BEHAVIOR ANALYSIS WORKSHEET

When he did a behavior analysis of his anger reactions, Sam found multiple internal triggers he hadn't expected.

SAM'S BEHAVIOR ANALYSIS WORKSHEET

1. Problematic emotion: *Rage at mother-in-law*

2. Precipitating event

    ■ External event: *Mother-in-law's visit. She looks disgusted when she sees my house.*

    ■ Thoughts: *House needs paint. The yard is full of weeds and run-down looking. Place is a dump.*

3. Secondary events

    a. Emotion: *Sadness*

        Thought: *I hate this place.*

    b. Emotion: *Shame*

        Thoughts: *Why do I spend my life in dumps like this? Why can't I do better than this? I know why—because I'm a loser who can't make any money.*

    c. Behavior: *Accused my mother-in-law of not helping us when we needed it, of not caring about our problems, and when she disagreed, blew up.*

Notice that the external event—the mother-in-law's visit—is only one step in a series. And most of the steps leading to the rage are internal—both thoughts and other painful feelings. If Sam is going to better regulate his anger, he may need to identify which steps in the triggering process he wants to change and then use problem solving to plan a different response.

The point here is that you *can* change or soften overwhelming emotions by changing what you do *before* the emotion sweeps you away. The first step, after completing your behavior analysis, is to decide which of the precipitating or secondary events you want to alter. This must be (1) an event you have control over (for example, your own thoughts or behavior) and (2) an event, if altered, that's likely to reduce your problematic emotion.

In Sam's case, he decided to do something about his shame-generating thoughts and the verbal attack. Sam realized that all too often over the years, this same pattern had repeated itself prior to his getting angry. He'd start with self-shaming thoughts, which would soon feel intolerably painful. Then he'd try to mask the shame by finding fault with others, which would trigger anger and eventually an attack.

Once you've identified the precipitating or secondary event(s) you want to change using your own Behavior Analysis Worksheet, the next step is to use the ABC Problem Solving technique.

BEHAVIOR ANALYSIS WORKSHEET

1.   Problematic emotion: _____

2.   Precipitating event (what happened before the emotion)

  ■   External event: Did something happen over which you have no control (losing a job, getting sick, disturbing news, and so on)? _____

  ■   Thoughts: What thoughts, prior to the emotion, might have triggered or intensified your reaction? _____

  ■   Emotion: Was there a prior and different emotion that triggered your reaction?
      _____

  ■   Behavior: Was something you or someone else did a trigger for your reaction?
      _____

3.   Secondary events: Identify what happened immediately after the precipitating event (but before the problematic emotion). Break it down into a series of steps (a, b, c).

  a.   Thoughts: _____

      Emotion: _____

      Behavior: _____

  b.   Thoughts: _____

      Emotion: _____

      Behavior: _____

  c.   Thoughts: _____

      Emotion: _____

      Behavior: _____

   When you complete a Behavior Analysis Worksheet, you'll see how emotions are built. Something always triggers them. Sometimes that trigger is internal—like your thoughts or feelings— and sometimes there are multiple causes, all of which need to be recognized and traced.

ABC Problem Solving

This is the second step of problem solving after you've completed your Behavioral Analysis Worksheet. It will teach you to identify the ABCs of problem solving:

A. *Alternatives.* Brainstorm alternative responses. How could you change precipitating or secondary thoughts or behaviors?

B. *Best ideas.* Evaluate your list and choose one or two of your best ideas to implement.

C. *Commitment to implementation.* Identify the time and place you'll try your new responses. Write out the new thoughts or behavior you'll use.

ALTERNATIVES: BRAINSTORMING

Let's go through the problem-solving steps with Sam as an example. Sam had two brainstorming lists—one to replace his shame-triggering thoughts and the other to change his attacking behavior.

SAM'S BRAINSTORMING IDEAS

Shame Thoughts	Attacking Behavior
■ *Think of things I do right.*	■ *Validate the person before saying anything negative.*
■ *Remind myself how crazy this makes me, how eventually I get angry.*	■ *Never say anything critical if I'm feeling upset or ashamed.*
■ *Distract myself; listen to music.*	■ *Give written, not verbal, feedback. I get too upset and say mean things.*
■ *Ask Millie [his wife] for support.*	■ *Remember how the other person would feel before saying anything.*
■ *Take a drive; take some pictures.*	■ *Check with Millie about whether I'm going off the deep end before giving criticism to anyone.*

BEST IDEAS: EVALUATION STEP

Sam evaluated the different ideas he'd come up with, and decided to try the following:

1. I'll distract myself with music or get involved in my photography.

2. I'll run things past Millie before getting on anyone's case; and I'll give thought-out, written feedback if I decide to say anything critical.

COMMITMENT TO IMPLEMENTATION

Finally, Sam decided to follow his plan with his mother-in-law for the rest of his visit, particularly whenever he was alone with her and she said something annoying.

Notice that Sam developed specific alternative behaviors to replace key actions that happened before he got angry, and he identified a situation where he was committed to using his new plan.

The most important thing about problem solving is to know *exactly* what you're going to do differently—and when and where you'll do it. The more concrete and specific you are, the better. Now, using your own example from your Behavioral Analysis Worksheet, work through the same steps, writing your ideas on a blank piece of paper, so that you can create a plan you can commit to following.

WEEKLY REGULATOR

Emotion regulation is best achieved when you employ your new skills on a regular basis. The Weekly Regulator Logsheet is essentially a reminder system to help you do that. Here are the skills you'll focus on:

- Managing physical vulnerability

- Managing cognitive vulnerability

- Noticing and remembering positive events

- Watching and accepting emotions

- Opposite action

- Problem solving

The Weekly Regulator Logsheet should be filled out every Sunday night. Make plenty of photocopies, and review the skills you've utilized during the past seven days. Checkmark the appropriate boxes to indicate when you used your skills.

WEEKLY REGULATOR LOGSHEET
PHYSICAL VULNERABILITY

	Mon	Tue	Wed	Thu	Fri	Sat	Sun
■ Took proactive steps to deal with physical illness/pain.							
■ Committed to balanced eating.							
■ Didn't use drugs/alcohol.							
■ Got enough sleep.							
■ Exercised.							
■ Used relaxation or mindfulness to cope with stress/tension.							

COGNITIVE VULNERABILITY

	Mon	Tue	Wed	Thu	Fri	Sat	Sun
■ Observed trigger thoughts.							
■ Used coping thoughts.							
■ Noticed at least one positive event.							

POSITIVE EVENTS THIS WEEK

Monday

1. _____

2. _____

3. _____

Tuesday

1. _____

2. _____

3. _____

Wednesday

1. _____

2. _____

3. _____

Thursday

1. _____

2. _____

3. _____

Friday

1. _____

2. _____

3. _____

Saturday

1. _____

2. _____

3. _____

Sunday

1. _____

2. _____

3. _____

WATCHING AND ACCEPTING EMOTIONS

	Mon	Tue	Wed	Thu	Fri	Sat	Sun
■ Watched the emotion.							
■ Didn't act on the emotion.							
■ Didn't judge the emotion.							

COPING WITH EMOTIONS

	Mon	Tue	Wed	Thu	Fri	Sat	Sun
■ Used opposite action.							
■ Used behavior analysis.							
■ Used problem solving.							

CHAPTER 8

Basic Interpersonal Effectiveness Skills

Interpersonal effectiveness skills are a composite of social-skills training (McKay, Davis, & Fanning, 1983), assertiveness training (Alberti & Emmons, 1990; Bower & Bower, 1991), and listening skills (Barker, 1990; Rogers, 1951) which have been combined by Linehan (1993a) for dialectical behavior therapy. In addition, we've added negotiation skills (Fisher & Ury, 1991) to complete the program.

Relationships are precious, and they are vulnerable. They bring love, companionship, and support. Yet, sometimes in a matter of moments, they can become broken beyond repair. Keeping your relationships healthy and alive requires interpersonal skills that you can learn in this chapter and the next. The most necessary and important of these skills is assertiveness, which is the ability to (1) ask for what you want, (2) say no, and (3) negotiate conflict *without damaging the relationship*. Before learning assertiveness, however, there are some key things you need to know.

MINDFUL ATTENTION

Relationships require attention. Whether it's a lover, friend, coworker, or merely a carpool companion, maintaining a good relationship depends on *noticing* the other person's feelings and reactions and then watching the process between you. Using the mindfulness skills you practiced in chapters 3 through 5, you can observe facial expression, body language, tone of voice, and choice of words during a conversation to get a fix on the mood and state of the relationship.

Paying attention means staying in the here and now—not thinking about what you want to say next or focusing on some memory. It means remaining present to what you see, hear, and sense emotionally. In the same way that you can breathe, walk, or even do dishes mindfully, you can also relate with full awareness to the present moment. When you pay attention, you notice trouble coming—before it overwhelms you—and also gain time to ask clarifying questions that can help you correct misconceptions.

Not paying attention—focusing away from the moment between you and others—has a heavy price. You'll end up doing one or more of the following:

- Missing vital cues about the other person's needs and reactions

- Projecting, inaccurately, your fears and feelings on the other

- Blowing up or running away when "surprised" by a negative response you could have seen coming

Mindful attention also involves watching your own experience in relation to others. Do you need something from the other person (for example, more attention or some help)? Do you need to change the process between you (for example, critical comments, demands, intrusive questions)? Do you have feelings that signal something important about what's going on (hurt, sadness, loss, shame, anxiety)? Noticing your feelings can help you figure out what needs to change in a relationship—before you blow up or run away.

In summary, then, the first interpersonal skill you need to cultivate is mindful attention because it helps you read important signals about the state of a relationship.

Exercise: Mindful Attention

In the very next conversation you have, practice being an observer of the moment by attending to the other person's physical and verbal behavior. If you find anything ambiguous or hard to read, ask a clarifying question. Here are some examples:

- How are you feeling? Are you doing okay?

- How are we doing? Are we okay?

- How are things between us?

- I notice _____ ; is that accurate?

- Is everything okay with you? With us?

Also notice your own needs and feelings in the interaction—do any of these require communication? How could you say it in a way that preserves the relationship?

Bill had noticed his girlfriend Gina looking away from him during dinner. When he asked "How are things between us?" she told him that she'd been hurt not to be invited to his office solstice party. This gave him a chance to explain that he hated company events and only planned to put in an appearance for a few minutes.

PASSIVE VERSUS AGGRESSIVE BEHAVIOR

These interpersonal patterns have a huge impact on your relationships. Being passive sometimes seems safe. You go along with what the other person expects. Long term, however, passivity is the royal road to interpersonal disaster. When you give in to others and abandon your own needs, it creates frustration and resentment that builds inside of you. Eventually, the relationship becomes so painful that you blow up, collapse into depression, or run away. The paradox of being passive is that in the short term, giving in seems to protect the relationship. Long term, however, the relationship takes a shape you can't stand—and you have to destroy it to stop the pain.

In comparison, aggressive behaviors also destroy relationships because they push people away. An aggressive interpersonal style derives from two sources. The first is a strong sense of the way things *should* be. In particular, you are acutely aware of how others ought to behave. You see clearly the right and wrong way to act in each situation. When others act in a way that violates your sense of what is appropriate or right, you may feel a strong need to punish them.

The second source of aggression is a need to control interpersonal events. Things have to go a certain way, and you expect certain outcomes to happen or not happen. So when the other person either violates your sense of what's right or fails to do what you expect, anger starts to roil up in you. You apply more pressure to control what happens. At times, you may feel so determined that you explode—and drive others away.

Passivity and aggression both destroy relationships. Either one of these patterns ends up being very painful for you—and those you care for. The assertiveness skills you'll be introduced to in the next chapter are a middle way. They will give you the tools to seek what you need in relationships, set limits, and negotiate conflicts—all without anger or coercive efforts to control.

Exercise: Identify Your Style

Think back over recent interactions in your five most significant relationships. Place a check (✓) next to the statements that reflect your typical behavior:

_____   1.   I go along with something, even if I don't like it.

_____   2.   I push people to do what's right, even if there's an upset.

_____   3.   I try to be pleasant and easygoing, no matter what people do or say.

_____   4.   I give people a piece of my mind when they deserve it.

_____   5.   I always try to be sensitive to what other people need and feel, even if my own needs get lost in the process.

_____   6.   I know what I want and insist on it, even if it means having to get angry.

_____   7.   When there's a conflict, I tend to give in and let things go the other person's way.

_____ 8.   When people don't do what's appropriate or reasonable, I don't let them get away with it.

_____ 9.   I'll pull away from a relationship rather than say anything that could be upsetting.

_____ 10. You can't let people continue being selfish or stupid; you have to shake them till they see what they're doing.

_____ 11. I leave people alone, let them be whatever they are.

_____ 12. If people ignore my needs or insist on things that don't work for me, I get more and more upset till they pay attention.

If you tended to mark _odd_ numbers, your predominant style is passive; if you checked _even_ numbers, you may have a tendency to an aggressive problem-solving style.

"I WANT–THEY WANT" RATIO

Every relationship consists of two people trying to get what they need. Sometimes they need the same thing—companionship, recreation, calm, and quiet—and it's easy. But when they need different things at the same time, or when one of them needs something the other doesn't want to give, there's trouble. For relationships to succeed you must be able to do the following:

■   Know and say what you desire.

■   Notice or find out what the other person desires.

■   Negotiate and compromise so you can get at least some of what you want.

■   Give what you can of what the other person wants.

If the "I want–they want" ratio isn't balanced, your relationship becomes unstable. Paying attention to what each person desires and using assertiveness skills to negotiate conflicts is vital to maintaining healthy relationships.

Exercise: "I Want–They Want"

The following exercise will help you assess the "I want–they want" ratio. Choose one relationship you want to evaluate. In the left-hand column, fill in the things you want and need in that relationship.

Under "Outcome," assess how well those needs are met. In the two right-hand columns, do the same for the other person. Now take a look at the outcomes on each side of the chart. Are more of one person or the other's needs being met? How does the relationship deal with those unmet needs? Are they ignored or negotiated? Are they sources of blame or withdrawal?

"I WANT–THEY WANT" ASSESSMENT

I Want	Outcome	They Want	Outcome

"I WANT–I SHOULD" RATIO

Every relationship requires keeping a delicate balance between seeking what you want to do and doing what you think you should do (for the good of the relationship or the other person). If most of your focus is directed toward getting and doing what you want with little attention to what must be done for the other, you'll soon earn resentment. If you're overbalanced on the side of "shoulds"—how you *should* act, what you *should* do for the other person—the relationship will begin to feel like a joyless burden, and you'll dream of escape.

For many, "shoulds" can become a controlling tyranny, forcing them to ignore important needs. They're so busy being good and giving that they fail to notice how depressed and desperate they've become. Sooner or later, the pain of denying yourself grows too big, and you have to escape or blow up the relationship.

Exercise: The "Shoulds"

Put a check (✓) next to the items that describe your beliefs or feelings:

_____   You should try to give everything that's asked of you in a relationship, even when it means putting your own needs aside.

_____   When someone is in pain, you should do anything required to help them.

_____   You should be caring and considerate at all times.

_____   You shouldn't ask for something if you know the other person doesn't want to give it.

_____   There is a right way to act with people, and it should be followed even if it means keeping quiet about your feelings and needs.

_____   You shouldn't say no to people; it's impolite.

_____   You shouldn't express feelings that might upset someone; it's wrong.

_____   You should respond to the needs of others because their needs are a high priority.

_____   You should never hurt or offend anyone.

_____   You should try not to disappoint others.

The more items you checked, the stronger your beliefs about the right and wrong way to relate with others and the more likely you are to deny your own needs in a relationship. There's nothing wrong with having values about how to treat others, but if those values overpower your ability to ask for what you want, you'll end up feeling helpless in any relationship.

SKILL BUILDING

Improving your interpersonal skills will take hard work. You don't need anyone to tell you how difficult it is to change relationship patterns. But you know why it's important—some relationships you value have blown up because you didn't know how to fix things that went wrong. This chapter and the next will give you new tools to manage how you function in relationships. Sometimes they'll work, sometimes they won't; and sometimes you may forget to use them. But you'll also be amazed how much they can improve a conversation or help to solve a problem.

It's hard, but it's okay if you fall down sometimes—if you blow up or withdraw—because it takes time to learn a new way. Practicing your new interpersonal skills will yield the following results:

- Help you be more effective in your dealings with people

- Improve your ability to get your needs met

- Help you negotiate conflicts without damaging a relationship

- Strengthen your self-respect by giving you alternatives to old, damaging patterns of anger or withdrawal

KEY INTERPERSONAL SKILLS

There are six core interpersonal skills that will change how your relationships feel:

1. *Knowing what you want.* How do you know what you want in a relationship? In some cases, you sense a yearning. Or you're aware of discomfort. The key is to pay attention and look for a way to describe, in your own mind, what you're feeling.

2. *Asking for what you want—in a way that protects the relationship.* The next chapter will give you an effective method and format for doing this. But for the moment, the basic idea is to put your needs into words that are clear, not attacking, and ask for specific behavioral change.

3. *Negotiating conflicting wants.* The willingness to negotiate starts with a clear commitment that there won't be winners or losers. It assumes that each person's needs are valid and understandable, and it draws on a willingness to compromise so that each person gets some of what he or she wants. A simple protocol for negotiating conflicting needs is provided in the next chapter.

4. *Getting information.* One of the most crucial of all interpersonal skills is finding out what the other person needs, fears, hopes for, and so on. The major blocks to getting

information are when you (1) falsely assume you know what the other person wants; (2) project your own fears, needs, and feelings on the other person; (3) fear appearing to pry; (4) fear hearing the worst possible answer; and (5) don't know how to ask or what to look for. The next chapter will give you some key strategies for getting information.

5. *Saying no—in a way that protects the relationship.* You can say no in three ways: (1) in a limp, powerless style that just gets overridden; (2) in a hard-edged, aggressive style that alienates people; or (3) in an assertive style that validates the other person's needs and desires while setting firm boundaries around what you will and won't do. The first two strategies undermine relationships because someone is going to end up feeling controlled and resentful. We'll describe how to implement the third strategy in the next chapter.

6. *Acting according to your values.* Being passive or aggressive in a relationship diminishes both your self-respect and the self-respect of others, because someone is losing out in the relationship—someone's needs and feelings are being ignored. Being clear about how you want to treat others is a critical step to interpersonal effectiveness. Ask yourself, "What type of relationships do I want with other people?" Do you want a loving relationship, a trustworthy relationship, or a committed relationship? Hopefully, as you've been using the skills and exercises in this workbook, you've begun to think about how you value your relationships. Acting in your relationships according to what you value is another crucial step that will determine the entire nature of your relationships. Don't be surprised when valueless relationships don't work out well. Try setting positive intentions and values for each of your relationships, and act in those relationships according to what you're trying to achieve.

Exercise: Identify Your Interpersonal Values

On the following lines, list any of your interpersonal behaviors that diminish self-respect. Include anything that emotionally damages you or another person. Also write down sins of omission—things you should have done, but didn't.

Example: *I get angry as soon as someone criticizes me.*

_____

_____

_____

_____

Now, in the space that follows, list your values regarding how people should be treated. These are your basic rules about what you and others are entitled to in a relationship.

Example: *It's important to me to hear that someone I love is hurting.*

_____

_____

_____

_____

When you compare the two lists, assess whether you're using interpersonal strategies that violate your values. Which core values do you disregard most frequently? How are your relationships impacted when you violate your values?

In the next chapter, you will learn interpersonal strategies that will help you be effective while at the same time preserving your self-respect.

BLOCKS TO USING INTERPERSONAL SKILLS

Despite how diligent you are about using your new interpersonal skills, there will still be many obstacles along the way that might temporarily block the success of your relationships. But don't worry—identifying these obstacles is half the battle. Once you know what they are, you can prepare to overcome them. Here are some of the most common blocks to using interpersonal skills:

- Old habits—of the aggressive kind

- Old habits—of the passive kind

- Overwhelming emotion

- Failure to identify your needs

- Fear

- Toxic relationships

- Myths

Old Habits—of the Aggressive Kind

In your family of origin, you observed how people solved interpersonal problems, and you began to model your own behavior on what you saw. If members of your family dealt with conflict using anger, blame, or withdrawal, these are the strategies you may have learned to use as well.

Techniques for influencing others that utilize fear, shame, or hurtful psychological pressure are called *aversive strategies*. There are eight of them:

1. *Discounting:* The message to the other person is that his or her needs or feelings are invalid and don't have legitimacy or importance. Here's an example: "You've been watching TV all day; why do you expect me to come home and do the bills?"

2. *Withdrawing/abandoning:* The message is "Do what I want or I'm leaving." The fear of abandonment is so powerful that many people will give up a great deal to avoid it.

3. *Threatening:* The message here is "Do what I want or I'll hurt you." The most typical threats are to get angry or somehow make the other person's life miserable. Here's an example: "Hey, okay, I won't ask you to help me again. Maybe I'll ask somebody else."

4. *Blaming:* The problem, whatever it is, becomes the other person's fault. Since they caused it, they have to fix it. Here's an example: "The reason we're running up our credit cards every month is that you never saw a store you didn't like."

5. *Belittling/denigrating:* The strategy here is to make the other person feel foolish and wrong to have a particular need, opinion, or feeling. Here's an example: "Why do you want to go to the lake all the time? All you ever do is get allergy attacks up there."

6. *Guilt-tripping:* This strategy conveys the message that the other person is a moral failure, that their needs are wrong and must be given up. Here's an example: "If you don't trust me, that tells me something is very wrong with our relationship."

7. *Derailing:* This strategy switches attention away from the other person's feelings and needs. The idea is to stop talking about them and instead talk about yourself. Here's an example: "I don't care what you want to do, right now I feel hurt."

8. *Taking away:* Here the strategy is to withdraw some form of support, pleasure, or reinforcement from the other person as punishment for something they said, did, or wanted. Here's an example: John said, "I'm not really in the mood for hiking; it's boring," after his partner was unwilling to invest in a new camera (adapted from McKay, Fanning, & Paleg, 1994).

As you review this list, are there strategies you recognize from your own behavior? Think back to times you've used aversive tactics—what was the impact on your relationship? Is this something you want to change? The best way to stop aversive behavior is to observe it closely.

Exercise: Conflict Log

The following Conflict Log will help you.

CONFLICT LOG

Date	My Need	My Behavior	Aversive Strategy	Consequences

Old Habits—of the Passive Kind

Some old habits are of the passive rather than aggressive variety. You may have learned in your family how to shut down or surrender when there is a conflict. You can use the same Conflict Log (using "Passive Strategy" rather than "Aversive Strategy" in column four to track conflicts when you withdraw or shut down.

After keeping the log, ask these questions:

■ What kind of needs or situations trigger your use of aversive or passive strategies?

■ Which strategies do you most frequently rely on?

■ Are you getting what you want using aversive or passive strategies?

■ What are the most frequent emotional consequences for using these strategies?

The assertiveness skills in the next chapter will give you more effective alternatives to the aversive and passive responses you've typically used.

Overwhelming Emotion

A third major block to using interpersonal skills is high emotion. Sometimes your best intentions and most carefully laid plans go up in smoke when you're upset. For some people, particularly those who have grown up in abusive homes, getting angry can cause a *dissociative fugue state*. In that frame of mind, they may do or say things that, on later reflection, seem to have been done by someone else. "It didn't feel like me telling my wife to get out," one man insisted. "I felt like I was possessed, in the control of some force outside myself."

There is good evidence that angry, dissociative states are responsible for a lot of emotional and even physical violence. What can you do when overwhelming emotion threatens to unravel your hard-won interpersonal skills? There are two things you can learn to do right now. First, pay attention to the red flags that indicate you're starting to lose control. Different people have different signals. Here are some that are typical:

■ Feeling hot or flushed

■ Heart pounding

■ Short of breath

■ Tension in your hands, arms, forehead, or shoulders

■ Talking more rapidly or more loudly than usual

■ Feeling a strong need to win, to crush someone, to make them feel bad

Exercise: Red-Flag Feelings and Behaviors

Make a list in the following space of red-flag feelings or behaviors that in the past signaled a loss of control:

_____

_____

_____

_____

_____

Now when conflicts arise, watch out for the red flags. If you notice them, you can use a second technique you've already learned: When you first notice that you're beginning to get overwhelmed by your emotions, start using your mindful breathing skills (see page 80). Take slow, diaphragmatic breaths, and put all of your attention on the physical experience of the breath. This will help to calm you and to disconnect the old neural pathways that made you feel overwhelmed.

Failure to Identify Your Needs

Interpersonal skills won't do you much good if you don't know what you want in a situation. If you can't clearly articulate your needs, all you're left with is frustration. The first section of the next chapter will offer you strategies for identifying what you want in terms of specific behavioral change from others. Once you can articulate a need to yourself, the sections on assertiveness and making a simple request will give you tools to say it out loud.

Fear

When you feel afraid of something, interpersonal skills often go out the window. You're just too full of catastrophic "what ifs" to think clearly. "What if I'm rejected? What if I lose my job? What if I can't stand this?" Catastrophic thoughts can scare you into using aggressive and aversive strategies. Or they can cause you to avoid a situation altogether. The net result is that you don't function well and aren't effective.

Wise-mind meditation (see page 87) can help you manage in the face of fear, as can mindful breathing. Another thing you can do is directly confront your catastrophic thoughts. There are two steps to this.

Exercise 1: Risk Assessment

Notice that the Risk Assessment/Risk Planning Worksheet on the next page is divided into four columns. In column one, write down your fear, and in column two list all the evidence you have that the fear will come true. In column three, write down all available evidence that the catastrophe won't occur. Now, after reviewing evidence for and against, write your estimate of the percentage of chance that the catastrophe will happen.

Exercise 2: Risk Planning

In the "Risk Planning" portion of the worksheet, imagine that the catastrophe you fear has actually happened. How would you cope? Do you have resources, family, or friends to help you? Do you have a plan for how you would do your best with the situation? What skills do you have to get you through?

The Risk Assessment/Risk Planning Worksheet is something you may want to photocopy and use again and again—whenever fear threatens to torpedo your relationship skills.

RISK ASSESSMENT

My Fear	Evidence For	Evidence Against	Percentage of Chance of Occurring

RISK PLANNING

Make a coping plan utilizing your skills and resources in the event your feared scenario comes true.

1. _____

2. _____

3. _____

4. _____

5. _____

6. _____

Toxic Relationships

Relationships where people use aversive strategies on you can make your interpersonal skills very difficult to use. No matter how determined you are to be assertive rather than aggressive or passive, people who blame, threaten, or belittle you can often trip you up and make you want to explode or run away.

The best solution is to get away from these folks. They're not going to change, and you'll never stop being vulnerable to their attacks. However, if these are people you can't avoid—for example, a boss or a family member—there are two things you *must* do to cope. First, you have to calm yourself before dealing with them. Use mindful breathing or wise mind to get centered. Second, based on past experience, you need to anticipate exactly how the toxic individual is likely to act, and then you need to make a specific plan—even a script—to deal with it. Planning ahead and developing a detailed response will keep you from falling back on old, ineffective patterns. See the assertiveness sections in the next chapter for the tools necessary to talk your way out of aversive traps.

Myths

The last of the major blocks to using interpersonal skills is found in the four paralyzing myths of relationship:

1. If I need something, it means there is something wrong or bad about me.

2. I won't be able to stand it if the other person gets mad or says no.

3. It's selfish to say no or ask for things.

4. I have no control over anything.

Each of these myths inhibits you from saying what you need and setting limits. Let's look at each of them.

- *Myth #1.* Every human being needs things from other human beings—whether it's attention, support, love, help, or just plain kindness. We are not sufficient unto ourselves, and our whole lives are spent negotiating with others for everything we require to survive—physically and emotionally. So needing things can't be shameful or wrong; it is basic to the human condition. In contrast to this myth, a healthy alternative coping thought is "*I have a right to want things.*"

- *Myth #2.* Hearing an angry refusal hurts. Sometimes it hits so hard and suddenly that it takes your breath away. But is it true you can't stand it? Think of the rejections you've suffered in your life—they were difficult, but you survived them. Refusals hurt, there's no doubt about it, but the worst thing is living with years of pain because you never asked for what you want. In contrast to this myth, a healthy alternative coping thought is "*I have a right to ask for things—even if the other person won't give them.*"

- *Myth #3.* You may feel that it's selfish to ask for things because of messages in your early family that said your needs didn't count or that your needs were less important than the needs of others. When you examine it, is this really true? Is there something flawed or wrong with you that makes your needs relatively unimportant? The truth is that everyone's needs are valid, and equally important. It isn't selfish to ask for things or set limits. It's normal. It's healthy and necessary. Our survival as individuals depends on knowing and saying what we want. Because if we don't, folks don't pay attention. A helpful coping thought is "*It's normal and healthy to ask for things.*"

- *Myth #4.* Control is relative. You can't control the behavior of others, even though some folks go nuts trying. What can be controlled is *your* behavior. Passive or aggressive styles often have bad outcomes. People ignore your needs or get angry and resist you. That's why you feel helpless—the strategies you're using aren't effective. Assertive behavior gets better results. People—more often than not—listen and respond positively. In contrast to this myth, a helpful alternative coping thought is "*I can choose to behave in more effective ways.*"

CHAPTER 9

Advanced Interpersonal Effectiveness Skills

This chapter contains all the applied skills of interpersonal effectiveness. Learning and practicing these skills will change your life because you'll have far less conflict and far more rewards in your relationships. Your connections to people will feel different—more satisfying than frustrating and more supportive than depriving. In this chapter, you'll learn the following specific skills:

- Knowing what you want

- Modulating intensity

- Making a simple request

- Making basic assertiveness scripts

- Using assertive listening skills

- Saying no

- Coping with resistance and conflict

- Negotiating

- Analyzing problem interactions

KNOWING WHAT YOU WANT

Interpersonal effectiveness has to begin with self-knowledge. You need to be clear about what you feel and want. Chapters 6 and 7 on emotion regulation will give you words for the nuances of what you feel and techniques to classify the emotion. For our purposes here, you can identify emotions through a simple decision-making process called a *decision tree*. It starts with the basic questions—is the feeling good or bad, painful or pleasurable? If the feeling is good, is it more like satisfaction, excitement, sexual attraction, love/affection, contentment, joy, pleasant anticipation, interest, or satiety? If the feeling is bad, is it more like anxiety, fear, anger, resentment, sadness, grief/loss, hurt, anger or disgust with oneself, embarrassment/shame, guilt, yearning/deprivation, or loneliness/emptiness? The decision tree looks like this:

EMOTIONS

Good	**Bad**
Satisfaction	Anxiety (for the future)
Excitement	Fear (of something now)
Sexual attraction	Anger
Love/affection	Resentment
Contentment	Sadness
Joy	Grief/loss
Pleasant anticipation	Hurt
Interest	Anger or disgust with oneself
Satiety	Embarrassment/shame
	Guilt
	Yearning/deprivation
	Loneliness/emptiness

Allan, for example, was aware that something felt wrong in his relationship with his father. When he looked at the list of feelings, the one that seemed closest was hurt—with a little bit of resentment. Allan could tell it somehow related to his father's planned visit. The man was coming to town with his new wife. Yet, in five days of sightseeing, his dad had scheduled just a single dinner with Allan. Once you can put words to what you feel, the next question becomes, what does this emotion make you want to change? And, more specifically, what is the behavior of others that you want to modify? Do you want them to do more or less of something? Do you want something to stop? Do you want new behavior that could make a difference in how you feel?

Now think about the behavior change in specific terms. When and where do you want to see this change? How often? What exactly would the new behavior look like?

Now let's condense this process into a series of steps.

Exercise: Knowing What You Want

Think of a recent experience where you had a bad feeling during an interaction. Getting from the feeling to a clear statement of desire would involve the following process:

1. Put the feeling into words: _____

   _____

2. What do you want the other person to change?

   ■ More of _____

   ■ Less of _____

   ■ Stop doing _____

   ■ Start doing _____

   ■ When _____

   ■ Where _____

   ■ Frequency _____

   Now put all this information into one or more clear sentences: _____

   _____

   _____

   _____

A woman whose sister frequently criticized how she parented a difficult child wrote this description of what she wanted changed: "I'd like Brenda to stop talking about Mike [my son] and stop talking about my 'needing a backbone' with him. I'd like her to stop it, in particular, when we're around people we know. Instead, I'd rather she ask me about other things—work, my photographs, my writing."

The problem with getting clear and specific about your desires is that it brings up anxiety. Do you deserve to ask for things? Do you dare trouble people with your needs? Are you allowed to disappoint, to annoy, to push people to make an effort on your behalf? The answer is yes. And the reason is that you are a human being who feels, who yearns for things, who hurts, who struggles with moments of pain. All of this entitles you to be heard.

Unfortunately, many people grow up in families that invalidate their needs. And all their lives they feel afraid to ask for things—as if they were bad or undeserving, as if their feelings and pain had no importance.

To remind you of your value and importance as a human being, we'd like you to review the following list of legitimate rights (adapted from McKay et al., 1983).

YOUR LEGITIMATE RIGHTS

1. You have a right to need things from others.

2. You have a right to put yourself first sometimes.

3. You have a right to feel and express your emotions or your pain.

4. You have the right to be the final judge of your beliefs and accept them as legitimate.

5. You have the right to your opinions and convictions.

6. You have the right to your experience—even if it's different from that of other people.

7. You have a right to protest any treatment or criticism that feels bad to you.

8. You have a right to negotiate for change.

9. You have a right to ask for help, emotional support, or anything else you need (even though you may not always get it).

10. You have a right to say no; saying no doesn't make you bad or selfish.

11. You have a right not to justify yourself to others.

12. You have a right not to take responsibility for someone else's problem.

13. You have a right to choose not to respond to a situation.

14. You have a right, sometimes, to inconvenience or disappoint others.

Put the rights that are most important or liberating to you on a file card, and tape it someplace where you'll see it frequently, like your bathroom mirror, in order to remind yourself.

MODULATING INTENSITY

How you ask for things depends on the situation. The intensity and level of insistence can vary based on two major factors:

1. How urgent is my need?

    Low urgency 1 2 3 4 5 6 7 8 9 10 High urgency

2. How vulnerable is the other person or the relationship?

Very vulnerable   1   2   3   4   5   6   7   8   9   10   Not vulnerable

Notice that you can assess each of these variables with a ten-point scale. The higher the total number, the more forceful it's appropriate to be. The lower the number, the more moderate and gentle you should be.

Exercise: Modulating Intensity

Think of some recent situations where you've needed another person to change. Evaluate them using these two key questions and the scoring method. What can you learn about the appropriate level of intensity and pressure? Did you use too much—or too little—in certain situations? Imagine what might have happened if you'd adjusted the intensity of your request based on (1) the urgency of need and (2) the level of vulnerability criteria.

Ask yourself these two questions during every situation where you need to express yourself. While you may not always have the time or inclination to use the 1 to 10 rating system, remembering "how urgent?" and "how vulnerable?" can help you make split-second decisions about how much strength, hardness, and volume to put into your voice.

During this exercise, Rachel evaluated some problematic discussions with her husband. One, in particular, had been very frustrating because she wanted him to attend a parent-teacher conference that was scheduled for 3:00—a time when he'd have to miss work. Her husband refused. But their son was having reading problems, and Rachel rated the urgency at an 8, while her husband's vulnerability was rated 7—not very vulnerable. Rachel realized that her gentle, easygoing approach had been a mistake.

MAKING A SIMPLE REQUEST

The skill of making a request is necessary to taking care of yourself. Asking for directions, asking to change tables at a restaurant, asking your mechanic to show you the parts he replaced on your car, asking someone not to smoke in your house—these requests are all about self-protection and quality of life. If you have trouble making such requests, you can easily end up feeling helpless or resentful.

There are four components to a brief request:

1. *A brief justification (optional).* Explain in one sentence what the problem is. "It's hot in here ... These bags are heavy ... It's a long way to walk ... These seem a little tight." Many situations don't need any justification; when they do, keep it simple.

2. *A softening statement.* This is an important piece because it establishes you as a reasonable person who's polite and nondemanding. Softening statements often start like this.

- "Would you mind if ..."

- "It would be helpful if you could ..."

- "I'd appreciate it if you would ..."

- (Said with a smile) "Could I have ..."

- "Hi, I was wondering if ..."

Notice that these openers are disarming. They're far less likely to encounter resistance than a hard-edged demand.

3. A *direct, specific question.* You say what you want clearly and exactly. Leave any charge or emotion out of your voice. Say what you want in a flat, matter-of fact-way. Don't blame or imply that anything's wrong with the other person. Present your request as normal and reasonable—something that anyone would be glad to accommodate. Keep the question to one sentence if you can—the more you elaborate and explain, the more resistance you'll tend to run into.

4. An *appreciation statement.* This reinforces the behavior of the other person saying yes to you. It makes them feel that you value what they're doing. Here are some examples:

- "This will really help me out."

- "Thanks for your effort with this."

- "This will make a real difference."

- "This is much appreciated."

When the components are strung together, simple requests can look like these:

- *In a restaurant:* "The sun's really bright. Would you mind lowering the shade a little? Thanks so much."

- *In a subway car:* "It's a bit tight here. Could you please move your briefcase off the seat to make some room? I really appreciate it."

- *Driving with a friend:* "I'm nervous to drive this close, especially at this speed. Would it be okay with you to leave a little more room between us and the car in front? Thanks for indulging me on this one."

Exercise: Making a Simple Request

If you sometimes find making requests challenging, you can practice in lots of everyday situations. Try some of these suggestions:

- *On the street:* Asking for the time, for directions, where someone bought a particular article of clothing, for change.

- *In stores:* Asking to examine merchandise, for information (for example, a return policy), to see something less expensive or in a different color, for advice regarding a purchase (for example, "Do these colors go together?"), for change.

- *At work:* Asking for information, for a little bit of help, for an extended deadline, for a moment of someone's time, for an opinion.

- *At home:* Asking for a change in schedule, for assistance, for time together, for help changing the environment ("Would you mind if we moved this chair to the kitchen?").

- *With friends and family:* Asking for a favor, for time, for a ride, for someone to stop something that's annoying.

- *With a teacher or therapist:* Asking for information, for help with a problem, for advice.

If you plan to work on this skill, choose *one* of the above options (or develop ones of your own) to work on *each day*. Either at breakfast or just before going to bed, identify the next day's challenge. Decide on the time and situation in which you plan to practice. Write it in your calendar to help you remember. Then do it.

ASSERTIVENESS SCRIPTS

As you read in the last chapter, assertiveness is a critical skill to maintaining healthy relationships. Without it, you'll be forced into passive or aggressive patterns that destroy the fabric of trust and intimacy.

Assertiveness is most easily learned by using a simple script. It will help you give structure to what you want to say and keep you focused. A script also has the advantage of permitting you to develop a statement in advance, practicing it by yourself or with someone you trust, and finally (at a time you choose) delivering it with greater confidence.

There are three basic components to an assertiveness statement and one optional component.

1. *"I think."* This part focuses on the facts and your understanding of what's going on. It should *not* include judgments or assumptions about the other person's motives. It should *not* in any way attack. "I think" is a clear description of events and experiences that you need to talk about—and perhaps change. Here are some examples:

    ■ "I think we haven't spent much time together lately—two nights last week, one the week before."

    ■ "You've billed me for a repair I didn't authorize."

    ■ "Looking back at the recent past, I think you've been late for the majority of our meetings."

    ■ "I'm getting back from the airport late—around 11:00 o'clock—and ..."

    Notice that there isn't much hint of emotion in these statements, and there's no disapproval in the statement of facts.

2. *"I feel."* This is an optional component that you'd likely use with a friend or family member but not with your garage mechanic. The purpose is to give a brief, nonpejorative description of any emotion triggered by the situation. Communication specialists call this component of assertiveness the "I" statement. That's because it's about you and your particular feelings. Appropriately, any sentence about your emotions should start with "I."

    ■ "I feel scared."

    ■ "I feel lonely."

    ■ "Lately, I feel sad about us."

    ■ "I feel hurt, with a twinge of giving up."

    ■ "I feel kind of lost and invisible and more and more disconnected."

    ■ "I feel rejected."

    ■ "I feel hopeful but nervous."

    Each example, while naming feelings of varied complexity, never makes the other person bad or wrong. That doesn't work—it just makes people defensive and less willing to give you anything. Accusations and blame statements often start with the word "you"—so they're called "you" statements.

    ■ "You're hurting me."

    ■ "You don't care about us."

- "You're always late."

- "You're ruining our business."

Some people dress up "you" statements to *look* like "I" statements. This charade is usually obvious because the sentence starts, "I feel that you ..."

- "I feel that you're selfish."

- "I feel that you're never home."

- "I feel that you manipulate me."

Notice that a judgment, not a feeling, forms the core of such communications. It's certainly safer than an "I" statement—because the speaker is less vulnerable—but it communicates nothing about your emotional experience.

3. *"I want."* This component is the whole point of assertiveness, and you need to think it through carefully. Here are some guidelines to follow:

   - *Ask for behavioral, not attitudinal, change.* You can't reasonably expect someone to change what they believe or feel just because you don't like it. Beliefs and feelings aren't usually in voluntary control. But you *can* ask someone to change how they act and what they do.

   - *Ask for one change at a time.* Don't give a laundry list. That overwhelms people and makes them feel pressured.

   - *Ask for something that can be changed now.* "The next time we go on vacation, I want you to ..." is a poor "I want" statement because it'll be long forgotten when the next vacation finally arrives.

   - *Be specific and concrete.* Vague requests like "Be nicer" don't get you anywhere because nobody has a very clear picture of what they mean. Describe what new behavior you expect, and say when and where you'd want it to occur. Asking someone for twenty minutes of help doing research on the Internet is more effective than requesting "technological assistance."

4. *Self-care solution (optional):* Just asking for things isn't always enough. Sometimes you need to give people encouragement (reinforcement) before they're motivated to do something for you. The encouragement that works best is a fourth (optional) component of your assertive script called the *self-care solution*. This amounts to nothing more than telling the other person what you'll do to take care of yourself if they don't comply with your request. The self-care solution isn't the same thing as threatening someone or punishing them. Its purpose is to give information and show that you're not helpless, that you have a plan to solve the problem. Here are some examples.

- "If you can't leave for the party on time, I'll take my own car."

- "If you can't help with the cleaning, I'll hire a maid and we'll divide that expense."

- "If you can't find a way to keep the party noise down, I'll ask the police to help you."

- "If you want to drive without insurance, I'll transfer the title to your name and you can take over the payments as well."

None of these self-care solutions are designed to hurt the other person; they're about protecting your rights and taking care of your own needs.

Integrating the Components of Being Assertive

Now, let's integrate the components of an assertive statement so you can see how they fit together. Here are some examples:

EXAMPLE #1

I think: *It's been three years since we've had a cost-of-living raise, and prices have increased more than 10 percent in that time.*

I feel: *I feel left out, because the company's doing well and I'm not participating in that.*

I want: *I'd like a 10 percent cost-of-living adjustment soon so my income can keep pace with inflation.*

Self-care: *If we can't work this out, I'm going to have to look for something else so I can better support my family.*

EXAMPLE #2

I think: *I've been working against a deadline tonight and haven't had time to cook dinner.*

I feel: *I'm pretty anxious and overwhelmed that I might not get this done.*

I want: *Could you whip something together from leftovers so I can keep going?*

Self-care: *If that doesn't work for you, I can order a pizza.*

One way to use your self-care solution is to hold it in reserve—only using it if the other person refuses your preferred solution. Saving the "big guns" for later is often an effective strategy.

Exercise: Developing Your Own Assertiveness Scripts

Now it's time to practice developing your own scripts. Start with identifying three situations in which something feels wrong and you want things to change. Write the information down in the space provided.

PROBLEM #1

1. The problem: _____

    _____

    _____

2. What I want changed: _____

    _____

    _____

PROBLEM #2

1. The problem: _____

    _____

    _____

2. What I want changed: _____

    _____

    _____

PROBLEM #3

1. The problem: _____

    _____

    _____

2. What I want changed: _____

    _____

    _____

Now let's turn this knowledge into actual scripts:

PROBLEM #1

I think: _____

_____

I feel: _____

_____

I want: _____

_____

How I'll take care of myself: _____

_____

PROBLEM #2

I think: _____

_____

I feel: _____

_____

I want: _____

_____

How I'll take care of myself: _____

_____

PROBLEM #3

I think: _____

_____

I feel: _____

_____

I want: _____

_____

How I'll take care of myself: _____

_____

ASSERTIVE LISTENING

Everyone knows that good communication is a two-way street. But what a lot of people don't know is that listening is an active rather than passive process. It requires a full commitment to really understand what the other person thinks and feels about the problem, and wants to do to change it. In other words, the same three things you're learning to express assertively, you'll also need to listen for and elicit with questions.

If, while listening, you have any uncertainty about the other person's feelings or wishes, ask a direct question. "I'm not really sure how you feel about that—could you tell me more?" "What do you think we should try to change in this situation?"

The more active your questions, the more you learn and the better equipped you'll be to find solutions and compromises that serve both people's needs. Key questions to ask others are as follows:

- "What's the central problem, as you understand it?"

- "How do you make sense of the situation? What do you think's happening?"

- "When you're struggling with (*name the problem*) _____, how does it make you feel?"

- "When you're dealing with (*name the problem*) _____, what does it make you want to do?"

- "What do you think needs to change?"

- "What would you like me to do to help with this?"

For example, Ron noticed that a coworker seemed irritated with a new order-processing system Ron had just initiated. When Ron asked, "What do you think needs to change?" he got a wealth of helpful feedback, and the whole emotional climate changed.

Assertive listening is extremely valuable, but remember—just because you found out what someone needs, it doesn't mean you have to give it to them.

Blocks to Listening

Here are ten ways that people sabotage their effective listening abilities (adapted from McKay et al., 1983). Right now, put a check (✓) by the listening blocks you're aware of using. But don't judge yourself—everybody does some of this.

_____ *Mind reading:* Assuming you know what the other person feels and thinks—without asking.

_____ *Rehearsing:* Planning what you want to say next and missing what's being said now.

_____ *Filtering:* Listening only to things that are important or relevant to you and ignoring the rest (even if it's important to the other person).

_____ *Judging:* Evaluating the other person and what they say rather than really trying to understand how they see the world.

_____ *Daydreaming:* Getting caught in memories or fantasies while someone is talking to you.

_____ *Advising:* Looking for suggestions and solutions instead of listening and understanding.

_____ *Sparring:* Invalidating the other person by arguing and debating.

_____ *Being right:* Resisting or ignoring any communication that suggests you are wrong or should change.

_____ *Derailing:* Flat out changing the subject as soon as you hear anything that bothers or threatens you.

_____ *Placating:* Agreeing too quickly ("I know … You're right … I'm sorry") without really listening to the other person's feelings or concerns.

Exercise: Listening Blocks

In the left-hand column of the following table, describe three situations where communications broke down between you and someone else. In the right-hand column, see if you can identify at least one of the listening blocks that kept you from hearing or understanding everything that was said.

LISTENING-BLOCK EXERCISE

Situation	Blocks to Listening
1.	
2.	
3.	

During the next week, notice how often you use your favorite listening blocks. Commit to replacing them with assertive listening (see key questions under Assertive Listening on page 211).

SAYING NO

The ability to say no is a vital part of healthy communication. Without it, any relationship is dangerous—it's like getting in a car with a gas pedal and no brakes. You have no control over what people do to you.

Saying no is simple and hard at the same time. The words are simple, but often it takes courage to say them. Let's start with the "how" of saying no. There are only two steps:

1. Validate the other person's needs or desires.

2. State a clear *preference* not to do it.

Here are some examples:

- "Action movies with a high body count are a lot of fun, but *I'd prefer* something calmer tonight."

- "I've seen chartreuse used to good advantage—it's a dynamic color—but *I'd prefer* something pastel in the bedroom."

- "I can see why you want to confront Ian (our son), but *I don't feel comfortable* with an approach that risks him turning his back on us."

■ "I can see why you want to go late, out of the hot sun, but *I'm not comfortable* trying to stay up so long after my bedtime."

Notice that the key phrases are "I'd prefer" and "I'm not comfortable." You don't offer a lot of justification for your position; you don't argue. You just validate and decline. The important thing is *not* giving the other person anything to use against you. No one can really argue with preferences or feelings.

Exercise: Building an Assertive Hierarchy

Learning assertiveness (including saying no) takes practice and willingness to take some risks. But you need to get your feet wet in low-risk situations, then work toward more anxiety-provoking encounters.

Make a list of situations where you want to make a change, say no, or set limits. Include problems with family, friends, people who work for or with you, authorities, and so on. Now rank the list from 1 to 10 in terms of risk and difficulty, with 1 being the least challenging and 10 being the most challenging situation.

ASSERTIVE SITUATION HIERARCHY

Rank	Situation

Now start with the lowest-ranked situations and do four things:

1. Write your script ("I think … I feel … I want").

2. Rehearse your script.

3. Identify the time and place you want to use it.

4. Commit yourself to making your assertive statement on a specific date.

When you've completed your first assertive goal, evaluate what worked and what needs improvement. For example, do you need to be firmer, with less arguing or excuse making? Whatever you learned from your first step, incorporate it into the preparations for the second-ranked situation. Keep moving up the hierarchy. As you do, you'll find your confidence and skill growing. And your relationships will become gradually more rewarding.

COPING WITH RESISTANCE AND CONFLICT

We looked earlier at how to improve your ability to hear others. But what happens if someone isn't listening to *you*? The answer is in the following five conflict management skills:

1. Mutual validation

2. Broken record

3. Probing

4. Clouding (assertive agreement)

5. Assertive delay

Mutual Validation

When people aren't listening to you, one of the most common reasons is that they feel invalidated. They don't experience that they're being heard, so they keep pouring on their arguments and assertions. You can short-circuit the problem with mutual validation. Validating someone doesn't mean agreeing with them. It means, instead, that you understand their *needs*, *feelings*, and *motivations*. You get it—you see how the other person could think and feel that way.

Thus mutual validation means you acknowledge and appreciate their experience, you understand where they're coming from, and then you validate your own experience as well. Here are some examples:

■ "*I understand* that it's scary to take a financial risk like this; you have every right to be cautious. *On my end*, I feel a pressure to make some higher-yield investments so we'll have a bit more when we retire. We're both coming from a reasonable place, just different."

- "*I understand* that my saying you're not pulling your weight hurt you. That would be hard for anyone—me included—to hear. *On my end*, I'm scared this project is in danger of going over budget and I'll have to answer for that. I need everyone to pull together."

- "*I understand* you're concerned about my safety, and that's why you replaced the part. I appreciate that very much. *On my end*, I've got a budget so tight I can't afford repair work that isn't literally keeping the car running. Safety isn't my highest concern right now."

Notice that each example of mutual validation includes a sentence that starts "I understand," and another one that begins "On my end." These two sentences establish that you appreciate both points of view.

Broken Record

You use this technique when someone isn't getting the message. Formulate a short, specific, easy-to-understand statement about what you want. Ideally, keep it to one sentence. Offer no excuses or explanations. Stand or sit straight, talk in a strong, firm voice. Then just keep repeating the statement as many times as necessary, varying a word here or there—but not much else.

Don't argue, don't get angry, and don't try to debate or refute anything the other person says. Don't answer any "why" questions ("Why do you want to . . .") because that just gives the other person ammunition for their arguments. Respond by saying "I just prefer it" or "That's just how I feel." Under no circumstances should you offer additional information or evidence for your point of view. Just repeat, politely and clearly, like a broken record. Here's an example:

Sam: Your tree has a large branch suspended over my roof. I'm concerned that the next big storm could bring it down on my house. I'd like you to get an arborist to cut off the limb.

Bill: It's been like that for years; I wouldn't worry about it.

Sam: I think that branch is a danger to my house, and I'd like you to have it removed.

Bill: Relax; that branch will still be up there long after we're pushing up daisies.

Sam: It's hanging over my roof, and I'm concerned about it. I'm asking you to remove it, Bill, before it falls.

Bill: Why have you gotten so nervous about it all of a sudden?

Sam: The branch is over my roof, Bill, and it needs to come down.

Probing

The key phrase here is this:

- ■ "What is it about (*name the situation*) _____ that bothers you?"

Just keep asking it until you get something useful.

For example, let's return to a previous example of a person who was accused of not pulling his weight. Imagine that you were criticized in that way. Here's how probing could help you.

Critic: You're not pulling your weight around here.

You: What is it about my work that bothers you?

Critic: Everybody else is working overtime. You waltz out every night at 5:00.

You: What is it that bothers you about me leaving the office on time?

Critic: The work has to be done. I'm responsible to see that it is. And you just work by the clock.

You: What is it that bothers you when I work by the clock?

Critic: Somebody else has to finish your work—often me. I want you to stay till it's done.

You: I appreciate your explaining to me.

If you wish to probe with more varied questions, review the sample queries in the Assertive Listening section.

Clouding

This technique allows you to "agree in part" with someone without accepting that everything they say is true. This calms people down and stops the win/lose arguing game.

The key is to find some part of what's being said that you can accept and then to acknowledge that the other person is right about that. Ignore the rest of their argument. One way to agree is to modify words of sheer exaggeration, such as "always" and "never."

EXAMPLE #1

Critic: You always get pissed off over little things.

You: It's true, there are times I find myself getting irritated.

EXAMPLE #2

Critic: You never support me when I need something.

You: It's true, there have been several times when I couldn't completely support what you were asking.

Notice how clouding steals your critic's thunder and neutralizes his or her argument. Now the door is open to real negotiation of legitimate, yet very different needs.

Assertive Delay

This technique gives you room to wait, particularly when things threaten to get hot and angry. People will often pressure you to make a decision or agree with a plan right away. Assertive delay allows you to take a break—whether for a few minutes or several hours. During the interval, you can calm down, think carefully about what's being said, and prepare a good response. "You've told me a lot, and I need time to sift through and see what I think." "Give me an hour. This is important, and I want to think carefully before I say anything."

HOW TO NEGOTIATE

When a conflict arises that requires negotiation between you and someone else, you need to start from the position that *each of you has valid needs*. The RAVEN checklist will keep you on track.

RAVEN stands for the following:

Relax. Accept conflict calmly. Take a deep breath before you say the next thing. Release tension as you exhale.

Avoid the aversive. Keep in mind the aversive strategies you might be tempted to use, and monitor what you say in order to avoid them.

Validate the other person's need or concern. Focus on a fair, mutually agreeable outcome where *both* people can get *some* of their needs met.

Examine your values. How do you want to be treated in a relationship—how do you want to treat others? What do you want to achieve, not only regarding the conflict, but in this relationship?

Neutral voice. Keep anger and contempt out of your voice.

Once you're committed to staying within the RAVEN guidelines, it's time to start the actual negotiation process. It begins by each person taking turns and offering solutions. Make sure that a solution you offer addresses at least some of the needs of the other person. If you aren't sure what those needs are—ask them.

Once you've each offered several alternative solutions—without agreement—it's time to look for a compromise. Here are some classic compromise solutions:

- *I'll cut the pie; you choose the first piece.* After the divorce, Sharon divided the artwork into two groups—but Lawrence got to choose which one he'd take.

- *Take turns.* Linda and Moe alternated between going to the mountains and the beach on their vacations.

- *Do both; have it all.* Take care of both people's needs simultaneously.

- *Trial period.* Agree to a solution only for a specific length of time, after which you'll reevaluate. If one party feels the solution isn't working, negotiations are reopened.

- *My way when I'm doing it; your way when you're doing it.* Each person, as he or she deals with a problem, gets to use their own method. Sam and Katrina were partners in a small boutique. Sam thought the big "come on in" sign that Katrina made was garish. They agreed he wouldn't use it on his days watching the store.

- *Tit for tat.* Roommates Jill and Denise agreed that if Jill cleaned the bathroom once a week, Denise would dust and vacuum once a week.

- *Part of what I want with part of what you want.* Two friends and coworkers planned to travel together to a convention. One wanted to relax on the train; one wanted to get there in a hurry by air. They agreed to fly one way and take the train the other.

- *Split the difference.* This often works with haggling over a price or how much time to spend doing something.

Exercise: How to Negotiate

Recall three recent conflicts where you had very different needs from someone else. For each conflict, work out two possible compromises from the above list. Describe specifically how you would implement them.

Conflict	Compromise
1.	a. b.
2.	a. b.
3.	a. b.

When working toward compromise, it's crucial to maintain flexibility. Holding a fixed, entrenched position makes negotiation difficult. Be open to creative, unexpected solutions. Be prepared to give something up to get something you want.

HOW TO ANALYZE PROBLEM INTERACTIONS

You need a way to figure out what happened when communications go wrong. Inevitably, problems and conflicts will show up in your relationships. Sometimes you will blow up or shut down. But the key is to learn from what happened and use that to polish your skills. No setback is completely negative if it helps you be more effective next time.

The following checklist will help you review interpersonal problems and become clearer about their causes.

COMMUNICATION EFFECTIVENESS CHECKLIST

1. Were you clear about your goals?

   _____ Did you know what you wanted?

   _____ Did you know what you *didn't* want—so you could say no?

   _____ Were you aware of your values, how you wanted to treat others, and how you'd like to be treated in return?

2. Did you use aversive strategies?

   _____ Discounting

   _____ Withdrawing/abandonment

   _____ Threats

   _____ Blaming

   _____ Belittling/denigrating

   _____ Guilt-tripping

   _____ Derailing

   _____ Taking away

3. Did you use passive strategies?

   _____ Avoiding/withholding

   _____ Shutting down/stonewalling

4. What were the blocking factors?

   _____ High emotion (see page 192)

   _____ Fear and "what ifs" (see page 193)

   _____ Toxic relationships (see page 196)

   _____ Myths (see page 196)

   - If I need something, it means there is something wrong or bad about me.
   - I won't be able to stand it if the other person gets mad or says no.
   - It's selfish to say no or ask for things.
   - I have no control over anything.

5. Intensity level

   _____ Too high?

   _____ Too low?

6. Assertiveness problems?

    ____ Judgments instead of facts (see page 206)

    ____ "You" statements instead of "I" statements (see page 206)

    ____ No specific behavioral description of what you want (see page 207)

7. Blocks to listening? (see page 212)

    ____ Mind reading

    ____ Rehearsing

    ____ Filtering

    ____ Judging

    ____ Daydreaming

    ____ Advising

    ____ Sparring

    ____ Being right

    ____ Derailing

    ____ Placating

8. Forgot the conflict management strategies?

    ____ Mutual validation (see page 215)

    ____ Broken record (see page 216)

    ____ Probing (see page 217)

    ____ Clouding (see page 217)

    ____ Assertive delay (see page 218)

9. Negotiation breakdown?

    ____ Did you forget to use RAVEN?

- **R**elax
- **A**void the aversive
- **V**alidate the other person's need or concern
- **E**xamine your values
- **N**eutral voice

    ____ Didn't use compromise solutions?

The Communication Effectiveness Checklist is a starting point to evaluate interactions that you wish could have gone better. Identify the problems first, then decide which ones you want to work on. Review the sections in this and the previous chapter regarding skills you want to improve. Finally, make a specific plan for how you are going to change your behavior *next time.* Don't try to fix too many things because you'll never remember it all. Just focus on a few changes that might lead to big improvements. Write down specifically what you're going to do differently and in which situations.

Here's an example. Laura used the Communication Effectiveness Checklist to evaluate an angry interaction with her boss. She had asked for lighter duties because of a sprained wrist. These are the items she checked as problems.

- Denigrating (*I told him the company didn't take very good care of its employees.*)

- High emotion (*I got quickly upset and forgot some of my skills.*)

- Myths (*I feel like there's something wrong with me if I ask for anything special.*)

- "You" statements (*I said, "I feel like you don't really care what happens to people."*)

- No behavioral description of need (*I didn't specify exactly what "light duty" I was asking for.*)

- Blocks to listening (*I used judging and sparring.*)

- Mutual validation (*I didn't validate his concerns.*)

- Probing (*I never found out his concerns.*)

Laura realized she couldn't deal with everything on her list, so she decided to focus on just a few things:

- Denigrating and "you" statements

- High emotion

- Behavioral description of need

- Probing

Here's Laura's written plan:

When I discuss this with Bob again, I'm going to do the following:

1. *Be extremely careful to make no critical statements about Bob or the company—no matter how upset I get.*

2. *Do a few minutes of mindful breathing to calm down before I talk to him.*

3. *Watch out for when I feel hot or I'm raising my voice—take a couple of deep breaths to calm down then.*

4. *Tell him I can do anything but collating, copying, and working with a mouse. I need to stop doing those things till my wrist is better.*

5. *If he objects, I'll ask what his concern is about temporarily changing my duties. Then I'll try to negotiate.*

The most important thing to remember about your new interpersonal skills is to keep working at them. Your persistence will benefit you. Shrug it off when things go wrong, figure out what happened, and then make a new plan. You have the ability to change your relationships and your life. All you have to do is keep trying.

CHAPTER 10

Putting It All Together

The skills you have learned in this book will grow stronger each day that you practice them. Conversely, if your skills aren't used, they'll slip further from your grasp. They'll cease to be real choices, real ways to change. Instead, they'll become mere ideas, vaguely recalled, with no power to help you.

Keeping and strengthening your skills will take sustained effort. There's an old saying that victory belongs to the most persevering, which is exactly what's needed now: a commitment to practice your skills daily—over time.

You may wonder—legitimately—where you'll find the motivation to keep doing something so challenging. And all this talk of perseverance may sound very nineteenth century and preachy. But there is a way to practice daily what you've learned, and it doesn't take a huge amount of willpower. What it requires is getting in the *habit* of spending about fifteen minutes a day practicing your skills.

DAILY PRACTICES FOR EMOTIONAL HEALTH

The *daily practices* are, in essence, an exercise regimen to maintain your emotional and psychological health. The practices have five parts:

1. Mindfulness

2. Deep relaxation

3. Self-observation

4. Affirmation

5. Committed action

The daily practices take a total of about fifteen minutes. They should be done, ideally, at the same time each day—so they can become a healthy habit. Choose a period in your day when you can be alone and have a little quiet. It could be just after your morning coffee or in your workspace just before going to lunch. It could be how you de-stress when you come home at night or part of your bedtime routine. Whatever time you choose, stick to it. Don't let other events or commitments interfere. Consider the time spent in daily practices as an appointment with yourself—no less important than all the other commitments that you keep.

Your daily practices will be assembled from a menu of choices. Here's how that works:

1. Mindfulness. *Three to five minutes.* Choose to do one of the following:

   ■ Mindful breathing (see chapter 3)

   ■ Wise-mind meditation (see chapter 4)

2. Deep relaxation. *Three minutes.* Choose to do one of the following:

   ■ Cue-controlled relaxation (see chapter 2)

   ■ Band of light (see chapter 3)

   ■ Safe-place visualization (see chapter 2)

3. Self-observation. *Three minutes.* Choose to do one of the following:

   ■ Thought defusion (see chapter 3)

   ■ Be mindful of your emotions without judgment (see chapter 7)

4. Affirmation. See chapter 2 for a list of self-affirmations or create a self-affirmation yourself. Repeat the affirmation five times while taking slow, long breaths. You can choose a different affirmation each day—or keep working on the same one.

5. Committed action. *Three minutes.* Choose to do one of the following:

   ■ Plan to implement today's (or tomorrow's) committed action (see chapter 2).

   ■ Plan for what you can do today (or tomorrow) to connect to your higher power (see chapter 2).

Each component of your daily practices is designed to strengthen one or more core skills. First and foremost are mindfulness skills because all of the others depend, to some degree, on mindful awareness. Deep relaxation is a key to distress tolerance, while self-observation and affirmation will help with emotion regulation. Finally, a plan for committed action will strengthen emotion regulation and interpersonal effectiveness skills.

The concept of committed action deserves special note. Your daily practices should include a plan for something you'll do—that day or the next—to solve a problem, deal effectively with a difficult situation or person, or strengthen awareness of your higher power. You can connect to your higher power through prayer, an act of kindness, or some giving of yourself to others. What you choose is up to you, but committed action—in some form—is necessary to make any real change in your life.

Right now, choose the five daily practices you will use tomorrow. Then, write them here as part of your commitment to really *do* them.

MY DAILY PRACTICES

Mindfulness: _____

Deep relaxation: _____

Self-observation: _____

Affirmation: _____

_____

Committed action plan: _____

_____

_____

What time each day will you do your practices? Please write that here: _____

_____

So far, so good—you know what you'll do for your daily practices and when you'll do them. But now comes the most important part: persevering—spending those fifteen minutes every day strengthening your skills.

How do you persevere? The answer is one day at a time—making sure that on *this* day, at the appointed time, you do your practices. And the next day you do the same thing ... and the next. A commitment isn't something you make once, and you're set for life. It's something you keep making, every day.

The daily practices will change your life because they will help you shape new responses to old struggles. Life isn't about hopes or intentions. It's about *doing*. It's about *being* effective. Now, as we close the book, we're asking you to live what you've learned. You can do this, maybe not perfectly, but enough to make real changes.

The poet and author Samuel Johnson once said: "The future is purchased by the present." Similarly, by investing in your dialectical behavior therapy skills and practices today, you can create a happier and healthier tomorrow.

References

Alberti, R. E., & Emmons, M. (1990). *Your perfect right* (6th ed.). San Luis Obispo, CA: Impact Press.

Anderson, W. P., Reid, C. M., & Jennings, G. L. (1992). Pet ownership and risk factors for cardiovascular disease. *Medical Journal of Australia, 157*(5), 298–301.

Babyak, M., Blumenthal, J. A., Herman, S., Khatri, P., Doraiswamy, M., Moore, K., et al. (2000). Exercise treatment for major depression: Maintenance of therapeutic benefit at 10 months. *Psychosomatic Medicine, 62*(5), 633–638.

Baer, R. A. (2003). Mindfulness training as a clinical intervention: A conceptual and empirical review. *Clinical Psychology: Science and Practice, 10,* 125–143.

Barker, L. L. (1990). *Listening behavior.* New Orleans, LA: SPECTRA.

Beck, A. T., Rush, A. J., Shaw, B. F., & Emery, G. (1979). *Cognitive therapy of depression.* New York: Guilford Press.

Bower, S. A., & Bower, G. H. (1991). *Asserting yourself: A practical guide for positive change* (2nd ed.). Reading, MA: Addison-Wesley Publishing.

Chodron, P. (2003, March). How we get hooked, how we get unhooked. *Shambala Sun,* 30–35.

Dodge, K. A. (1989). Coordinating responses to aversive stimuli: Introduction to a special section on the development of emotion regulation. *Developmental Psychology, 25*(3), 339–342.

Feldman, C. (1998). *Thorsons principles of meditation.* London: Thorsons.

Fisher, R., & Ury, W. (1991). *Getting to yes: Negotiating agreement without giving in* (2nd ed.). New York: Viking Penguin.

Greenwood, K. A., Thurston, R., Rumble, M., Waters, S. J., & Keefe, F. J. (2003). Anger and persistent pain: Current status and future directions. *Pain, 103*(1–2), 1–5.

Hayes, S. C., Strosahl, K. D., & Wilson, K. G. (1999). *Acceptance and commitment therapy: An experiential approach to behavior change.* New York: Guilford Press.

Inayat Khan, P. V. (2000). *Awakening: A Sufi experience.* New York: Tarcher/Putnam.

Johnson, S. M. (1985). *Characterological transformation: The hard work miracle.* New York: W. W. Norton & Company.

Kabat-Zinn, J. (1982). An out-patient program in behavioral medicine for chronic pain patients based on the practice of mindfulness meditation: Theoretical considerations and preliminary results. *General Hospital Psychiatry, 4,* 33–47.

Kabat-Zinn, J. (1990). *Full catastrophe living: Using the wisdom of your body and mind to face stress, pain, and illness.* New York: Delacorte.

Kabat-Zinn, J. (2003). Mindfulness-based interventions in context: Past, present, and future. *Clinical Psychology: Science and Practice, 10*(2), 144–156.

Kabat-Zinn, J., Lipworth, L., & Burney, R. (1985). The clinical use of mindfulness meditation for the self-regulation of chronic pain. *Journal of Behavioral Medicine, 8,* 163–190.

Kabat-Zinn, J., Lipworth, L., Burney, R., & Sellers, W. (1987). Four-year follow-up of a meditation-based program for the self-regulation of chronic pain: Treatment outcomes and compliance. *Clinical Journal of Pain, 2,* 159–173.

Kabat-Zinn, J., Massion, M. D., Kristeller, J. L., Peterson, L. G., Fletcher, K. E., Pbert, L., et al. (1992). Effectiveness of a meditation-based stress reduction program in the treatment of anxiety disorders. *American Journal of Psychiatry, 149,* 936–943.

Kerns, R. D., Rosenberg, R., & Jacob, M. C. (1994). Anger expression and chronic pain. *Journal of Behavioral Medicine, 17*(1), 57–67.

Kristeller, J. L., & Hallett, C. B. (1999). An exploratory study of a meditation-based intervention for binge eating disorder. *Journal of Health Psychology, 4,* 357–363.

Linehan, M. M. (1993a). *Cognitive-behavioral treatment of borderline personality disorder.* New York: Guilford Press.

Linehan, M. M. (1993b). *Skills training manual for treating borderline personality disorder.* New York: Guilford Press.

Marra, T. (2005). *Dialectical behavior therapy in private practice: A practical and comprehensive guide.* Oakland, CA: New Harbinger Publications.

McKay, M., Davis, M., & Fanning, P. (1983). *Messages: The communication skills book.* Oakland, CA: New Harbinger Publications.

McKay, M., Davis, M., & Fanning, P. (1997). *Thoughts and feelings: Taking control of your moods and your life.* Oakland, CA: New Harbinger Publications.

McKay, M., Fanning, P., & Paleg, K. (1994). *Couple skills: Making your relationship work.* Oakland, CA: New Harbinger Publications.

McKay, M., Rogers, P. D., & McKay, J. (2003). *When anger hurts: Quieting the storm within* (2nd ed.). Oakland, CA: New Harbinger Publications.

Merton, T. (1960). *Spiritual direction and meditation.* Collegeville, MN: Order of St. Benedict.

Olerud, J. C., & Wilson, K. G. (2002, May). *Evaluation of an ACT intervention in a preventive program for chronic pain at the worksite.* Paper presented at the meeting of the Association for Behavior Analysis, Toronto, Canada.

Pinson, D. (2004). *Meditation and Judaism: Exploring the Jewish meditative paths.* Northvale, NJ: Jason Aronson.

Rahula, W. (1974). *What the Buddha taught* (2nd ed.). New York: Grove Press.

Rogers, C. R. (1951). *Client-centered therapy.* New York: Houghton Mifflin Company.

Salzberg, S. (1995). *Lovingkindness: The revolutionary art of happiness.* Boston: Shambhala.

Salzberg, S. (1997). *A heart as wide as the world: Living with mindfulness, wisdom, and compassion.* Boston: Shambhala.

Salzberg, S. (2005). *The force of kindness: Change your life with love & compassion.* Boulder, CO: Sounds True.

Segal, Z. V., Williams, J. M. G., & Teasdale, J. D. (2002). *Mindfulness-based cognitive therapy for depression: A new approach to preventing relapse.* New York: Guilford Press.

Serpell, J. (1991). Beneficial effects of pet ownership on some aspects of human health and behaviour. *Journal of the Royal Society of Medicine, 84*(12), 717–720.

Shapiro, S. L., & Schwartz, G. E. (2000). The role of intention in self-regulation: Toward intentional systemic mindfulness. In M. Boekaerts, P. R. Pintrich, & M. Zeidner (Eds.), *Handbook of self-regulation* (pp. 253–273). New York: Academic Press.

Suzuki, S. (2001). *Zen mind, beginner's mind: Informal talks on Zen meditation and practice.* New York: Weatherhill.

Tart, C. T. (1994). *Living the mindful life: A handbook for living in the present moment.* Boston: Shambhala.

Teasdale, J. D., Segal, Z. V., Williams, J. M. G., Ridgeway, V. A., Soulsby, J. M., & Lau, M. A. (2000). Prevention of relapse/recurrence in major depression by mindfulness-based cognitive therapy. *Journal of Consulting and Clinical Psychology, 68,* 615–623.

Wilson, K. G. (2002). The Valued Living Questionnaire. Available from the author at Department of Psychology, University of Mississippi, University, MS.

Wilson, K. G., & Murrell, A. R. (2004). Values work in acceptance and commitment therapy: Setting a course for behavioral treatment. In S. C. Hayes, V. M. Follette, & M. M. Linehan (Eds.), *Mindfulness and acceptance: Expanding the cognitive-behavioral tradition* (pp. 120–151). New York: Guilford Press.

Matthew McKay, Ph.D., is a professor at the Wright Institute in Berkeley, CA. He is coauthor of **The Relaxation and Stress Reduction Workbook, Thoughts and Feelings, Messages, Self-Esteem,** and others. His books combined have sold more than 2 million copies. He received his Ph.D. in clinical psychology from the California School of Professional Psychology. In private practice, he specializes in the cognitive behavioral treatment of anxiety, anger, and depression.

Jeffrey C. Wood, Psy.D., lives and works in the San Francisco Bay Area. He specializes in cognitive behavioral treatments for depression, anxiety, and trauma, as well as assertiveness and life-skills coaching. He can be reached at **www.drjeffreywood.com.** He is author of **Getting Help**.

Jeffrey Brantley, MD, is a consulting associate in the Duke Department of Psychiatry and the founder and director of the Mindfulness-Based Stress Reduction Program at Duke University's Center for Integrative Medicine. He has represented the Duke MBSR program in numerous radio, television and print interviews. He is the best-selling author of **Calming Your Anxious Mind** and coauthor of **Five Good Minutes: 100 Morning Practices to Help You Stay Calm and Focused All Day Long.**